A Book Forged in Hell

TRACTATUS
THEOLOGICO-
POLITICUS

Continens

Diſſertationes aliquot,

Quibus oſtenditur Libertatem Philoſophandi non tantum
ſalva Pietate, & Reipublicæ Pace poſſe concedi: ſed
eandem niſi cum Pace Reipublicæ, ipſaque
Pietate tolli non poſſe.

Johann: Epiſt: I. Cap: IV. verſ: XIII.

*Per hoc cognoſcimus quod in Deo manemus, & Deus manet
in nobis, quod de Spiritu ſuo dedit nobis.*

HAMBURGI,
Apud *Henricum Künraht.* cIɔ Iɔ cLXX.

The title page of Spinoza's *Tractatus Theologico-Politicus*, 1670; photo-
graph courtesy of the Rare Books Division; Department of Rare Books
and Special Collections, Princeton University Library

A Book Forged in Hell

Spinoza's Scandalous Treatise and the Birth of the Secular Age

Steven Nadler

Princeton University Press
Princeton and Oxford

Published by Princeton University Press, 41 William Street, Princeton, New Jersey 08540
In the United Kingdom: Princeton University Press, 6 Oxford Street, Woodstock,
Oxfordshire OX20 1TW
press.princeton.edu

Jacket art: Benedict Spinoza (1632–77), (oil on canvas) by Dutch School, Herzog August
Bibliothek, Wolfenbuttel, Germany / The Bridgeman Art Library
Jacket illustration: courtesy of Shutterstock

Library of Congress Cataloging-in-Publication Data
Nadler, Steven M., 1958–
  A book forged in hell : Spinoza's scandalous treatise and the birth of the secular age / Steven
Nadler.
    p. cm.
  Includes bibliographical references (p. 267) and index.
  ISBN 978-0-691-13989-0 (hardcover : alk. paper)
  1. Spinoza, Benedictus de, 1632–1677. Tractatus theologico-politicus. 2. Philosophy and
religion. 3. Religion and politics. I. Title.
  B3985.Z7N34 2011
  199'.492—dc22   2011005960

British Library Cataloging-in-Publication Data is available

This book has been composed in Garamond 3
Printed on acid-free paper. ∞
Printed in the United States of America

10 9 8 7 6 5 4 3 2 1

For Larry Shapiro
amicus currens optimus

The vilest hypocrites, urged on by that same fury which they call zeal for God's law, have everywhere prosecuted men whose blameless character and distinguished qualities have excited the hostility of the masses, publicly denouncing their beliefs and inflaming the savage crowd's anger against them. And this shameless license, sheltering under the cloak of religion, is not easy to suppress.

—Baruch Spinoza, *Theological-Political Treatise*

Contents

Preface

Writing in May 1670, the German theologian Jacob Thomasius fulminated against a recent, anonymously published book. It was, he claimed, "a godless document" that should be immediately banned in all countries. His Dutch colleague, Regnier Mansveld, a professor at the University of Utrecht, insisted that the new publication was harmful to all religions and "ought to be buried forever in an eternal oblivion." Willem van Blijenburgh, a philosophically inclined Dutch merchant, wrote that "this atheistic book is full of abominations . . . which every reasonable person should find abhorrent." One disturbed critic went so far as to call it "a book forged in hell," written by the devil himself.

The object of all this attention was a work titled *Tractatus Theologico-Politicus* (*Theological-Political Treatise*) and its author, an excommunicated Jew from Amsterdam: Baruch de Spinoza. The *Treatise* was regarded by Spinoza's contemporaries as the most dangerous book ever published. In their eyes, it threatened to undermine religious faith, social and political harmony, and even everyday morality. They believed that the author—and his identity was not a secret for very long—was a religious subversive and political radical who sought to spread atheism and libertinism throughout Christendom. The uproar over the *Treatise* is, without question, one of the most significant events in European intellectual history, occurring as it did at the dawn of the Enlightenment.[1] While the book laid the groundwork for subsequent liberal, secular, and democratic thinking, the debate over it also exposed deep tensions in a world that had seemingly recovered from over a century of brutal religious warfare.

The *Treatise* is also one of the most important books of Western thought ever written. Spinoza was the first to argue that the

Bible is not literally the word of God but rather a work of human literature; that "true religion" has nothing to do with theology, liturgical ceremonies, or sectarian dogma but consists only in a simple moral rule: love your neighbor; and that ecclesiastic authorities should have no role whatsoever in the governance of a modern state. He also insisted that "divine providence" is nothing but the laws of nature, that miracles (understood as violations of the natural order of things) are impossible and belief in them is only an expression of our ignorance of the true causes of phenomena, and that the prophets of the Old Testament were simply ordinary individuals who, while ethically superior, happened also to have particularly vivid imaginations. The book's political chapters present as eloquent a plea for toleration (especially "the freedom to philosophize" without interference from the authorities) and democracy as has ever been penned.

The reputation of a philosopher from the past is often at the mercy of what is popular among contemporary practitioners. The canon of classical philosophers, while relatively stable at its core for a long time (like the permanent members of the United Nations Security Council), has seen its share of additions and dismissals. And for a long time, especially in the Anglo-American philosophical world in the first half of the twentieth century, Spinoza did not make the cut. While he may have continued to enjoy honorary status as one of the great Western thinkers, he was not considered to be a relevant one, and his works were rarely studied even in survey courses in the history of philosophy. It certainly did not help that his metaphysical-moral magnum opus, the *Ethics*, while composed in the "geometric style," was extremely opaque (contrary to the clarity of thinking and writing prized, at least in principle, by analytic philosophers), and that in that work he propounded doctrines that seemed to many to border on the mystical.

Spinoza's rehabilitation in the latter half of the twentieth century progressed as metaphysics and epistemology came to dominate academic philosophy. The metaphysics in fashion was not the system-building kind of earlier periods, including that of Spinoza or the idealist sort favored by the latter-day Hegelians of Cambridge in the late nineteenth and early twentieth centuries, but rather precise analytic investigations into mind, matter, causation, and universals. Meanwhile, modern epistemologists, like Plato and Descartes before them, inquired into the nature of belief, truth, justification, and knowledge. And these were all topics on which, it was believed, Spinoza (despite his grander pretensions) had something interesting and relevant to say. Moreover, his unorthodox view of God and his ingenious approach to the mind-body problem made him seem, in some respects, much more modern than his more religiously inclined seventeenth-century contemporaries.

The somewhat problematic result of this was that Spinoza (again, like Descartes) came to be seen as someone who was primarily engaged in metaphysics and epistemology, and who was interested only in such questions as the nature of substance and the mind-body problem and in addressing the skeptical challenges to human knowledge. The focus, in teaching and in scholarship, was on the first two parts of the *Ethics*, in which are found Spinoza's monistic view of nature, his account of understanding and will, and the mind-body parallelism that is supposed to be his response to the difficulties faced by Descartes's dualism. Parts Three, Four, and Five of the *Ethics*—his theory of the passions and his moral philosophy—were seldom discussed at all (and even less frequently taught). This produced a very incomplete and misleading picture of Spinoza's philosophical project; one was left wondering why the work is called *Ethics*.

Spinoza's *Theological-Political Treatise* (*Tractatus Theologico-Politicus*) received even worse treatment in this period; indeed, it was all but ignored by philosophers in the twentieth century. The neglect came not only from those working in metaphysics and epistemology but also, and more surprisingly, from scholars of political philosophy and of religion.[2] Very few histories of political thought discuss Spinoza, and works on the philosophy of religion rarely mention his name. Even today, one would be hard-pressed to find the *Treatise* taught in a philosophy course.[3]

Despite all this, outside the walls of academia there continued to be widespread fascination with Spinoza's thought. And the interest was not so much in what he had to say about substance or mind-body relations, which may be topics that only professional philosophers can get excited about, but in his views on God, religion, miracles, the Bible, democracy, and toleration. Nonphilosophers—the kind of people who will show up in great numbers on a Sunday afternoon for a public lecture about Spinoza—are deeply curious about his radical ideas on these questions, especially in the light of his well-known excommunication from Judaism. They may have some passing familiarity with—as well as a good many romantic and innocent notions about—what Spinoza had to say, but few have actually read the *Treatise*, even though it is a much more accessible work than the intimidating and heavy-going *Ethics*.

The last two decades have been much kinder to the *Treatise*. There have been a number of important books and many fine articles devoted to elucidating its theses and arguments, as well as its historical context. Most of these works, however, are of a specialized nature, and they tend to be devoted to this or that aspect of Spinoza's religious and political thought. Useful as they are in furthering our understanding of the *Treatise*, these scholarly studies are directed to an academic readership. Thus, they seem to have done little to sate what appears to be a real longing among general readers for information on a book about which they have heard or read such extraordinary things.

With this study, I hope to bring Spinoza's *Theological-Political Treatise* to a larger audience. My focus is broad: the composition, contents, and context of the *Treatise*. What exactly does Spinoza say in this book that so scandalized early modern Europe? What moved him to write such an incendiary treatise? What was the reaction to its publication, and why was it so vicious? And why is the *Treatise*, almost three and a half centuries after its publication, still of great relevance?

This is not a book on Spinoza's philosophy as a whole. Nor is it even a study of Spinoza's religious and political philosophy; I have considered the philosophical theology and political themes of the *Ethics*, as well as his late and unfinished *Political Treatise*, only insofar as they are relevant to my project of elucidating the *Theological-Political Treatise*. Nor do I investigate the considerable and very important reception of the *Treatise* beyond the immediate response to it by Spinoza's contemporaries. The legacy of the *Treatise*—from 1670 to our own time—is a rich and fascinating topic, one deserving thorough study in its own right.[4]

What I *am* interested in is simply understanding what Spinoza is saying in the *Treatise* and why he is saying it, as well as showing why the book occasioned such a harsh backlash. Spinoza has a rightful place among the great philosophers in history. He was certainly the most original, radical, and controversial thinker of his time, and his philosophical, political, and religious ideas laid the foundation for much of what we now regard as "modern." But if we do not give the *Theological-Political Treatise* the attention it deserves, then we do not really know Spinoza.

Acknowledgments

I am grateful to friends and colleagues who generously provided help in the research and writing of this book. In the Netherlands, my thanks to Piet Steenbakkers, Henk van Nierop, and Odette Vlessing for being so helpful in pursuing the answers to various questions I had, and to Henriette Reerink for assistance with some research matters, and especially for her continuing friendship. I also want to thank Daniel Schneider, a graduate student in the Department of Philosophy at the University of Wisconsin–Madison, for research on the publication history of the *Tractatus Theologico-Politicus*. Above all, I am indebted to Ed Curley and Michael Della Rocca, who took time away from their own work to read and comment on the entire manuscript. Their critical remarks and suggestions were extraordinarily valuable, and I deeply appreciate their generosity.

At Princeton University Press, Rob Tempio has been a superb and supportive editor. I am very grateful for his enthusiasm for this book, as well as other projects, and it has been a true pleasure working with him. And without the efforts of Andrew Stuart, of the Stuart Agency, this book would not have found such a fine home. My thanks, too, to Marjorie Pannell for her expert copy editing.

I have benefited greatly from support provided by the College of Letters and Science and the Graduate School at the University of Wisconsin–Madison. This includes a sabbatical and a semester's leave at the Institute for Research in the Humanities, as well as research funds accompanying the award of a Wisconsin Alumni Research Foundation professorship, which I was able to name after the late William Hay. Bill, who had retired just before I arrived at the university in 1988, was very kind and generous to me in my first years there. I was also honored by the Mosse/Weinstein Center for Jewish Studies to be the holder of the Weinstein/Bascom Professorship in Jewish Studies while working on this book, and the research funds provided by that position were much appreciated.

Parts of this book were presented in the fall of 2010 as lectures at the University of Amsterdam's Center for the Study of the Golden Age; I would like to thank audiences there for their questions and comments, and especially the center's director, Lia van Gemert, for allowing me the honor of giving the annual Golden Age Lecture. My thanks as well to audiences at the Spinoza Workshop at the University of Groningen, the Catholic University of America (Washington, D.C.), the Southwest Seminar in Early Modern Philosophy at the University of New Mexico, and the Bradshaw Conference at Claremont Graduate University.

Much of the writing of the book took place during the first year of our "empty nest." My wife Jane and I miss our children, Rose and Ben, dearly. Still, I have to admit, it was kind of nice to have the extra time to finish this project.

Finally, I dedicate this book to Larry Shapiro, my good friend and colleague and longtime running companion and fellow Ironman (who, it needs to be said publicly, beat me by four and a half minutes). Whatever he knows about Spinoza he's heard from me, and by now he's probably tired of hearing it.

A Book Forged in Hell

Chapter 1

Prologue

On the morning of July 28, 1670, Philips Huijbertsz[1] said goodbye to his wife, Eva Geldorpis, and left his home on the Nieuwendijk in Amsterdam. On this summer day, however, the fifty-six-year-old silk merchant was not on his way to the shop he had inherited from his father. It was Sunday, and he had more spiritual matters to attend to—matters of grave concern to the religious and moral well-being of his community.

Just four days earlier the consistory, or church council, of Amsterdam's Reformed Church had commissioned Brother Huijbertsz and his colleague, Brother Lucas van der Heiden, also in the silk trade, to represent it at the upcoming meeting of the Amsterdam regional *classis*.[2] This was the larger district synod at which preachers from local church communities in Amsterdam and surrounding villages would regularly gather to address issues of common interest. (The Amsterdam *classis* was one of fourteen in the province of Holland.) Philips and Lucas were given the responsibility of making the members of the district synod aware of the Amsterdam consistory's worries, expressed at their meeting of June 30, about some recently published materials:

> Because some grievances now confront our church, an inquiry was
> undertaken in order to bring these forward to the district synod
> and accordingly to the provincial synod, should that be approved
> by the district synod and it has agreed that there is nothing new in
> this matter. Our church requests only that, under [the rubric of] the
> old grievances [*gravamina*], attention should especially be paid to

the impudence of the papacy, Socinian and licentious book publications, and in particular the harmful book with the name *Theological-Political Treatise*.[3]

The "old grievances" that the consistory is now asking the Amsterdam *classis* to refer to in considering these new publications is an edict that the States of Holland—the chief legislative body of the province, and arguably the most powerful body in the nation—enacted in 1653 forbidding the printing and dissemination of certain "irreligious" books. The Amsterdam church elders would like the preachers sitting in the district synod to declare that the 1653 ban should be applied in this new case. The *classis* should then refer the matter to the Synod of North Holland, the provincial church council—there was another for South Holland—in whose jurisdiction the Amsterdam district, along with five others, lay.

Amsterdam was not the first Reformed consistory to take notice of "a profane, blasphemous book titled *Theological-political treatise concerning the freedom of philosophizing in the state.*" Already by May 1670 the church consistories of Utrecht, Leiden, and Haarlem had asked their town councils to seize any existing copies of the work and to take steps to prevent further publication or distribution. And the book had been published only in January of that year! Amsterdam was a bit slower in responding. However, as the most important city in the Netherlands, an urgent appeal brought forward from its Reformed leaders would certainly have great influence with the *predikanten* in the district and provincial synods.

Philips Huijbertszoon ("Huijbert's son") may have been charged with this important diplomatic task because he was a person of some reputation and trust in the community. Twenty years earlier he had acted as warranty for an exchange of Dutch citizens who, while abroad, had been captured as slaves and were being ransomed for a large sum of money.[4] Or, as a member of the local church leadership, he may have been among those who were particularly upset by the writings in question. He was familiar with at least some of the contents of the *Theological-Political Treatise* that the consistory was asking the synod to consider. Soon after his arrival that day in the Nieuwe Kerk, where the Amsterdam *classis* held its meetings in the same room as the local consistory, he would read to its members some of the particularly offensive passages, in the hope of getting them to see the danger.

The presentation had its desired effect. That very afternoon, the Amsterdam district synod came to the conclusion that

> licentious book publishing and especially the harmful book titled *Theological-Political Treatise* should be dealt with under the old griev-ances [i.e., those covered by the 1653 edict]. . . . The *classis*, having heard from its committee various enormous and abominable samples contained in that book, has proclaimed that book to be blasphemous and dangerous.[5]

It then forwarded the matter to the North Holland Synod, which was due to meet one week later. On August 5, the provincial body issued its own judgment:

> The *classis* of Amsterdam desires that . . . licentious book publish-ing and especially the harmful book titled *Theological-Political Trea-tise* should be dealt with under the old grievances. . . . Regarding the blasphemous book, the *Theological-Political Treatise*, the deputies have taken all the necessary steps against that book with the first council in the Court [of Holland], and are awaiting the outcome. The Christian Synod, heartily abominating that obscene book, gives its thanks to the honorable gentlemen from Bennebroeck for their offer to suppress this writing as much as they can, and to the Broth-ers from Amsterdam for their reading of their extracts from the book. Thanks also to the deputies for their performed service, and [the synod] entrusts them together with the deputies from South Hol-land to present all this to their honorable Mightinesses [the States of Holland] and to seek their help against [the book] with powerful suppression of it, and also to seek an edict to forbid this and all other blasphemous books.[6]

It was just the result Philips Huijbertszoon and his colleagues from Amsterdam's consistory were hoping for.

While these machinations were taking place in Amsterdam, the author of the scandalous book that so troubled the city's church leaders was leaving behind life in the peaceful countryside and relocating to the city of The Hague, the administrative and legislative capital of the Dutch Republic. There, in some rooms on the upper floor of a house owned by the widow Van der Werve on a back wharf called *De Stille Verkade* (the Quiet Ferry Quay), he would quietly continue his philosophical and political writing.

Bento de Spinoza was born on November 24, 1632, to a prominent merchant family among Amsterdam's Portuguese Jews.[7] This Sephardic community was founded by former New Christians, or *conversos*—Jews who had been forced to convert to Catholicism in Spain and Portugal in the late fifteenth and early sixteenth centuries—and their descendants. After fleeing harassment by the Iberian Inquisitions, which doubted the sincerity of the conversions, many New Christians eventually settled in Amsterdam and a few other northern cities by the early seventeenth century. With its generally tolerant environment and greater concern for economic prosperity than religious uniformity, the newly independent Dutch Republic (and especially Holland, its largest province) offered these refugees an opportunity to return to the religion of their ancestors and reestablish themselves in Jewish life. There were always conservative sectors of Dutch society clamoring for the expulsion of the "Portuguese merchants" in their midst.[8] But the more liberal regents of Amsterdam, not to mention the more enlightened elements in Dutch society at large, were unwilling to make the same mistake that Spain had made a century earlier and drive out an economically important part of its population, one whose productivity and mercantile network would make a substantial contribution to the flourishing of the Dutch Golden Age.

The Spinoza family was not among the wealthiest of the city's Sephardim, whose wealth was in turn dwarfed by the fortunes of the wealthiest Dutch. They were, however, comfortably well-off. Spinoza's father, Miguel, was an importer of dried fruit and nuts, mainly from Spanish and Portuguese colonies. To judge both by his accounts and by the respect he earned from his peers, he seems for a time to have been a fairly successful businessman.

Bento (or, as he would have been called in the synagogue, Baruch) must have been an intellectually gifted youth, and he would have made a strong impression on his teachers as he progressed through the levels of the community's school. He probably studied at one time or another with all of the leading rabbis of the Talmud Torah congregation, including Menasseh ben Israel, an ecumenical and cosmopolitan rabbi who was perhaps the most famous Jew in Europe; the mystically inclined Isaac Aboab da Fonseca; and Saul Levi Mortera, the chief rabbi of the congregation, whose tastes ran more to rational philosophy and who often clashed with Rabbi Aboab over the relevance of kabbalah, an esoteric form of Jewish mysticism.

Spinoza may have excelled in school, but, contrary to the story long told, he did not study to be a rabbi. In fact, he never made it into the upper levels of the educational program, which involved advanced work in Talmud. In 1649, his older brother Isaac, who had been helping his father run the family business, died, and Spinoza had to cease his formal studies to take his place. When Miguel died in 1654, Spinoza found himself, along with his other brother, Gabriel, a full-time merchant, running the firm Bento y Gabriel de Spinoza. He seems not to have been a very shrewd merchant, however, and the company, burdened by the debts left behind by his father, floundered under their direction.

Spinoza did not have much of a taste for the life of commerce anyway. Financial success, which led to status and respect within the Portuguese Jewish community, held very little attraction for him. By the time he and Gabriel took over the family business, he was already distracted from these worldly matters and was devoting more and more of his energies to intellectual interests. Looking back a few years later over his conversion to the philosophical life, he wrote of his growing awareness of the vanity of the pursuits followed by most people (including himself), who gave little thought to the true value of the goods they so desperately sought.

> After experience had taught me that all the things which regularly
> occur in ordinary life are empty and futile, and I saw that all the
> things which were the cause or object of my fear had nothing of
> good or bad in themselves, except insofar as [my] mind was moved
> by them, I resolved at last to try to find out whether there was any-
> thing which would be the true good, capable of communicating
> itself, and which alone would affect the mind, all others being re-
> jected—whether there was something which, once found and ac-
> quired, would continuously give me the greatest joy, to eternity.

He was not unaware of the risks involved in abandoning his former engagements and undertaking this new enterprise.

> I say that "I resolved at last"—for at first glance it seemed ill-advised
> to be willing to lose something certain for something then uncer-
> tain. I saw, of course, the advantages that honor and wealth bring,
> and that I would be forced to abstain from seeking them, if I wished
> to devote myself seriously to something new and different; and if by
> chance the greatest happiness lay in them, I saw that I should have
> to do without it. But if it did not lie in them, and I devoted my en-
> ergies only to acquiring them, then I would equally go without it.[9]

By the early to mid-1650s, Spinoza had decided that his future lay
in philosophy, the search for knowledge and true happiness, not in
the importing of dried fruit.

Around the time of his disenchantment with the mercantile
life, Spinoza began studies in Latin and the classics. Latin was still
the lingua franca for most academic and intellectual discourse in
Europe, and Spinoza would need to know the language for his
studies in philosophy, especially if he planned on attending any
university lectures. He had to go outside the Jewish community
for instruction in these disciplines, and found what he needed
under the tutelage of Franciscus van den Enden, a former Jesuit
and political radical whose home seemed to function as a kind
of salon for secular humanists, arch-democrats, and freethinkers.
(Van den Enden himself was later executed in France for his par-
ticipation in a republican plot against King Louis XIV and the
monarchy.) It was probably Van den Enden who first introduced

Spinoza to the works of Descartes, who would prove so important to Spinoza's philosophical development, and of other contemporary thinkers. While pursuing this secular education in philosophy, literature, and political thought at his Latin tutor's home, Spinoza seems also to have continued his Jewish education in the yeshiva (or academy) Keter Torah (Crown of the Law), run by Rabbi Mortera. It was probably under Mortera that Spinoza first studied Maimonides and other Jewish philosophers.

Although distracted from business affairs by his studies and undoubtedly experiencing a serious weakening of his Jewish faith as he delved ever more deeply into the world of pagan and gentile letters, Spinoza kept up appearances and continued to be a member in good standing of the Talmud Torah congregation throughout the early 1650s. He paid his dues and communal taxes, and even made the contributions to the charitable funds that were expected of congregants.

And then, on July 27, 1656, the following proclamation was read in Hebrew before the ark of the Torah in the crowded synagogue on the Houtgracht:

> The gentlemen of the *ma'amad* [the congregation's lay governing board] hereby proclaim that they have long known of the evil opinions and acts of Baruch de Spinoza, and that they have endeavored by various means and promises to turn him from his evil ways. But having failed to make him mend his wicked ways, and, on the contrary, daily receiving ever more serious information about the abominable heresies that he practiced and taught and about his monstrous deeds, and having numerous trustworthy witnesses who have reported and borne witness to this effect in the presence of the said Espinoza, they have become convinced of the truth of this matter.

The board, having consulted with the rabbis, consequently decided that the twenty-three-year-old Spinoza

> should be excommunicated and expelled from the people of Israel. By decree of the angels and by the command of the holy men, we excommunicate, expel, curse, and damn Baruch de Espinoza, with the consent of God, Blessed be He, and with the consent of the

entire holy congregation, and in front of these holy scrolls with the 613 precepts which are written therein; cursing him with the excommunication with which Joshua banned Jericho and with the curse which Elisha cursed the boys and with all the castigations which are written in the Book of the Law. Cursed be he by day and cursed be he by night; cursed be he when he lies down and cursed be he when he rises up. Cursed be he when he goes out and cursed be he when he comes in. The Lord will not spare him, but then the anger of the Lord and his jealousy shall smoke against that man, and all the curses that are written in this book shall lie upon him, and the Lord shall blot out his name from under heaven. And the Lord shall separate him unto evil out of all the tribes of Israel, according to all the curses of the covenant that are written in this book of the law. But you that cleave unto the Lord your God are alive every one of you this day.

The document concludes with the warning that "no one is to communicate with him, orally or in writing, or show him any favor, or stay with him under the same roof, or come within four cubits of his vicinity, or read any treatise composed or written by him."[10]

It was the harshest writ of *herem*, or religious and social ostracism, ever pronounced on a member of the Portuguese Jewish community of Amsterdam. The community leaders sitting on the *ma'amad* that year dug deep into their books to find just the right words for the occasion.[11] Unlike many of the other bans issued in the period, this one was never rescinded.

We do not know for certain why Spinoza was punished with such extreme prejudice. That the punishment came from his own community—from the congregation that had nurtured and educated him, and that held his family in high esteem—only adds to the enigma. Neither the *herem* itself nor any document from the period tells us exactly what his "evil opinions and acts" were supposed to have been, or what "abominable heresies" or "monstrous deeds" he is alleged to have practiced and taught. He had not yet published anything, or even composed any treatise. Spinoza never refers to this period of his life in his extant letters and thus does not offer his correspondents (or us) any clues as to why he was expelled.[12] All we know for certain is that Spinoza received, from the community's leadership in 1656, a *herem* like no other in the period.

Three relatively reliable sources, however, provide suggestive clues as to the nature of Spinoza's offense. According to the chronology of the events leading up to the *herem* provided by Jean-Maximilien Lucas, Spinoza's earliest biographer and writing just after Spinoza's death, there was much talk in the congregation about his opinions; people, especially the rabbis, were curious about what the young man, known for his intelligence, was thinking. As Lucas tells it, "among those most eager to associate with him there were two young men who, professing to be his most intimate friends, begged him to tell them his real views. They promised him that whatever his opinions were, he had nothing to fear on their part, for their curiosity had no other end than to clear up their own doubts."[13] They suggested, trying to draw Spinoza out, that if one read Moses and the prophets closely, then one would be led to the conclusion that the soul is not immortal and that God is material. "How does it appear to you?" they asked Spinoza. "Does God have a body? Is the soul immortal?" After some hesitation, Spinoza took the bait.

> I confess, said [Spinoza], that since nothing is to be found in the Bible about the nonmaterial or incorporeal, there is nothing objectionable in believing that God is a body. All the more so since, as the Prophet says, God is great, and it is impossible to comprehend greatness without extension and, therefore, without body. As for spirits, it is certain that Scripture does not say that these are real and permanent substances, but mere phantoms, called angels because God makes use of them to declare his will; they are of such kind that the angels and all other kinds of spirits are invisible only because their matter is very fine and diaphanous, so that it can only be seen as one sees phantoms in a mirror, in a dream, or in the night.

As for the human soul, Spinoza reportedly replied that "whenever Scripture speaks of it, the word 'soul' is used simply to express life, or anything that is living. It would be useless to search for any passage in support of its immortality. As for the contrary view, it may be seen in a hundred places, and nothing is so easy as to prove it."

Spinoza did not trust the motives behind the curiosity of his "friends"—with good reason—and he broke off the conversation as soon as he had the opportunity. At first his interlocutors thought he was just teasing them or trying merely to shock them by expressing scandalous ideas. But when they saw he was serious, they started talking about Spinoza to others. "They said that the people deceived themselves in believing that this young man might become one of the pillars of the synagogue; that it seemed more likely that he would be its destroyer, as he had nothing but hatred and contempt for the Law of Moses." Lucas relates that when Spinoza was called before his judges, these same individuals bore witness against him, alleging that he "scoffed at the Jews as 'superstitious people born and bred in ignorance, who do not know what God is, and who nevertheless have the audacity to speak of themselves as His People, to the disparagement of other nations.'"[14]

While some scholars doubt Lucas's reliability, his report is broadly consistent with an earlier account, given shortly after the *herem* but not discovered in the archives until the mid-1950s. Brother Tomas Solano y Robles was an Augustinian monk who was in Madrid in 1659, just after a voyage that had taken him through Amsterdam in late 1658. The Spanish inquisitors were interested in what was going on among the former New Christians now living in northern Europe, most of whom had once been in its domain and still had *converso* relatives—and business contacts—back in Iberia. They interviewed the friar, as well as another traveler to the Netherlands, Captain Miguel Pérez de Maltranilla, who had stayed in the same house in Amsterdam, and at the same time, as Brother Tomas. Both men claimed that in Amsterdam they had met Spinoza and a man named Juan de Prado, who had been banned by the Jewish community shortly after Spinoza. The two apostates told Brother Tomas that they had been observant of Jewish law but had "changed their mind," and that they had been expelled from the synagogue because of their views on God, the soul, and the law. They had, in the eyes of the congregation, "reached the point of atheism."[15] According to Tomas's deposition, they were saying that the soul was not immortal, that the law of Moses was "not true," and that there was no God except in a "philosophical" sense.[16] Maltranilla confirms that, according to Spinoza and Prado, "the law . . . was false."[17]

The Amsterdam Portuguese Jewish community poet-historian David Franco Mendes is the final witness on this matter. Although he was writing many years later than Lucas, his work undoubtedly represents a repository of communal record and memory. He insists, in his brief report on the case, that Spinoza not only violated the Sabbath and the laws governing the festivals but also was filled with "atheistic" ideas, and was punished accordingly.[18]

"God exists only philosophically," "the law is not true," "the soul is not immortal." These are rather vague and indeterminate propositions. Ordinarily there is no more telling what is intended by them than what is meant by the notoriously ambiguous charge of "atheism." But in Spinoza's case we have some fair basis for knowing what he would have meant, for they are likely just the views that he would at least begin elaborating and arguing for in his written works within five years of the *herem*. To be sure, we cannot be certain that what we find in those writings is exactly what he was saying within the community. But the report by Lucas and the testimony by Brother Tomas indicate that the metaphysical, moral, and religious doctrines that are to be found in his mature philosophical works were already in his mind, and apparently also on his tongue, in the mid-1650s.

According to Lucas, Spinoza took his expulsion in good stride. "All the better," he quotes Spinoza as saying, "they do not force me to do anything that I would not have done of my own accord if I did not dread scandal. . . . I gladly enter on the path that is opened to me."[19] By this point, he was certainly not very religiously observant, and must have had grave doubts about both the particular tenets of Judaism and, more generally, the value of sectarian religions. Besides the opportunity it afforded him to maintain the family business and earn a living, membership in good standing in the Portuguese community seems to have mattered little to him.

Within a couple of years, Spinoza had left Amsterdam. By 1661 he was living in Rijnsburg, a small village just outside Leiden, grinding lenses for a living and working on various elements of what he was then calling "my Philosophy." These included, in good Cartesian tradition, a treatise on philosophical method, the *Treatise on the Emendation of the Intellect*, in which Spinoza addresses some basic problems concerning the nature and varieties of human knowledge and the proper means to achieving true understanding, all in the context of a broad conception of what constitutes "the good" for a human being. He also composed around this time his *Short Treatise on God, Man and His Well-Being,*[20] which contains in embryonic form many themes and ideas that will reappear in more mature versions and in a more orderly and perspicuous format in his philosophical masterpiece, the *Ethics*. Spinoza did not finish these early works, and neither of them would be published in his lifetime. The *Short Treatise*, however, represents Spinoza's first serious attempt to lay out what he takes to be the metaphysics of God and nature, the proper conception of the human soul, the nature of knowledge and freedom, the status of good and evil, and the human being's relationship to nature and the means to true happiness.

Over the years, Spinoza kept up with his circle of friends in Amsterdam, who were soon asking him for an accessible general introduction to the philosophy of Descartes, on which they considered him an expert. Thus, in 1663, shortly after moving from Rijnsburg to Voorburg, a small village not far from The Hague, he composed for their benefit the only work he published in his lifetime under his own name, *Parts One and Two of the Principles of Philosophy of René Descartes Demonstrated According to the Geometric Method*. This was based on some tutorials on Descartes's *Principles of Philosophy* that Spinoza had been giving to a young man who was living with him for a time in Rijnsburg. In the written version, Spinoza re-presents the metaphysics, epistemology, and basic physics of Descartes's "textbook" of philosophy into a geometric method involving axioms, definitions, and demonstrated propositions. (By this point he had decided that the Euclidean format was the best way to present these parts of philosophy.) The *Principles* brought Spinoza fame as an expositor of Cartesian philosophy, and (quite misleadingly) even earned him a reputation as a leading Cartesian; this would later, as Spinoza's infamy grew, cause a good deal of trouble for Descartes's true followers.

The exposition of Descartes, however, was primarily a distraction for Spinoza from what, in the early to mid-1660s, was his main preoccupation, a rigorous presentation of his own highly original philosophical thoughts. Having aborted the *Short Treatise*, which clearly did not satisfy him, Spinoza took up his pen to begin what would be his philosophical masterpiece and one of the greatest works in the history of philosophy, the *Ethics*.

Still, in essence, a treatise on God, man, and his well-being, the *Ethics* was an attempt to provide a fuller, clearer, and more systematic layout in "the geometric style" for his grand metaphysical and moral project. When finished, many years later, Spinoza's five-part magnum opus would offer a rigorous demonstration of the way to human happiness in a world governed by strict causal determinism and filled with obstacles to our well-being, obstacles to which we are naturally prone to react in not entirely beneficial ways.

Spinoza begins the *Ethics* by arguing that at the most basic ontological level, the universe is a single, unique, infinite, eternal, necessarily existing substance. This is what is most real, and he calls it "God or Nature" (*Deus sive Natura*). Spinoza's God is not some transcendent, supernatural being. He—or, rather, It—is not endowed with the psychological or moral characteristics traditionally attributed to God by many Western religions. Spinoza's God does not command, judge, or make covenants. Understanding, will, goodness, wisdom, and justice form no part of God's essence. In Spinoza's philosophy, in other words, God is not the providential, awe-inspiring deity of Abraham. Rather, God just is the fundamental, eternal, infinite substance of reality and the first cause of all things. Everything else that is belongs to (or is a "mode" of) Nature.[21]

All things within Nature—that is, everything—are invariably and necessarily determined by Nature. There is nothing that escapes Nature's laws; there are no exceptions to its ways. Whatever is, follows with an absolute necessity from Nature's necessary universal principles (God's attributes). There are thus no purposes for Nature or within Nature. Nothing happens for any ultimate reason or to serve any goal or overarching plan. Whatever takes place does so only because it is brought about by the ordinary causal order of Nature. And because God is identical with the universal, active causal principles of Nature—the substance of it all—it follows that the anthropomorphic conception of God that, as Spinoza sees it, characterizes sectarian religions, and all the claims about divine reward and punishment that it implies, are nothing but superstitious fictions.

Spinoza then turns to the nature of the human being and its place in Nature. Nature, as infinite substance, has infinite attributes or essences, each constituting a kind of universal nature of things. We know of only two of these attributes: Thought (or thinking essence, the stuff of minds) and Extension (material essence, the stuff of bodies). The course of Nature is one, since Nature is one substance, a unity. But for just this reason it proceeds under each attribute in parallel coordination with its unfolding in every other attribute. Any individual thing or event is only a "mode" of Nature appearing under the different attributes. One and the same thing or event, then, manifests itself in Thought (as a mental or thinking thing or event), in Extension (as a material or bodily thing or event), and so on through the other attributes. Thus, the human mind and the human body are one and the same thing in Nature, manifesting itself under Thought and Extension, respectively. Their unity in a human being and the correlation of their respective states is a function of their ultimate metaphysical identity in Nature. The upshot is that human beings are as much a part of Nature as any other thing and do not inhabit some separate "dominion" in which they are exempt from its laws. Every individual, human or otherwise, is subject to the same causal determinism that governs all of Nature's events. This explains how Spinoza can propose to treat human thoughts, emotions, desires, and volitions "just as if it were a question of lines, planes, and bodies."[22]

Spinoza's account of human nature is accompanied by a psychology that reflects the various ways in which human beings are affected by the world around them and that investigates the striving to persevere in existence in the face of these external forces that characterizes human beings' (and any being's) essence. Human mental life is made up of various passions and actions. The former are our affective responses to the ways in which external objects causally impinge on us; the latter derive from our own inner resources. Both represent ways in which our powers are increased or decreased by the causal nexuses within which we exist. The picture of human life that emerges from Spinoza's catalogue of the passions is a tormented one in which a person is emotionally tossed about and at the mercy of things and forces beyond his or her control.

The remedy for such a life mired in the passions lies in virtue, that is, in the pursuit of knowledge and understanding. No human being can ever be entirely free from the passions, since all beings are necessarily a part of Nature and always subject to external influences. Human beings can, however, achieve some degree of autonomy and freedom from their turmoil to the extent that they are active and guided by reason and thereby acquire an understanding of the way in which everything in Nature must happen as it does, including acts of human volition. In this way, the power of the passive affects is at least diminished.

> Human power is very limited and infinitely surpassed by the power of external causes. So we do not have an absolute power to adapt things outside us to our use. Nevertheless, we shall bear calmly those things which happen to us contrary to what the principle of our advantage demands, if we are conscious that we have done our duty, that the power we have could not have extended itself to the point where we could have avoided those things, and that we are a part of the whole of nature, whose order we follow. If we understand this clearly and distinctly, that part of us which is defined by understanding, i.e. the

better part of us, will be entirely satisfied with this, and will strive to persevere in that satisfaction.[23]

The ideal of the free, rational individual presented in the *Ethics* provides a model for a virtuous human life liberated from various illusions and seeking what is truly in its best interest (as opposed to those things that merely cause transitory pleasure).

The highest form of knowledge, "as difficult as it is rare," is a thorough understanding of Nature and its ways. This includes an intellectual intuition of how the essence of anything (especially of oneself and all of one's mental and bodily states) follows from Nature's most universal elements—or, since God and Nature are one and the same, how the essence of anything relates to God. Spinoza concludes the *Ethics* with an examination of the ultimate benefits of such deep insight. The true rewards of virtue, he insists, lie not in some otherworldly recompense for an immortal soul. There is no such thing as personal immortality; it is a fiction used by manipulative ecclesiastics to keep us in a perpetual condition of hope and fear and thus control us. Rather, "blessedness" and "salvation" consist in the well-being and peace of mind that understanding brings us in this life. The virtuous person sees the necessity of all things, and is therefore less troubled by what may or may not come his way. He regards the vicissitudes of fortune with equanimity, and his happiness is not subject to circumstances beyond his control.

Spinoza worked on the *Ethics*—or, as he called it at this point, *Philosophia*—steadily for a number of years, through his move to Voorburg in 1663 and on into the summer of 1665. He appears to have had a fairly substantial draft in hand by June 1665. Indeed, he felt confident enough of what he had written so far to allow a select few to read it, and there were Latin and Dutch copies of parts of the manuscript circulating among his Amsterdam friends. He may even have contemplated publishing it in the near future.

By late 1665, however, in what seems an abrupt change of project, Spinoza put the *Ethics* aside to concentrate on more pressing matters, matters that required something more than metaphysical, epistemological, and psychological inquiry.

Chapter 2

The Theological-Political Problem

In the early spring of 1661, Henry Oldenburg, the corresponding secretary for the Royal Society in England, was on one of his periodic trips to the continent. He passed through Amsterdam and Leiden, visiting with old friends and making new contacts to broaden his already considerable circle of acquaintances and scientific collaborators. While in the Dutch Republic, he heard of a gifted young philosopher and lens grinder—and ostracized Jew—who used to live in Amsterdam but now resided in a small village just outside Leiden. His interest no doubt piqued, in part by what he must have heard about this fellow's work on lenses and the refraction of light, Oldenburg went out of his way to pay Spinoza a visit soon after he had settled in Rijnsburg. The two men shared many philosophical and scientific interests, including recent developments in chemistry and optics (they discussed, among other things, Robert Boyle's experiments), and soon a fruitful correspondence ensued. The first extant letters we have from Spinoza are an extended series of exchanges with Oldenburg in the fall of 1661. In one of his letters, the Englishman urges that the two of them "bind ourselves to one another in unfeigned friendship, and let us cultivate that friendship assiduously, with every kind of good will and service."[1]

Despite this initial ardor, the intervening years saw only occasional letters. Moreover, the assiduous cultivation of friendship was complicated by the Anglo-Dutch war that broke out in March 1665. Communication between London and Voorburg, where Spinoza was now living, was difficult. Still, in April of that year Oldenburg took the initiative once again and managed to get a letter across the North Sea, looking to renew the correspondence and expressing his hope that Spinoza was "alive and well and remembered your old Oldenburg." Interested in hearing how Spinoza's work on the *Ethics* was coming along, he was probably surprised to learn that his friend had put that treatise aside and taken on an entirely different project.[2] Writing from London in September 1665, there is some concern in his voice as he good-naturedly teases Spinoza about his decision to turn to new and potentially treacherous topics. "I see that you are not so much philosophizing as theologizing, if one may use such terms, for you are recording your thoughts about angels, prophecy, and miracles."[3] In his reply, Spinoza explains the reason for his change of plans.

> I am now writing a treatise on my views regarding Scripture. The reasons that move me to do so are: 1. The prejudices of theologians. For I know that these are the main obstacles that prevent men from giving their minds to philosophy. So I apply myself to exposing such prejudices and removing them from the minds of sensible people [*prudentiorum*]. 2. The opinion of me held by the common people, who constantly accuse me of atheism. I am driven to avert this accusation, too, as far as I can. 3. The freedom to philosophize and to say what we think. This I want to vindicate completely, for here it is in every way suppressed by the excessive authority and egotism of preachers.[4]

The *Ethics* is a very wide-ranging work. Its most profound and lasting contribution is perhaps in the realm of metaphysics. Through its rigorously demonstrated propositions and explanatory scholia, Spinoza proposes an audaciously radical rethinking of the nature of God, the cosmos, and the human being. However, the *Ethics* is also, even primarily, a work of moral philosophy. The metaphysics, theory of knowledge, and psychology of Parts One through Three pave the way for Spinoza's account of human freedom and virtue and the path to happiness. Spinoza's goal is to illuminate what constitutes the good life, how to achieve some degree of flourishing in a deterministic universe that is indifferent to human happiness. In this respect, and despite the evident impersonality of its style, the *Ethics* makes its appeal on a very personal and egoistic level. It is about what it means for any individual, motivated as all creatures are by self-interest and the will to persevere in existence, to reach a condition of well-being in this lifetime as he confronts a world of exterior forces, many of which oppose his own striving (*conatus*) for increased power.

Spinoza also broaches some questions of social ethics and political philosophy in the *Ethics*. Since all individuals, in the quest for survival and flourishing, are striving to maintain and even augment their own power, there will naturally be conflict, particularly when this striving is governed by the passions and directed at external goods coveted by others. People will experience envy, jealousy, love, hate, hope, and fear as they compete for the things they value. The virtuous person who is governed by reason, however, will not only see that these transitory goods contribute nothing to real happiness but will also recognize that his own well-being is best fostered when he is surrounded by other virtuous people who are living according to reason—that is, other people who know what the true goods are and pursue them, and who therefore are flourishing. Thus, he will act toward others in such a way that he benefits them and helps them move toward such an ideal condition. Nonetheless, the civil state is necessary, Spinoza argues, because not everyone in fact acts according to reason. To avoid a "state of nature," a hostile environment characterized by each person's unbridled pursuit of what he wants and what he believes (usually falsely) to be in his own best interest, and to increase the security of our possessions and even create the conditions for living better, more rational lives and achieving human perfection, individuals transfer many of their rights to a political authority that is charged with establishing and enforcing laws.

The *Ethics* is not really a treatise in political philosophy, however. Such topics are treated only briefly and superficially in Part Four. Spinoza is more concerned in this work with individual "salvation" and "blessedness," with what a person can do through his own devices to maximize his freedom (understood as rational autonomy, living according to the knowledge of what is truly good) and happiness. Indeed, Spinoza's view is that were all human beings rational, virtuous, and free, there would be no need for the state.

The *Theological-Political Treatise*, on the other hand, whose origins Spinoza was explaining to Oldenburg in the fall of 1665, is a very different kind of work. Like the *Ethics*, as well as almost all his correspondence, he wrote it in Latin. But the forbidding geometric presentation of his metaphysical-moral treatise has given way to something more recognizable, to a kinder, gentler style. It remains, in its own way, a rather difficult book. But as opposed to the dense Euclidean architecture of definitions, axioms, propositions, and demonstrations of the *Ethics*, the *Treatise* offers a more discursive and approachable presentation. Rather than spare deductive arguments aided by the occasional scholium, it relies on a variety of methods to make its points: biblical commentary, literary hermeneutics, historical inquiry, philology, empirical observation, philosophical and theological reflection, legal analysis, and both theoretical and practical political thinking. In the *Treatise*, Spinoza offers his understanding of the lessons of ancient Israelite history, considers the moral core of the teachings of Jesus, and speculates on the purposes of God's commandments, making it clear, albeit in a very careful way, that all of this has implications for the contemporary Dutch scene.

In short, the *Treatise* is no less broad in its ambitions than the *Ethics*, perhaps even bolder in its conclusions, and seemingly more open in drawing them. Spinoza's goal, as he states in the work's subtitle, is to show that "freedom of philosophizing can be allowed in preserving piety and the peace of the Republic; but that also it is not possible for such freedom to be upheld except when accompanied by the peace of the Republic and piety themselves." The *Treatise*, in other words, is an extended argument for freedom of thought and expression in the modern state, as well as for the separation of philosophy and religion as a means to such liberty. The end of philosophy is truth and knowledge, the end of religion is pious behavior, or "obedience." Reason, therefore, must not be the handmaiden of theology, or vice versa, and religion oversteps its bounds when it tries to limit intellectual inquiry and the free expression of ideas.

To achieve this polemical and highly political goal, Spinoza must do some serious debunking of various dogmatic pillars of the religious establishment. He needs to undermine or at least illuminate the true meaning of those fundamental principles that were used by manipulative ecclesiastics (especially in the Dutch Republic) to gain power over public and even private life. Thus, in the *Treatise* Spinoza offers a deflationary account of prophecy and miracles, reveals the superstitious beliefs that support sectarian religions, claims that rites and ceremonies have nothing to do with "true piety," and—perhaps most audaciously of all—argues that the Bible, perhaps the most powerful tool wielded by clerics to exercise control over their flocks, is nothing but a work of human literature, one composed over time by many authors, who often disagreed with one another.

Naturally, such a project would be troubling to many of Spinoza's seventeenth-century contemporaries. What made it even more worrisome, however, was the fact that the *Treatise*, while written in Latin, was, in its conception and style, a relatively accessible and therefore highly dangerous book. While the copious quotation and analysis of Hebrew passages in certain chapters would make some of Spinoza's arguments opaque to many educated (and skilled Latin) readers of the time, it would not have been too difficult to divine his overall message.

The *Ethics* was composed for a fairly narrow audience: philosophers, primarily, particularly those schooled in the Cartesian tradition (and including Spinoza's friends in Amsterdam who had studied his treatise on Descartes's *Principles of Philosophy*), but also the neo-Aristotelians and latter-day Scholastics, who occupied most of the positions on the university faculties in the Netherlands and elsewhere. They would have had the background necessary to understand the vocabulary of Spinoza's system (substance, attributes, modes, and so on) and the skills required to follow and evaluate the proofs for its propositions.[5] In fact, the doctrines of the *Ethics* constitute, in part, a demonstration that if one adopts the most fundamental categories of earlier metaphysics, shared by Aristotelians and Cartesians, and follows them to their ultimate logical conclusions, then one will be led inexorably to Spinoza's doctrines. Thus, the classical idea that substance is what "exists in itself and not in something else," if applied strictly and consistently, ultimately implies that there is only one substance, and it is God or Nature.

The audience for the *Treatise*, by contrast, while it includes philosophers, is much broader.[6] First, there are the theologians— not just those teaching on the university faculties but also the religious leaders of the Dutch Reformed Church (and would-be social and political leaders of the Dutch Republic). It is these doctrinal authorities whose "prejudices" are responsible for constricting the minds of citizens and whose strict moral policies would, if put into effect, constrict their everyday behavior as well. Just below them in the ecclesiastic hierarchy are the *predikanten*, the conservative Reformed foot soldiers, whose self-serving weekly sermons appeal to people's superstitious beliefs and manipulate their passions. These preachers are the ones who can inflame their congregants when the need arises—for example, to oppose a city's tolerant policies. Spinoza does at one point say that he does not "commend this treatise" to an ecclesiastic audience, "for I have no reason to expect them to approve it in any way," mainly because he knows "how deeply rooted in the mind are the prejudices embraced under the guise of piety."[7] He was certainly not naive enough to expect a friendly reception for the book among conservative Reformed leaders and clerics; indeed, he knew they would harshly attack it. But if Spinoza did not write the *Treatise* expressly for the Reformed theologians, he must have at least composed it with them partly in mind. He would have seen them as an educated and influential audience that would certainly read the book and possibly understand (if not accede to) its arguments. Perhaps he even nourished some small, maybe vain hope that it might have an effect—that they, like the philosophers, might "derive great profit" from it.[8]

More important, there are the Dutch regents, the Republic's relatively liberal elite who governed many of the cities and towns in the provinces. These scions of wealthy professional, manufacturing, and merchant families in Amsterdam and elsewhere had the political upper hand in the 1650s and 1660s and, through the States of Holland and the States General (a federal body to which the provincial states sent representatives), were responsible for something resembling national policy. They tended to resent ecclesiastic meddling in public affairs. They also generally favored a tolerant attitude in intellectual, cultural, and religious matters, and are among the "sensible" people, the *prudentiorum*, whom Spinoza, in his letter to Oldenburg, sees as the work's primary audience. Although in many respects still a conservative faction wedded to the political status quo from which they profited, members of the regent class would be sympathetic to much of the theological-political message of the *Treatise*. As we shall see, if Spinoza intends the work to have practical consequences for the way the Dutch Republic is governed—and particularly for the relationship between political and religious authority and the defense of religious and intellectual toleration—this is the camp he must enlist.

Finally, the lessons of the *Treatise* are directed at, to use Spinoza's own form of address, the "philosophical reader" (*philosophe lector*). This means the philosopher in the strict sense, of course, including members of university faculties and independent intellectuals, although Spinoza suspects they already know and recognize the importance of what he has to say. "I believe," he says at the beginning of the book, "the main points are adequately known to philosophers."[9] But the term also includes any learned reader who approaches the book without the prejudices that govern the minds of the multitude and make them condemn things impulsively. This is the person "who would philosophize more freely if he were not prevented by this one thought: that reason ought to serve as handmaid to theology."[10] A relatively open-minded individual, he is ready to engage seriously in philosophy once he is reassured that it does not undermine piety and threaten his salvation. He simply needs to learn that his love of God and respect for the Bible are perfectly consistent with, even independent of, the free inquiry into truth.

This category extends as well to Spinoza's own friends and their religious and philosophical fellow travelers in Amsterdam and elsewhere. Some of these individuals were true freethinkers, secular intellectuals who had little use for religion in any guise. Most, however, were fairly devout but (from the standpoint of the Dutch Reformed hierarchy) highly unorthodox in their religious views. They have been called *Chrétiens sans église*,[11] and belonged to some of the dissenting Reformed sects that flourished in the Netherlands in the seventeenth century. These Collegiants, Quakers, Anabaptists, and Mennonites were true religious reformers, and perhaps the most sympathetic audience for Spinoza's new work. They were opposed to the authoritarian hierarchy and dogmatic sectarianism of the official church and sought a more egalitarian and inward approach to spiritual matters. They shared the belief that true Christianity was nonconfessional. In their view, it consisted in an evangelical love for one's fellow human beings and for God, as well as an obedience to the original words of Jesus Christ, unmediated by any theological commentary. The Collegiants in particular, among whom Spinoza counted several close friends, insisted that beyond the few simple and general truths contained in Jesus' teachings, each individual had the right to believe what he or she wanted and no right to harass others for what they believed. Salvation was attained not through any superstitious rites or signs or by belonging to any organized cult but only by a heartfelt inner faith. The Collegiants had no use for pastors, and they rejected any doctrines of predestination as incompatible with Christian liberty. Anticlerical to the core, they sought to liberate Christianity from the restraints imposed on worship and deed by institutionalized religions. Moral action was, for most of these dissenting sects, more important than any set of dogmas. They had much to lose if the orthodox Calvinists—who had already effected a purge of the Dutch Reformed Church in 1618 with the condemnation of the Remonstrants at the Synod of Dordrecht—succeeded in increasing their influence and imposing their ways even further on Dutch society.

The *Treatise*, then, was intended for a diverse readership, one that included both the political leadership to which it is directly making its appeal and the religious dissenters and progressive intellectuals—actual and potential "philosophers"—who would benefit from the success of that appeal.

There is one group, however, for which the *Treatise* was definitely not intended: the masses. Or, at least, so Spinoza says.

> I know that the masses [*vulgus*] can no more be freed from their superstitions than from their fears. . . . I know that they are unchanging in their obstinacy, that they are not guided by reason, and that their praise and blame is at the mercy of impulse. Therefore I do not invite the common people to read this work, nor all those who are victims of the same emotional attitudes. Indeed, I would prefer that they disregard this book completely rather than make themselves a nuisance by misinterpreting it after their wont.[12]

Spinoza did not fully trust the ordinary public—the retail merchants, laborers, artisans, and tavern-keepers who made up a good part of the population of cities like Amsterdam. These citizens were governed too much by the passions. Even those who could read and understand the message of the *Treatise* would not be able to make a fair and balanced judgment of it.

The breadth of Spinoza's intended audience for the *Treatise* indicates his great ambitions for the work, but it also made his task a rather complicated, even dangerous one. Composed not only of political liberals and philosophical progressives, his audience ranged from atheists to pious believers, from democrats to monarchists. It was, above all, a Christian audience. Lest he alienate any segment of it, he had to be careful in how he made his points in a work intended to effect a radical rethinking and bring about serious theological-political change.

A theological-political treatise is, in many respects, a distinctly early modern (i.e., postmedieval) product. This is because the problem it addresses—the theological-political problem—arises in Europe with the greatest urgency at the political and religious crossroads of the sixteenth century. Early modern rulers sought to

use religion in the form of an official church to shore up their regimes and, through confessional uniformity, strengthen the bonds
among their subjects. There was nothing new in this, of course,
as it was a part of imperial and royal practice in late antiquity and
the Middle Ages. But the fifteenth and sixteenth centuries saw
a gradual transition from small kingdoms and principalities to
nation-states and the centralization of political power over larger
territories, while the Reformation introduced greater religious diversity (and division) among populations. This gave sovereigns all
the more reason to put religion in the service of political unity and
loyalty. As one historian writes, "a shared religion was supposed
to weld rulers and subjects together under the Divine Protection
that depended on an orderly religious life regulated by true doctrine, a well-ordered church organization, decent public worship,
and pious public conduct."[13]

The game had to be played carefully, however, and a proper balance struck. As useful as religion was for political purposes, a too
powerful church could become a hindrance, even a threat, to the secular regime as an alternative dominion within a dominion. Indeed,
by the mid-seventeenth century, and especially in a republic like the
Netherlands and a constitutional commonwealth like England, secular institutions began to grow suspicious of ecclesiastic encroachment on civic life. Dutch liberals, for example, while upstanding
members of the Reformed Church, were always on guard against
their conservative and more orthodox opponents seeking to make
the Republic a rigorously Calvinist state. At the same time, religious
authority, which in Europe had reached the pinnacle of its political
and social influence in the Middle Ages, now feared being marginal-
ized by an increasingly independent political authority. Church leaders saw themselves losing control over the lives of ordinary citizens.
The support and protection that an official religion enjoyed in a confessional state was welcome, but the clerics, jealous of political and
moral influence, also struggled to regain the upper hand.

These historical developments encouraged greater theoretical
attention to the role of religion in the state. In the competition
between civil and religious authority for state power, as well as for

the hearts and minds (and bodies) of the people, thinkers on both sides raised the question as to what ought to be the proper relationship between the theological and the political. Should the political be subservient to the theological, with a nation ultimately governed by its clerics and its laws restricted, even commanded, by theological principles? Or, on the other hand, should a polity's religious life, like its other aspects, be controlled by the secular authorities? Should the church rule the state or the state rule the church? Or should one have nothing whatsoever to do with the other?

The seventeenth century saw the publication of a number of important and influential treatises on the theological-political question. One such work, the poet John Milton's *Areopagitica* (*Hill of Ares*), published in England in 1644, was primarily a plea for freedom of speech and the press. But Milton feared that the harsh attacks against an earlier treatise in which he defended divorce, as well as Parliament's subsequent promulgation of a censorship law, were religiously motivated and instigated by ecclesiastic authorities (the law was indeed supported by English divines). This kind of church influence in public affairs and over the expression of ideas was much too papal for Milton's taste.

The theological-political question was particularly acute in a new nation like the Netherlands. Having recently liberated themselves from Spain's Catholic rule, the Calvinist provinces of the northern Low Countries not only continued to debate what form of government would be best for them but also had to decide what was going to be the place of religion in their society. Article thirteen of the Union of Utrecht (1579), which served as a kind of founding constitution for the Republic, explicitly stated that "every individual should remain free in his religion, and no man should be molested or questioned on the subject of divine worship." By the mid-seventeenth century, and especially in liberal cities like Amsterdam, Catholics, Jews, and other minority religious groups (such as Lutherans) were allowed to worship freely— if not always openly, at least with an understanding wink and without the kind of persecution that minority religions suffered elsewhere in Europe. The myth of the Dutch Golden Age as an era of openness for all faiths may be an exaggeration, but it is nonetheless true that the Republic was an unusual model of religious toleration in the period.[14] Still, the Reformed Church dominated Dutch life. It enjoyed enormous advantages over other confessions and constituted the Republic's privileged (if not official) denomination. Public worship, as well as public office, was for a long time limited to its members.

Pierre de la Court (or, in Dutch, Pieter van den Hove), a textile manufacturer in Leiden who would gain an international reputation for his political writings, was perhaps the most important Dutch writer before Spinoza to take on the theological-political question. His book, *The Interest of Holland* (published in 1662 in French and Dutch editions), was primarily an argument against the institution of stadholder, a province-wide leadership position and a holdover from the days when the Low Countries were governed in absentia by the Dukes of Burgundy. When held by the same person in several major provinces (which was usually the case), the stadholdership effectively centralized political power in the Republic, much like a monarchy. De la Court argued that peace and economic prosperity were best fostered not only by a decentralized, republican system of government but also by a separation of church and state. Indeed, the well-being of society, he insisted, required that the church—in this case, the Reformed leadership—keep to its proper sphere, the spiritual condition of its flock, and not be allowed any influence in the political arena. While De la Court believed that some supervision of minority confessions was necessary, he argued that freedom of religion was essential if the Republic was to flourish.[15]

Milton's pamphlet is subtle in its approach to the theological-political problem, and De la Court is focused primarily on the situation in the Netherlands. But there is nothing subtle or parochial about Thomas Hobbes's *Leviathan*. Published in English in 1651 (and in Dutch translation in 1667, and in a Latin edition in 1668), *Leviathan: The Matter, Forme and Power of a Common Wealth Ecclesiasticall and Civil* offers an extended examination of human nature, political society, and religious institutions, all undertaken to show that the most secure and powerful state is one in which power is granted to a single sovereign (preferably an individual monarch). Hobbes's account, as we shall see,[16] grounds the commonwealth in the psychology of human beings living in the state of nature, a precivil condition where anyone may do whatever he can to survive. Led by reason to seek means that will preserve their lives and secure their possessions, these individuals voluntarily enter into a covenant and transfer all their rights of self-defense to a sovereign. This sovereign, to fulfill such a role, should be all-powerful and have total control over the laws and institutions of the state. There are no freedoms other than those proclaimed by the sovereign.

Hobbes is concerned about the place of religion in the commonwealth he describes. This is because ecclesiastic institutions so often constitute a second (and allegedly higher) locus of power and loyalty in a state and thus threaten the unity that is essential to its survival. If the state is to enjoy both internal peace and a common defense against external enemies, there can be one and only one sovereign, and its authority must be absolute. There is therefore to be a "consolidation" of political and religious power in the civil sovereign.

> There are Christians in the dominions of several princes and states, but every one of them is subject to that commonwealth whereof he is himself a member, and consequently cannot be subject to the commands of any other person. . . . Temporal and spiritual government are but two words brought into the world to make men see double and mistake their lawful sovereign. It is true that the bodies of the faithful, after the resurrection, shall be not only spiritual, but eternal; but in this life they are gross and corruptible. There is, therefore, no other government in this life, neither of state nor religion, but temporal; nor teaching of any doctrine, lawful to any subject, which the governor, both of the state and of the religion, forbiddeth to be taught. And that governor must be one, or else there must needs follow faction and civil war in the commonwealth: between the Church and State . . . between the sword of justice and the shield of faith.[17]

The monarch's authority extends to religion within his domain, and he is to function as chief pastor to all citizens; he controls the outward practices of religion and the doctrines proclaimed to be faith. He owes fealty to no other authority, not even the pope. The alternative can lead only to divided loyalties and "great troubles."

Hobbes makes his case at great length, by considering both the grounds of political obligation and the roots of religion in human psychology. In this and other respects, *Leviathan* very closely resembles Spinoza's *Treatise*. The Englishman, like his Dutch counterpart, investigates the nature of prophecy and the truth about miracles, and he takes on the ever dangerous question of the status and interpretation of Scripture. His views on many issues are, from the perspective of a seventeenth-century divine and the loyal members of his congregation, highly unorthodox, even blasphemous. A materialist about nature and human beings, Hobbes goes so far as to deny that there can be such a thing as an "incorporeal substance," thereby ruling out not only incorporeal human souls but also an incorporeal God. Hobbes's tone is often mocking, and he clearly does not have much respect for sectarian religions, especially Catholicism.[18] Part Four of the book, titled "The Kingdom of Darkness," is not about the otherworldly domain of Lucifer but the realm of ecclesiastics in this life, "a confederacy of deceivers that, to obtain dominion over men in this present world, endeavor by dark and erroneous doctrines to extinguish within them the light, both of nature and of the gospel, and so to disprepare them for the kingdom of God to come."[19]

It is no wonder that so many of the attacks against Spinoza's *Treatise* also saw fit to include Hobbes's theological-political masterpiece among recent publications that should be seized and banned. As for Hobbes's own response to the *Treatise*, it is very telling. His early biographer tells us that he, the author of what is undeniably an extraordinarily bold book, was himself taken aback by Spinoza's audacity. The author of the *Treatise*, he said, "had outthrown him a bar's length, for he durst not write so boldly."[20]

Spinoza clearly read *Leviathan* (although it would had to have been the Dutch or Latin translation), as well as De la Court's *On the Interest of Holland.*[21] What he found in these works certainly inspired him and contributed to this thinking about the state, his view of religion, and his opinion of what needed to be done about clerical meddling in political affairs.

Spinoza does not begin the *Theological-Political Treatise* by directly addressing the theological-political question. But what he does have to say in the early chapters about a number of theological, religious, and historical matters lays the groundwork for his eventual conclusions about the proper relationship between political sovereignty and ecclesiastic power in the modern state.

The *Treatise* opens with a brief natural history of religion and an account of the psychology of traditional theism. Religion as we know it, Spinoza argues in the work's preface, is nothing more than organized superstition. Power-hungry ecclesiastics prey on the naïveté of citizens, taking advantage of their hopes and fears in the face of the vicissitudes of nature and the unpredictability of fortune to gain control over their beliefs and their daily lives. The preface of the *Treatise* both makes clear Spinoza's contempt for sectarian religions and opens the way for his reductive and naturalistic explanations of central doctrinal and historical elements of the Judeo-Christian traditions.

As we shall see, Spinoza begins his attack by targeting standard religious ways of thinking about prophecy, miracles, God's "election" of the Jewish people, and, above all, the Bible. The ancient prophets, Spinoza insists, were not especially learned or gifted individuals, and certainly not philosophers; rather, they were nothing more than charismatic figures with particularly vivid imaginations who were capable of inspiring others with their moral messages. And miracles, understood as supernatural divine interventions, are, strictly speaking, impossible. Every event has a natural cause and explanation, and the laws of nature, as the supreme expression of God's attributes, cannot possibly admit of any exceptions; the belief in true miracles is grounded in ignorance, not piety. As to the divine "vocation" of the Jews, Spinoza claims that it consists not in any special metaphysical or moral endowment but rather in an extended period of wise political organization and good fortune.

Perhaps Spinoza's boldest, most influential, and (to his contemporaries) most shocking conclusion in the *Treatise* is that Holy Scripture is, in fact, a work of human literature. It is not, therefore, necessarily a source of truth, although it is a useful tool for motivating obedience to God—that is, for leading the masses to moral behavior. Spinoza will go on to conclude that we therefore need to examine the Bible anew and find within it the doctrine of the "true religion," namely, the very basic moral imperative that we love others and live by justice and charity. Only then will we be able to delimit exactly what we need to do to show proper respect for God and obtain blessedness.

Spinoza believes that his analyses will contribute to undermining both the practical ability of religious authorities to control our emotional, intellectual, and physical lives and the theoretical justifications they employ for doing so. The lessons of the *Treatise*, if given a fair hearing and taken to heart by the leaders of the Republic, will also, in his view, pave the way for reinstating a proper and healthy relationship between the state and religion and thus create an environment conducive to the individual pursuit of virtue and well-being.

Spinoza may have had to put the *Ethics* aside in order to compose the *Treatise*, but this does not mean that he abandoned, even temporarily, that work's metaphysical and moral concerns. If there is one theme that runs throughout *all* of Spinoza's writings, it is the liberation from bondage, whether psychological, political, or religious. The *Treatise* and the *Ethics* are part of the same overall philosophical and political project: to liberate the minds of individuals from superstition and the lives of citizens from ecclesiastic authority. His goal is a tolerant democratic society of individuals whose deeds are guided by the true (moral) religion.

Both works are devoted to the pursuit of freedom, understood as autonomy or self-government. In the case of the *Ethics*, it is freedom from irrational passions such as hope and fear and the superstitious beliefs and actions to which they give rise. As one moves toward a condition of greater rationality, toward an adequate understanding of nature and one's place in it, the power of the passive affects diminishes and one becomes a more autonomous individual. What one does results less from the random way that external things happen to affect one and more from one's grasp of the truth about the world. The free individual described in the *Ethics* acts from knowledge, not emotion.

The *Treatise* is an extended plea for freedom in the civic realm: freedom of thought and expression, and especially freedom of philosophizing and freedom of religion (at least to the extent that it does not involve public activities). These latter two freedoms are most definitely not to be confused with each other: one regards the pursuit of truth, the other is about encouraging moral behavior. The argument of the *Treatise* proceeds by undermining the various means used by religious authorities to control people's minds and actions and to usurp power in the state.

The *Ethics* and the *Treatise* thus complement each other. To the extent that a person becomes more free as an individual and more rational in his beliefs, the less likely he is to fall prey to superstition and indenture himself to religious sectarians. And the more a state is liberated from ecclesiastic influence and governed by liberal democratic principles, the more freedom there will be for citizens to engage in philosophy and discover the truths that will liberate their minds. Both the *Treatise* and the *Ethics*, in working together to make this case, offer a profound critique of religion: the former from a theological, political, and historical perspective, the latter from a metaphysical and moral one.

Because the two works were composed around the same time—after completing the *Treatise* Spinoza went back to working on the *Ethics*—it is not surprising to find the doctrines of each reflected in the other. The political propositions in Part Four of the *Ethics*, for example, constitute a truncated version of the account of the state in the *Treatise*; it is unlikely that these propositions would have been formulated as they are without Spinoza in the interim having read Hobbes and written the *Treatise*. On the other hand, Spinoza's conception of God in the *Ethics* informs his explanation of divine providence in the *Treatise*: "God's decrees and commandments, and consequently God's providence, are in truth nothing but Nature's order."[22] The *Treatise*, in effect, draws out the theological, religious, and political implications of what the *Ethics* has established about God, nature, the human being, and society. What Spinoza wants to see is a politics of hope (for eternal reward) and fear (of eternal punishment) replaced by a politics of reason, virtue, freedom, and moral behavior. The *Treatise* and the *Ethics* each makes its own particular contribution to this goal.

It is thus not so much a new project that Spinoza has taken on in the summer of 1665 as a continuation of the same overall mission, although from a different direction and by different means. Indeed, among the many religious and political issues that he addresses in the *Treatise*—the status and interpretation of Scripture; the divine election of the Jewish people; the origins of the state; the nature, legitimacy, and bounds of political and religious authority; and the imperative for toleration—are ones that there is reason to believe were of concern to Spinoza as far back as the period of his ban from the Amsterdam Jewish community. The testimonies about his religious beliefs from around 1655–57, including the depositions by Captain Maltranilla and Brother Tomas, all mention views on Scripture that are, if the generally hostile witnesses are to be trusted, essentially those of the *Treatise*. And a long-lost *Apologia* (or *Defense*) for his "departure" from the Jewish religion that Spinoza allegedly wrote soon after the *herem*—described in one early report as a "dissertation against the Old Testament"—is said to have contained much of the material that later appears in the *Treatise*, including the denial of the divine origin of the Torah and claims about "the election of the Hebrew nation."[23] Thus, just as the *Ethics* represents Spinoza's attempt, after abandoning the *Short Treatise*, to give adequate expression to his metaphysical and moral ideas, so the *Theological-Political Treatise* offers a mature and extended articulation of the religious views that accompanied the loss of faith he experienced as a young man.

Unlike the cool and detached tone of the *Ethics*, however, the *Treatise* is a very passionate, even angry work. One cannot help but notice a zeal and an urgency subtly (and sometimes not so subtly) running through its chapters. This is because the *Treatise* is a response to recent developments that both touched him personally and, in his eyes at least, represented an ominous sign of deterioration in the Dutch Republic's commitment to its own fundamental principles. Dark clouds were forming on the political horizon in late 1665, and things would soon get much worse.

Chapter 3

Rasphuis

In the Middle Ages, much of the outermost wall of Amsterdam was surrounded by a canal. The Singel (girdle), as it was called, was a moat that protected the city from the west, south, and east. By the middle of the seventeenth century, when the municipality had expanded by reclaiming more land from the surrounding marshes in order to house its growing population, the Singel had become but the first of several concentric canals, or *grachten*, forming a broad series of belts around upscale neighborhoods.

The Singel begins at the bay from the Ij River and today follows a half-ring course that goes along Amsterdam's flower market and the famous red-light district. Just before it passes the Muntplein and ends by flowing into the Amstel River, it runs past a short, narrow street called the Heiligeweg. From 1596 until the middle of the nineteenth century, this street, whose two blocks stretch across the tip of one of the long islands making up the oldest part of the city, enjoyed some notoriety as the home of Amsterdam's house of correction, the Tuchthuis. Formerly the site of the Cloister of the Sisters of St. Clare—which had been cleansed of all Catholic traces in the great Calvinist iconoclasms of the sixteenth century—the Tuchthuis (literally "House of Correction") was a large rectangular building with an open central courtyard that, at least according to maps from the time, towered over surrounding houses.

One passed through two gates to get to the prison's inner yard. Above the ornate outer gate was a bas-relief by the sixteenth-century artist Hendrick de Keyser, "the Michelangelo of Amsterdam," showing a charioteer driving a wagon of timber and whipping a team of lions and other wild beasts. Above this frieze, engraved in stone, is a quotation from Seneca: *Virtutis est domare quae cuncti pavent*, "It is a virtue to tame those things of which all are afraid." (By the end of the seventeenth century, this would be crowned with an imposing sculpture group showing the Maid of Amsterdam, identified by the shield of the city in her hand, subduing two prisoners in chains. Beneath her is the motto *Castigatio*, "Punishment.")

The Tuchthuis was originally conceived not, in fact, to administer *castigatio* but as a house of moral correction and spiritual rehabilitation. The original proposal for its establishment stated that its aim should be "not sore punishment, but the improvement and correction of those who do not realize its usefulness to them and would try to avoid it."[1] The idea was to instill virtue among those members of the city's population who may have lost their way, especially "young people who had got on the wrong path and are headed for the gallows, so that they can be saved therefrom and kept at honest labor and a trade in the fear of God."[2] By the mid-seventeenth century, however, the Tuchthuis had become a place of punishing labor for all kinds of criminals and other deviants. Thieves, beggars, drunks, wifebeaters, and murderers all were confined within its walls. The prison did not discriminate on the basis of age or offense. Violent and nonviolent offenders, youthful pickpockets and old debtors, by the 1650s there were well over a hundred inmates, some as young as ten years. Only women were excluded; there was a separate house of correction for the city's female delinquents (including prostitutes).

The prison was more generally known, in Amsterdam and among the city's many foreign tourists (for whom it was a popular site to visit), as the Rasphuis. This nickname derived from one of the primary chores assigned to inmates: pulverizing (*raspen*) brazilwood to produce sawdust. It was backbreaking work involving a heavy, multibladed cross-saw. The prison had not completely abandoned its project of edification; manual labor was regarded as beneficial for the criminal soul, and over the inner gate leading to the courtyard was a life-size sculpture depicting two half-naked prisoners sawing wood. (The women's prison became known as the Spinhuis because spinning wool was believed to have a restorative effect on the female character.) There was also good economic sense behind this particular toil. The city had granted the institution a monopoly on brazilwood powder, whose bright color made it useful for producing pigment dyes for the textile industry.

Rasping was but one of the varieties of toil to which the prisoners were sentenced. The regents of the Rasphuis were also not averse to more severe means of correction, including deprivation of food, corporal punishment (especially whipping), and even prolonged torture.

In September 1668, among the more unfortunate prisoners languishing in the cells of the Rasphuis was Adriaan Koerbagh, a thirty-five-year-old lawyer and medical doctor who lived on the Oude Nieuwstraat. Koerbagh came from a good if not particularly prosperous family—his father was in the ceramics trade—and he was, at least nominally, a member of the Dutch Reformed Church.[3] He had fallen afoul of the religious and civil authorities, however, and received an unusually severe punishment. Unaccustomed to the harsh conditions of the prison and probably already suffering from illness when delivered to its gates, he would not survive long enough to serve even one-tenth of his full sentence.

Two years earlier, Adriaan and his younger brother Johannes, a Reformed preacher, had been interrogated by the Amsterdam consistory. Johannes was, with good reason, considered to be harboring unorthodox, even heretical opinions, while Adriaan was regarded as leading a life of debauchery, in part because he had fathered a child out of wedlock. The consistory grilled Johannes on his beliefs about God and other matters and gave Adriaan a warning about his immoral behavior. While there continued to be suspicion around the brothers, no action was taken at that time. In February 1668, however, around the same time that Johannes was once again called before his ecclesiastic superiors to answer for his antitrinitarian views, Adriaan went ahead and published *Een Bloemhof van allerley lieflijkheyd* (A Flower Garden Composed of All Kinds of Loveliness). In this book, Adriaan, perhaps the more politically engaged (and intemperate) of the Koerbagh brothers, and who had an interest in the history and usage of the Dutch language, undertook to set forth his anticlerical views under the guise of a lexicon that clarified foreign words that had crept into the legal, medical, devotional, and colloquial vocabularies of Dutch. His intention was clearly to criticize, even mock, nearly all organized religions, including the Dutch Reformed variety, and his tone alternates between sarcasm and contempt. He took particular delight—and probably not too much to the displeasure of Calvinists—in deriding what he saw as the superstitions of Catholicism.

> Altar: A place where one slaughters. Among those of the Roman Catholic faith, they are even holy places, where priests daily celebrate the divine service. But it no longer consists in the slaughter of animals, as among the Jews or pagan, but in a more marvelous affair, that is, in the creation of a human being. For they can do what even God cannot do, at any hour of the day: make a human creature from a small piece of wheatcake. This piece of cake remains what it was beforehand, and they give it to someone to eat while saying it is a man—not simply a man, but the God-Man. What an absurdity![4]

Throughout all of Koerbagh's writings there is, underneath the ridicule, a serious metaphysical theology and a philosophy of religion that he shared with other radical figures of the time. Among other things, Koerbagh denied the divine authorship of the Bible. It is, he insisted, a work of human literature, compiled from a variety of other writings by "Esdras" (Ezra). And the proper method for interpreting the meaning of Holy Scripture is, as for any book, a naturalistic one that relies mainly on its language and on the historical context of its authors and texts. For grasping the *truth* contained in Scripture, on the other hand, nothing more is needed than human reason.

> Bible: . . . In general, a book, of any sort, including the story of Renard [the fox] or Eulenspiegel. . . . One cannot know who the

authors of the Jewish writings were. Among the most famous theologians, some think that a certain Esdras compiled them from other Jewish writings. . . . Meanwhile, there is, in Scripture, something that is certain and that agrees with reason, the sole thing that I hold as scripture, and that must have served for the composition of other writings. But the rest is, for us, useless and vain, and can be rejected without difficulty.[5]

Both in the *Bloemhof* and in a book he composed later that same year but never got the chance to publish, *Een Ligt schijnende in duystere plaatsen* (A Light Shining in Dark Places), Koerbagh attacked the irrationality of most religions, with their superstitious dogmas, rites, and ceremonies. The real teaching of God, the "true religion," is simply a knowledge of and obedience to his word and a love of one's neighbor. Fearlessly inviting the charge of Socinianism—an antitrinitarian movement that initially enjoyed a strong following in Poland but slowly made inroads across Europe—Koerbagh denied that Jesus was literally divine. God, he argued, is one, being nothing but the eternal substance of the universe. Indeed, God, on Koerbagh's view, is identical with nature itself understood as a necessary and deterministic system. Miracles, considered as divinely caused departures from the laws of nature, are thus impossible, and divine providence is just the ordinary course of nature.[6]

Koerbagh seems not to have been a particularly religious man. He was a committed rationalist, and believed that human flourishing was achieved through the exercise of natural reason. While he maintained a God-oriented conception of human happiness, it was a fairly reductive one. He argued that our *beatitudo* is found in the knowledge of God. But this apprehension of the divine is not some mystical insight of a supernatural being; rather, it is reason's intellectual grasp of the eternal, immutable reality that is nature itself. On this basis, Koerbagh argued against irrational theology, superstitious religious practices, and ecclesiastic repression. True religion, he insisted, is an inner, personal matter.

In the political domain, Koerbagh was a radical democrat and secularist. He believed strongly in the virtues of a tolerant, liberal republic and warned of the dangers of the usurpation of state power by church authorities. In Koerbagh's ideal commonwealth, there is a well-defined boundary between the public and private domains, and politics and religion are to be kept separate. He was also in favor of a decentralized state. In a pamphlet published in 1664, he argued (like De la Court before him) against consolidating political power in the Dutch Republic in the hands of a stadholder and presented the case for a federation of sovereign and autonomous provinces, as well as for the subordination of ecclesiastic to civil authority.[7]

None of this was to the liking of Amsterdam's Reformed leaders. Ordinarily, there was little they could do besides complain to the secular authorities—they did not have the power to incarcerate anyone; and, unlike his brother, Adriaan was not a member of the clergy whom they could discipline. Moreover, such complaints often fell on deaf ears. The regents of Amsterdam, frequently at loggerheads with the more conservative leaders of the consistory and recognizing the economic benefits of the city's liberal and tolerant cosmopolitanism, were reluctant to punish people for their political or religious ideas. Their typical response was that those who held heretical views could not be penalized if they did not publish or otherwise publicly proclaim their ideas. According to one magistrate, "in our country, in the absence of public gatherings or writings, we do not take much interest in the opinions that people hold with respect to the church."[8] In 1665, the members of the city council dragged their heels when urged by the consistory to put an end to the assembly of a local group of Collegiants who were meeting in a private home; two years after the local pastors had complained, the meetings were still taking place, "more numerous and more often than before."[9]

Koerbagh had made a critical mistake, however. He not only published his blasphemous views, he did so in Dutch, and thus made them readily accessible to the general (and impressionable) public. He also made it easier for the church authorities to pursue him—and harder for the civic authorities to feign indifference—by putting his name on the book's cover. This time the consistory pushed hard. The Amsterdam city council was again reluctant to get too deeply involved in theological matters. They ordered copies of the book to be seized, but handed prosecution of the affair over to the city sheriff, Cornelis Witsen. Johannes, who was initially believed to have had a hand in writing both the *Bloemhof* and *Een Ligt*, was arrested; he was later released when the judges concluded that he, while not abjuring his views and probably sympathetic to the ideas in those works, was not the author of either treatise. Adriaan had already gone into hiding in Leiden (reportedly disguised with a black wig). He was betrayed by a "friend," however, who had found his attacks on religion offensive (and who also had an interest in the bounty of fifteen hundred guilders being offered). By July, Adriaan was back in Amsterdam, in chains and under close guard.

After a series of interrogations, Koerbagh confessed not only to being the sole author of the books in question but also to denying the divinity of Jesus and the virginity of Mary. "We do not really know who was, in truth, the father of this Savior (Jesus). That is why some ignorant people have affirmed that it was God, the God of eternity, and a son of the God of eternity, and that he was born of a virgin without the intervention of man. But these theses, too, are foreign to Scripture and contrary to the truth."[10] The city magistrates handed down their decision: Adriaan Koerbagh was to be sent to prison for ten years; afterward, he was to be banished from Amsterdam for another ten years, as well as pay a fine of four thousand guilders.[11] This was, in fact, somewhat more lenient than the punishment recommended by Sheriff Witsen, who wanted to see Koerbagh publicly tortured by having his right thumb cut off and his tongue pierced by a hot iron, followed by thirty years in prison.

Koerbagh actually spent less than two months, in the fall of 1668, in the Rasphuis. He was probably confined in the "private section" reserved for the sons of good families and those guilty of ideological or political offenses.[12] While these privileged prisoners were spared hard labor, Koerbagh was still clearly suffering. He was ill, and so was moved to Het Willige Rasphuis, another prison in the city that had more tolerable conditions and an infirmary. Koerbagh's health did not improve, however, and on October 5, 1669, just a few days after a visit by a pastor concerned for the state of Koerbagh's soul, his body gave out. He was buried in the Nieuwe Kerk.

Spinoza was deeply touched by Koerbagh's death. Both brothers were members of the philosophical circle in Amsterdam with which Spinoza kept in touch from Voorburg. Its progressive members discussed, among other things, Spinoza's own writings (including the manuscript of the *Ethics*). The Koerbaghs may, in fact, have been among the most radical in this group on religious and political questions. But·Spinoza and Adriaan were also good friends. They most likely met in Leiden in the late 1650s or early 1660s, when Adriaan was studying medicine at the university and Spinoza was living in nearby Rijnsburg. Koerbagh and Spinoza may have both attended the lectures on Descartes being given there by Johannes de Raey, a professor in the medical faculty. They also had several close acquaintances in common, including Franciscus van den Enden, Spinoza's erstwhile tutor in Latin and philosophical topics.

By the mid-1660s, Spinoza and Koerbagh seem to have developed an intimate, mutually influential intellectual relationship. Spinoza shared Koerbagh's political views and his attitude toward organized religion. And there is an unmistakable strain of Spinoza's metaphysical doctrines, as these are found in the *Ethics*, in Koerbagh's ideas about God and nature. As we shall see, Spinoza's *Theological-Political Treatise* also has much in common with Koerbagh's opinions on the state and on Scripture; these were topics which the two men must have discussed at length on many occasions.[13] Koerbagh and Spinoza were, on philosophical, theological, and religious questions, kindred spirits.

This appears to have been something intuited by the authorities. By 1668, Spinoza's own radical thinking, including his ideas

about the Bible, was sufficiently well known and worrisome—
even though the only thing he had published up to this point was
his critical exposition of Descartes's *Principles*—that Koerbagh's
interrogators pursued his possible connections to the excommunicated Jew. When questioned about who shared his opinions,
Koerbagh replied, rather implausibly,

> No one, to his knowledge. He added that he had not spoken about
> them with [Abraham] Van Berckel [another friend of Spinoza's
> and the Dutch translator of Hobbes's *Leviathan*] nor with anyone
> else, not even with Spinoza or with his brother. . . . He admitted to
> having spent some time with Spinoza, to having gone to his home
> on different occasions, but he had never spoken of this affair with
> him. . . . The accused admitted to having had relations with Van
> Berckel and others, but affirms that he never spoke of this doctrine
> with Spinoza.[14]

When Koerbagh died in late 1669, Spinoza lost a good companion, a philosophical and political fellow traveler, and an intrepid
ally in his campaign against sectarianism and superstition. It was
not merely a personal tragedy, however. He also saw Koerbagh's
incarceration as a betrayal of the ideals of Amsterdam and the
principles of the Dutch Republic.

For many years, the United Provinces of the Netherlands enjoyed
just the kind of decentralized federation favored by Koerbagh.
When William II, the stadholder of Holland and other major
provinces, died suddenly in 1650, a "Great Assembly" was called
to debate the political future of the republic. Johann de Witt,
at the time the town pensionary of Dordrecht and thus its permanent deputy to the States of Holland, argued forcefully at the
gathering for eliminating a quasi-monarchical office that, in the
view of many, was nothing but a medieval relic. Three years later,
the Republic's major stadholdership was still empty. After the res-
ignation of the sitting grand pensionary of the States of Holland,

Jacob Cats, and then the death of his immediate successor, Adriaan Pauw, De Witt found himself occupying the highest and most influential political office in the land.

De Witt, perhaps the most important political personality of the Dutch Golden Age, was a true republican. He was devoted to the Netherlands as a constitutional federation without any centralized, all-powerful office whose authority extended throughout many provinces (although he was willing to let each province decide for itself whether or not to appoint a stadholder). In De Witt's view, the governing bodies of the Republic's towns and provinces—the city councils and the provincial states—had the right to choose anyone they wished for local and provincial office and to represent them at the federal level in the States General. Ushering in the period known as the "True Freedom," after nearly a century of stadholders, De Witt pressed for the devolution of Dutch politics. Each province was to be sovereign over its own affairs. The States General should exercise only those powers granted to it by the Union of Utrecht: waging war and making international treatises. All other powers belonged properly to the provincial states, each of which in turn derived its powers and prerogatives from the towns that sent it their deputies.

Along with this devolution of state power came a general (but not absolute) toleration in the social, cultural, intellectual, and religious domains. While not quite willing to proclaim "Let a hundred tulips bloom!," De Witt was reluctant to impose the kind of oversight and censorship demanded by his conservative opponents. He was himself a talented mathematician and a proponent of the new science of the sort pursued by such contemporaries as Descartes, Huygens, and Anton van Leeuwenhoek. He defended the freedom to philosophize, within limits, when he intervened in the university debates over Cartesianism in 1656 and forestalled attempts by the academic old guard to forbid the teaching of any philosophy other than that of Aristotle. De Witt also favored freedom of religious belief and expression, while insisting on respect for the preeminence of the Reformed faith over all others. De Witt's policies represented the relatively progressive values of the merchant and professional class that supported him; they were policies that he believed were most conducive to Dutch flourishing.

De Witt was not a democrat, however. Like other members of the regent class, he was wedded to the self-perpetuating oligarchic system in which true power was in the hands of Dutch society's wealthy elite families. And his commitment to religious and philosophical toleration, impressive as it was, had its limits. He was not willing to do away with all censorship and practical restraints on intellectual and religious dissent. The grand pensionary had a very clear vision of the limits beyond which authors were expected not to trespass. De Witt's commitment was, above all, to the security, political stability, and economic prosperity of Holland and the other provinces, and not necessarily to abstract political ideals.

Still, radical democrats like Spinoza and Koerbagh, who were extreme secularists and defenders of an extensive conception of liberty, were natural political allies of De Witt and his "States" faction against their "Orangist" opponents, who favored the return of the stadholder system and more centralized rule. (The term "Orangist" derives from the fact that the stadholders, from William the Great on, were traditionally members of the House of Orange.) Spinoza and De Witt stood on the same side of the great ideological divide that characterized Dutch society in the seventeenth century. Spinoza was a true believer in the True Freedom, if a guarded one. He knew the pressures that De Witt was under, particularly when the Dutch Republic was at war with England in the late 1660s and the Orangists were clamoring for a stadholder to serve as military (and, by implication, political) leader. And he probably regarded with nervousness the compromises that De Witt had to make to keep the domestic peace.

There was a religious dimension to these deep and principled political differences in the Dutch Republic. The States faction favored a relatively secular commonwealth. While the regents who, during De Witt's tenure, governed the cities and provinces were for the most partisans if not formal members of the Dutch Reformed Church, they did not think that the state and society, including foreign policy, should be determined according to the rigorous Calvinist principles preached from the altar. They tended to resent political and cultural meddling by the *predikanten*, whose power they wished to see limited to the ecclesiastic sphere. The Orangist camp, by contrast, found great support among the more orthodox (and more intolerant) Reformed clergy. The pastors known as "Voetians"—so-called because they were inspired by Gisbertus Voetius, the firebrand rector of the University of Utrecht—especially were chafing against the limitations that the State's party, under the True Freedom, sought to impose on their authority. They decried the lack of "godliness" and moral fiber in everyday lifestyles, as well as the lax observance of the Sabbath. The Lord's Day, they argued, was for rest and prayer, not ice-skating parties along the rivers. The call for the reinstatement of a stadholder from the House of Orange—in particular William III, nephew to Charles II of England—was strong within this segment of the Church, which expected such a leader to be sympathetic to its socio-religious aims and willing to work against the States of Holland and the overly tolerant (and therefore theologically suspect) regents who controlled it.

To be sure, there were liberals among the clergy who supported—and in turn were supported by—De Witt and his program. These "Cocceians" (who took their lead from the principles of Johannes Cocceius, a professor of theology at the University of Leiden) resisted the "Calvinization" of everyday life and, conversely, the politicization of the church. Cocceians favored a true separation of church and state, and saw the States party leaders as allies who would help check the growing influence—within the Reformed Church, as well as within society at-large—of the more conservative clergy. Among the views that so inflamed their Voetian opponents was the idea that a strict observance of the Sabbath, including abstinence from work, was no longer necessary. (At one point, the controversy between Cocceians and Voetians over Sabbath protocol had reached such a ferocious level—"wretched disputes and growing dissension which have weighed so oppressively on the churches in these provinces, through the publications of professors and preachers regarding the observance of the Lord's Day"—that the States of Holland had to intervene and order an end to all discussion of the issue.)[15]

Cocceians also argued for a separation between philosophy and theology. They took a nonliteral approach to Scripture, and tended to be supporters of Descartes's followers in the universities and their progressive scientific program. The Cartesians claimed that just as philosophers must not presume to pronounce on theological matters, so theologians should remain quiet when it is not a question of an article of faith and allow the philosophers and scientists freedom to pursue their inquiries through reason alone.

For De Witt's faction, the separation of the two disciplines—and, within the universities, between the two faculties, Arts and Theology—was especially important for reducing the influence of the theologians. To limit their sphere of control, it was necessary to support, and even expand, the freedom to philosophize. If philosophy and theology were kept distinct, then there would be clear and well-defined boundaries beyond which theologians must not tread. The Voetians, by contrast, argued that if theology were not placed above philosophy and allowed to exercise control over the realm of ideas, then eventually philosophy would subordinate theology. The resulting freethinking, they insisted, would lead only to an increase in blasphemies and heresy.

Adriaan Koerbagh's treatment by the Amsterdam magistrates at the instigation of the local consistory represented a small but significant victory for the *predikanten*. A man was to be incarcerated and then banished from the city—a city whose alias on the title page of many early modern books published there was "Eleutheropolis," or "City of Freedom"—because of his ideas! For Spinoza and like-minded thinkers, conscious of all the stress that the young Republic was under, including the menace of foreign enemies, this was an ominous sign of things to come. Freedom to philosophize—about God, nature, and human flourishing—was under threat, primarily because the civil authorities had given in to pressure from the ecclesiastic realm. And things would only get worse. Within two years of the publication of the

Theological-Political Treatise, De Witt would be brutally assassinated by a rabid mob and William III installed as stadholder. The days of the True Freedom were numbered.

Something else was worrying Spinoza in the mid-1660s when he put aside his metaphysical and moral treatise and turned to theological-political matters. It started out as a local affair among his Calvinist neighbors but it threatened to grow into something more dangerous for him personally.

Things were not always quiet in the rustic little hamlet of Voorburg. In 1665, just as Spinoza was finishing a draft of the *Ethics*, a dispute broke out in the local church over who would succeed Jacob van Oosterwijck as preacher. A man from Zeeland named Van de Wiele had the support of the congregation's nominating committee, the diocese's bishop, and a group of liberal members— including some Collegiants. On the other side stood the congregation's more orthodox faction. These conservatives accused the nominating committee of deliberate provocation in naming Van de Wiele, whom they presumably found too liberal for their tastes, and appealed to the city magistrates of Delft to seat their own candidate for pastor.

From the conservatives' petition to the Delft authorities, it appears that they believed Spinoza to have been a partisan of, even the moving force behind, their liberal opponents. While there was probably little truth to this suspicion, since it is hard to believe that Spinoza would have been willing to get involved in church business, he nevertheless was known to associate with the local Collegiant group. As a result, in the minds of many of his Reformed neighbors in Voorburg, Spinoza, that man "born of Jewish parents," now had a reputation. He was, even more so than his alleged liberal accomplices in this affair, a danger to society: "[He] is now (so it is said) an atheist, or someone who mocks all religions and thus surely is a harmful instrument in this republic, as many learned individuals and preachers can attest."[16]

Spinoza was always deeply offended by the accusation that he was an atheist, particularly if the charge meant, as his Voorburg opponents claimed, that he "mocks all religions." Spinoza did not oppose *all* religions, only those that were led by ambitious clergymen and that introduced divisive sectarian loyalties into society. In reply to one correspondent's accusation that Spinoza has "renounced all religion," Spinoza writes, "Does that man, pray, renounce all religion who declares that God must be acknowledged as the highest good, and that he must be loved as such in a free spirit? And that in this alone does our supreme happiness and our highest freedom consist?"[17] Spinoza's philosophy does rule out an anthropomorphic God and the providential theology of the Judeo-Christian traditions that, in his view, follows from it. But, he insists, he certainly does believe in what he calls the "true religion," that is, the basic rational moral principles that lead to human flourishing, to "blessedness" and "salvation."

Despite Spinoza's protests, the label stuck. And his sensitivity to the charge of atheism was one of the motivating factors behind his decision to put aside the *Ethics* for a while in order to compose a treatise on theological and political matters. As we have seen, this much is clear from his September 1665 letter to Oldenburg, in which he lays out the reasons for "writing a treatise on my views regarding Scripture." Among other concerns—combating "the prejudices of theologians," and defending "the freedom to philosophize and to say what we think" from being "suppressed by the excessive authority and egotism of preachers"—he includes "the opinion of me held by the common people, who constantly accuse me of atheism. I am driven to avert this accusation, too, as far as I can."[18]

The *Theological-Political Treatise* is a public-minded book. Much more so than the *Ethics*, it is grounded in an immediate, very concrete, and potentially dangerous situation. Its arguments are directed at a broad audience that, Spinoza hopes, shares his concerns about the political future of the Republic and the place of religion in Dutch society.

Spinoza fully appreciates the advantages that he and others enjoy by living in the Netherlands: "We have the rare good fortune to live in a commonwealth where freedom of judgment is fully granted to the individual citizen and he may worship God as he pleases, and where nothing is esteemed dearer and more precious than freedom."[19] There must be a good deal of irony in this statement, given the treatment recently given to Koerbagh. If the Dutch Republic were really as free as Spinoza here pretends, then there would have been no need to write the *Treatise*. Still, there can be no doubt that Spinoza also recognizes that Holland allows its citizens more freedom than anywhere else in Europe (much as Socrates recognized, as Athens was putting him to death, that there was no other city-state where he could have enjoyed the philosophical life to such a degree). He is, however, worried about the growing influence of ecclesiastic authorities in civic affairs and about the weakening of De Witt's True Freedom and the threat to his nation's republican and tolerant traditions. But the *Treatise* also a very personal book. It is a response to the loss of a dear friend, and his reply to what he perceived to be the calumnies increasingly being leveled against him.

Chapter 4

Gods and Prophets

The Wars of Religion that ravaged Europe in the aftermath of the Reformation may have been over by the middle of the seventeenth century, at least according to signed treaties and various social-political accommodations, but their repercussions extended for many more decades. Political rivalries among the superpowers of the period—especially France, England, Spain, and the Netherlands—were stoked by religious differences, and vice versa. It seems that the only thing Catholics, Anglicans, Lutherans, and Calvinists agreed on was that the real threat to society and the souls of its members lay in "godless" works such as Spinoza's *Theological-Political Treatise* and Hobbes's *Leviathan*.

To the charge that he was an irreligious man, a dangerous atheist whose goal was to subvert piety and morality, Spinoza believed he had a ready philosophical response. Like the *Ethics*, the *Treatise* is a defense of what Spinoza considers "true religion." As we shall see, this turns out to be a simple code of moral behavior accompanied by an understanding of what constitutes the best condition for a human being and how to achieve it. However, rather than rigorously establishing by geometric demonstration the metaphysical, cognitive, and ethical grounds of authentic piety (the love of God), as he does in the *Ethics*, Spinoza approaches the issue in the *Treatise* by considering in a critical manner what passes for religion among his contemporaries. His focus is especially on the major organized religious traditions that seem to have been a source not of peace and happiness but of strife and misery throughout history (and especially in early modern Europe). Thus, more so than the

Ethics, the *Treatise* is a polemical work that addresses the historical, psychological, textual, and political foundations of traditional or popular religion.

The religions that Spinoza is primarily interested in, of course, are Christianity and Judaism, two of three major Abrahamic traditions. Since the final expulsion of the Muslims from Spain in the fifteenth century, Christianity governed the spiritual (not to mention the worldly) life of Western Europe. And while Jews were still officially banned from many European countries for most of the seventeenth century (including England, France, and Spain), significant Jewish communities existed in Italy, the Netherlands, and the German lands, as well as in Central and Eastern Europe. These traditions, he explains in the preface to the *Treatise*, where he offers a brief natural history of religion, are basically nothing but organized superstition. They are grounded not in reason but in ignorance and the emotions—in particular, the passions of hope and fear.[1]

A particular feature of life for human beings in this world that has been consistently remarked upon by philosophers and poets since antiquity is the role that fortune plays in our happiness. We do not have very much control over the conditions of our existence, and particularly whether various goods and evils come our way. It is generally not up to us whether we shall have prolonged enjoyment of the people to whom we are attached and the external things we value. Death quickly robs us of a loved one, while wealth or honor gained one day is easily lost the next. Moreover, the pursuit of the goals we set ourselves and hope to accomplish is often frustrated by circumstance. In short, the world poses innumerable and often unpredictable obstacles to our well-being, and the achievement of happiness and a good life is subject to good and bad fortune. Even if one should be fortunate enough to obtain some degree of satisfaction, there is no guarantee that it will last. As the ancient Greek tragedians recognized, there is a good deal of luck in human flourishing.[2]

As Spinoza sees it, our natural response in the face of the slings and arrows of outrageous fortune is superstition. As long as things are going well, we are content to rely on our own resources; a

person who is satisfied with his lot does not generally seek supernatural aid, or even the help of other mortals. "If men were able
to exercise complete control over all their circumstances, or if continuous good fortune were always their lot, they would never be
prey to superstition." But once our hopes are dashed and our fears
realized, as we are "reduced to such straits as to be without any
resource," we quickly turn to certain modes of behavior calculated
to reverse the course of events and make things go our way again.

> When fortune smiles at them, the majority of men, even if quite un-
> versed in affairs, are so abounding in wisdom that any advice offered
> to them is regarded as an affront, whereas in adversity they know not
> where to turn, begging for advice from any quarter; and then there
> is no counsel so foolish, absurd or vain which they will not follow.

To those down on their luck or afraid of what lies ahead, the most
trivial occurrences will appear as harbingers of good or bad fortune, while unusual phenomena will be taken to reveal the benefi-
cent or malevolent will of the deities. "They read extraordinary
things into Nature as if the whole of Nature were a partner in
their madness." The course of events as directed by hidden powers
appears to such individuals as something that they can, with a
little effort, manipulate, and they will even regard it as pious to do
so. They thus offer sacrifices to avert impending disaster and make
vows that they hope will bring back whatever goods they have
lost. As Spinoza says, "fear . . . engenders, preserves and fosters
superstition" and is the origin of "spurious religious reverence."[3]
   But fear and hope are very unstable emotions. Thus, the superstitions grounded in them are inconstant and variable. As soon
as things start going well again, people will typically cease those
practices they had believed would bring better circumstances in
their train. Those who have the most to gain from the continuation
of such superstitious practices—diviners, soothsayers, priests—
therefore take great pains to stabilize them and give them some
permanence. They do this primarily by exaggerating the importance of these activities and surrounding them with impressive
and dignified ceremonies. This will ensure that, even when things

are going well, people will continue to pay due respect to the gods and, more important, to their earthly ministers. The result is organized sectarian religion.

> This inconstancy [in superstitious practices] has been the cause of many terrible uprisings and wars, for . . . "the multitude has no rule more potent than superstition." So it is readily induced, under the guise of religion, now to worship its rulers as gods, and then again to curse and condemn them as mankind's common bane. To counteract this unfortunate tendency, immense efforts have been made to invest religion, true or false, with such pomp and ceremony that it can sustain any shock and constantly evoke the deepest reverence in all its worshippers.[4]

For the adherents of these codified superstitions, life is a state of "bondage," coerced obedience in body and in mind. They live in a state of "deception" and are prevented (sometimes by force) from exercising free judgment. True worship has been replaced by flattery of God, the pursuit of knowledge by servitude to false dogma, and freedom of thought and action by persecution of heterodoxy and nonbelievers. "Piety and religion . . . take the form of ridiculous mysteries, and men who utterly despise reason, who reject and turn away from the intellect as naturally corrupt—these are the men (and this is of all things the most iniquitous) who are believed to possess the divine light!" Spinoza concludes that if these self-appointed guardians of piety "possessed but a spark of the divine light, they would not indulge in such arrogant ravings, but would study to worship God more wisely and to surpass their fellows in love, as they now do in hate."[5]

To those of his contemporaries who were already familiar with Hobbes's description of the origins of religion in his *Leviathan*, Spinoza's account in the *Treatise* would sound very familiar (which no doubt explains why the two works were so often condemned in the same breath by ecclesiastic authorities). Like Spinoza, Hobbes locates the motivation toward religious devotion in irrational human emotions—above all, "anxiety," or fear and hope in the face of uncertainty about the future—as well as in ignorance of the true causes of things. The superstitious beliefs and practices to which these passions give rise are easily manipulated by secular and sectarian leaders for the sake of "keeping the people in obedience and peace." Indeed, as Hobbes sees it, the credulity of the masses is extremely useful for political authorities, who prefer to see their subjects occupied by religious obligations. This keeps them distracted from political affairs and unable to engage in too close an examination of the governance of the state. The ancient Romans, for example, knew well that "by these [ceremonies, supplications, sacrifices, and festivals, by which they were to believe the anger of the gods might be appeased] and such other institutions," rulers can ensure that "the common people in their misfortunes, laying the fault on neglect or error in their ceremonies, or on their own disobedience to the laws, were the less apt to mutiny against their governors. And being entertained with the pomp and pastime of festivals and public games, made in honor of the gods, need nothing else but bread to keep them from discontent, murmuring, and commotion against the state."[6]

While Hobbes's most critical remarks are reserved for Roman Catholicism—he examines its structures and ceremonies in Part Four of *Leviathan*, provocatively titled "The Kingdom of Darkness"—he clearly has no more respect for organized religion in general than does Spinoza.[7]

In Spinoza's account, behind the major organized religions lies a certain convenient but ultimately irreverent and harmful conception of God. The superstitious rites and ceremonies of Judaism and Christianity, calculated to win God's favor and avoid his wrath, rest on the false assumption that God is very much a rational agent, endowed as we are with a psychological life and moral character. God is, in other words, supposed to be a kind of person, possessed of intelligence, will, desire, and even emotion. The Judeo-Christian deity is a wise and just God, a transcendent providential being who has purposes and expectations, makes commands and judgments, and is capable of great acts of mercy and vengeance.

It is precisely this traditional religious picture of God that Spinoza elsewhere rejects as foolish anthropomorphism. In the *Ethics*, he inveighs against "those who feign a God, like man, consisting of a body and a mind, and subject to passions. But how far they wander from the true knowledge of God, is sufficiently established by what has already been demonstrated."[8] Having established that Nature is an indivisible, infinite, uncaused, substantial whole—in fact, the *only* substantial whole; that outside of Nature there is nothing; and that everything that exists is a part of Nature and is brought into being by and within Nature with a deterministic necessity through Nature's laws, Spinoza concludes that God and Nature—the substantial, unique, unified, active, infinitely powerful, necessary cause of everything—are one and the same thing.

When Spinoza draws out the religious implications of this metaphysical theology in the subsequent propositions of the *Ethics*, it becomes clear that his *Deus sive Natura* is totally unsuitable for the role that the Judeo-Christian deity is ordinarily called on to play. Because of the necessity inherent in Nature, there are no purposes for or within the universe, outside the projects that human beings may set for themselves. God or Nature does not act for any ends, and things within Nature are not created for the sake of anything. God or Nature does not *do* things to achieve any goals. The order of things just follows from God's (Nature's) attributes with necessity. All talk of God's intentions, preferences, or aims is just a pernicious fiction.

> All the prejudices I here undertake to expose depend on this one: that men commonly suppose that all natural things act, as men do, on account of an end; indeed, they maintain as certain that God himself directs all things to some certain end, for they say that God has made all things for man, and man that he might worship God.[9]

God is not some goal-oriented planner who then judges things by how well they conform to his purposes. Things happen only because of Nature and its laws. "Nature has no end set before it. . . .

All things proceed by a certain eternal necessity of nature." To believe otherwise is precisely what leads to those superstitions that are so easily manipulated by preachers and rabbis.

> [People] find—both in themselves and outside themselves—many means that are very helpful in seeking their own advantage, e.g., eyes for seeing, teeth for chewing, plants and animals for food, the sun for light, the sea for supporting fish. . . . Hence, they consider all natural things as means to their own advantage. And knowing that they had found these means, not provided them for themselves, they had reason to believe that there was someone else who had prepared those means for their use. For after they considered things as means, they could not believe that the things had made themselves; but from the means they were accustomed to prepare for themselves, they had to infer that there was a ruler, or a number of rulers of nature, endowed with human freedom, who had taken care of all things for them, and made all things for their use. And since they had never heard anything about the temperament of these rulers, they had to judge it from their own. Hence, they maintained that the Gods direct all things for the use of men in order to bind men to them and be held by men in the highest honor. So it has happened that each of them has thought up from his own temperament different ways of worshipping God, so that God might love them above all the rest, and direct the whole of Nature according to the needs of their blind desire and insatiable greed. Thus this prejudice was changed into superstition, and struck deep roots in their minds.[10]

In a letter to one of his more troublesome correspondents, a rather pietistic grain merchant and regent from Dordrecht named Willem van Blijenburgh, Spinoza emphasizes the absurdity of conceiving of God in this way. The language of traditional theology, he says, represents God "as a perfect man" and claims that "God desires something, that God is displeased with the deeds of the impious and pleased with those of the pious." In all philosophical rigor, however, "we clearly understand that to ascribe to God those attributes which make a man perfect would be as wrong as to ascribe to a man the attributes that make perfect an elephant or an ass."[11] Some years later, in another letter, this time to Hugo

Boxel, the former pensionary of Gorinchem, Spinoza turns to sarcasm to make his point:

> When you say that you do not see what sort of God I have if I deny him the actions of seeing, hearing, attending, willing, etc. and that he possesses those faculties in an eminent degree, I suspect that you believe that there is no greater perfection than can be explicated by the aforementioned attributes. I am not surprised, for I believe that a triangle, if it could speak, would likewise say that God is eminently triangular, and a circle that God's nature is eminently circular.[12]

A judging God who has plans and acts purposively is a God to be obeyed and placated. Spinoza's God, by contrast, is shorn of the anthropomorphic fantasies that, he insists, are unworthy of the kind of being God is. "This doctrine [which would have God act as humans act] takes away God's perfection."[13] There is no comfort to be found in Spinoza's God. It is not a being to which one would turn in times of trouble, or to which one would pray for the satisfaction of one's hopes or the avoidance of what one fears.

This, at least, is the God of the *Ethics*. None of the early readers of the *Treatise* would have read the *Ethics* (there was no opportunity to do so until 1678, when it was posthumously published with Spinoza's other writings).[14] And Spinoza is more cautious in the *Treatise* about revealing his considered philosophical view about God. He is prepared in this work to speak of God's will and providential care, of God doing things and having thoughts, plans, and preferences. However, as we shall see, these ways of speaking can be given a proper Spinozistic reading. The God of the *Ethics*—what Spinoza considers the true conception of God—does indeed inform the *Treatise* in many important and unmistakable ways. And Spinoza often makes this clear to the reader, even if he is, for the sake of accommodating his Christian audience, hesitant to proclaim it too loudly.

The organized religions that, in Spinoza's view, have brought so much trouble to society and so enslaved the minds of individuals are also grounded in a particular view of the source of religious knowledge and the communication of divine truths. Central to all faiths in the Abrahamic tradition is prophecy, or the idea that certain people are endowed with the special gift to receive and pass on the word of God. Like the power of diviners and seers of pagan antiquity, this endowment is usually construed as the ability to access information not available to others or by ordinary means. The prophet may be someone who is the direct recipient of divine revelation, a beneficiary of angelic mediation, or simply an inspired interpreter of signs that God has placed before humankind. He may have a real foreknowledge of the future, or a less infallible but still reliable ability to predict what the outcome of events will be, based perhaps on special interpretive powers to read the significance of past and present states of affairs. Prophetic power may, on some accounts, be a supernatural gift or it may be grounded in natural faculties.[15] The information can come to the prophet by way of visions or dreams, or (in the rarest instance) it might result from an unmediated encounter with God himself.

Among the prophets of Judaism, only Moses is supposed to have spoken directly to God, face to face; the other prophets received their prophecies in visions or dreams, through images or voices. According to Islamic tradition, Mohammed's initial revelation came through the archangel Gabriel. In Christianity, Jesus' possession of prophetic powers is regarded as unique because he, while human, is to be identified with God. Moses, Jesus, and Mohammed were each charged with bringing the supreme law from God to the people, while other prophets served as interpreters of those principles, foretold the rewards that come from its observance, and issued warnings of the doom that follows disobedience. Thus, Ezekiel, speaking on behalf of God, proclaims that the kingdom of Judah will suffer for its "rebellious ways" and "abominable deeds," and particularly for the idolatry that its people, like their ancestors, continue to practice. He predicts the certain downfall of Jerusalem and the exile of the Israelites from the land, a fact accomplished by the Babylonians in 586 BCE:

These are the words of the Lord God: Are you defiling yourselves as
your forefathers did? Are you wantonly giving yourselves to their
loathsome gods? . . . I will pass you under the rod and bring you
within the bond of the covenant. I will rid you of those who revolt
and rebel against me. I will take them out of the land where they are
now living, but they shall not set foot on the soil of Israel. Thus shall
you know that I am the Lord. (Ezekiel 20.30–38)

The prophet tells the people of God's anger and the harsh punishment that is coming their way.

These are the words of the Lord: I am against you; I will draw my
sword from the scabbard and cut off from you both righteous and
wicked. It is because I would cut off your righteous and your wicked
equally that my sword will be drawn from the scabbard against all
men, from the Negev northwards. All men shall know that I the
Lord have drawn my sword; it shall never again be sheathed. Groan
in their presence, man, groan bitterly until your lungs are bursting.
(Ezekiel 21.3–6)

Ezekiel reminds the children of Israel, however, that God is merciful and faithful to his covenant. He foresees that they will return
to the land and that the city of Jerusalem will be restored and the
Temple rebuilt.

A prophet, then, has a kind of wisdom. He knows many things
of great importance for the flourishing of those to whom he is
speaking, and one disregards him at great risk. His words should
be heeded because what he says is reliable and relevant. But what
exactly is the nature of that wisdom? Is the prophet a philosopher?
Does he have theological knowledge about the nature of God?
Does he have scientific understanding of the cosmos and of the
natural world? Is he an authority on human nature and an expert
in politics and history? In short, what kind of truths, if any, does
a prophet convey in his prophecies?

These are precisely the questions that Spinoza addresses in the
opening chapters of the *Treatise*. While they are also dealt with
by many medieval and early modern thinkers, there is one earlier

philosopher who is of particular importance for Spinoza's discussion of prophecy. Spinoza clearly intends his analysis to be a direct critique of the view of Maimonides, the twelfth-century rabbi and physician and the author of perhaps the most important work in the history of Jewish philosophy, the *Guide of the Perplexed*. Spinoza was greatly influenced by Maimonides in many ways: his metaphysics, his philosophical theology, and his moral philosophy all reflect a close reading of the *Guide* and other writings. Sometimes what Spinoza has to say—in the *Ethics*, for example, about the relationship between virtue, reason, and happiness, or about the connection between knowledge and immortality—seems like a logical, if radical, extension of Maimonides' own intellectualist views.[16] On other occasions, Spinoza turns Maimonides' account on its head and uses it to attack his Jewish rationalist forbear and the philosophically (if not religiously) more conventional position he represents; this is the case with Spinoza's discussion of prophecy in the *Treatise*.

In the *Guide*, Maimonides insists that there are several conditions that must obtain before an individual becomes a prophet. First, he must be in good physical condition, enjoying a "perfection of his bodily faculties"; this is both because an infirm body and a disruptive temperament will cause too many distractions from the life of the mind and because the imagination, which is central to prophecy as Maimonides understands it, is a part of the body (namely, the brain). Second, he must have perfected his moral character and attained a high state of virtue; a wicked or even an imperfectly ethical person can never be a prophet. A prophet must be a moral paragon and be able to lead others toward goodness. He must show the requisite "renunciation of and contempt for bodily pleasures." Indeed, one sure way of determining that a person is, despite his pretensions, *not* a prophet is if he does not lead an ethically austere life, if he is easy prey for worldly temptations.

Possession of the best temperament and bodily constitution and supreme moral virtue, however, are not sufficient to make one a prophet. If they were, then prophecy would be a relatively easy and, in principle, widespread phenomenon. Two further conditions are necessary:

Know that the true reality and quiddity of prophecy consist in its being an overflow from God, may He be cherished and honored, through the intermediation of the Active Intellect, toward the rational faculty in the first place and thereafter toward the imaginative faculty. This is the highest degree of man and the ultimate term of perfection that can exist for his species; and this state is the ultimate term of perfection for the imaginative faculty. This is something that cannot by any means exist in every man. And it is not something that may be attained solely through perfection in the speculative sciences and through improvement of moral habits, even if all of them have become as fine and good as can be. There still is needed in addition the highest possible degree of perfection of the imaginative faculty in respect of its original disposition.[17]

A person of fine body and outstanding morality becomes a prophet only when he also reaches perfection in his intellect and his imagination. He perfects (or "actualizes") his intellect through the pursuit of "knowledge and wisdom"—that is, science and philosophy. In acquiring "a perfect and accomplished human intellect," this individual has connected with and comes to enjoy the intellectual bounty that overflows from God, who is the supreme intellect of the universe. The speculative knowledge belonging to the Creator now reaches his rational faculty. If this is where it ended, if the overflow went only so far as the rational faculty, then such a person, with his perfected intellect, would belong to "the class of men of science engaged in speculation"—that is, he would be a philosopher.

However, if this individual is also perfect in his imagination, which is therefore capable in turn of receiving the overflow from the rational faculty, then he is endowed with the ability to prophesize. Prophecy itself occurs when the senses are at rest and the onrush of material from the external world is quieted. This allows the imagination to receive the overflow from the rational faculty and rework its content and translate it into images. The result is visions and "veridical dreams" informed by the speculative knowledge of the overflow.

Now there is no doubt that whenever—in an individual of this description—his imaginative faculty, which is as perfect as possible,
acts and receives from the intellect an overflow corresponding to his
speculative perfection, this individual will only apprehend divine
and most extraordinary matters, will see only God and His angels,
and will only be aware and achieve knowledge of matters that constitute true opinions and general directives for the well-being of men
in their relations with one another.[18]

A prophet, in other words, is someone who knows everything that
the philosopher knows but grasps it by way of concrete images.
(The only exception to this is Moses, who communicated with
God directly and not by means of images.) He also has the additional skill of being able to communicate such matters to others
in the more accessible form of imaginative narratives (such as parables), rather than in abstract theories.

The case in which the intellectual overflow overflows only toward the
rational faculty and does not overflow at all toward the imaginative
faculty—either because of the scantiness of what overflows or because
of some deficiency existing in the imaginative faculty in its natural disposition, a deficiency that makes it impossible for it to receive
the overflow of the intellect—is characteristic of the class of men engaged in speculation. If, on the other hand, this overflow reaches both
faculties—I mean both the rational and the imaginative . . . and if
the imaginative faculty is in a state of ultimate perfection owing to
its natural disposition, this is characteristic of the class of prophets.[19]

The role that the imagination plays actually gives the prophet an
advantage over the philosopher. Because of the imaginative way in
which he receives the content of the overflow, through dreams and
visions, he perceives things that the more abstract and theoretically inclined philosopher does not. He can see "what will happen and [apprehend] those future events as if they were things
that had been perceived by the senses."[20] The imagination allows
the prophet to grasp connections between things that the philosopher might miss, "for all things bear witness to one another and

indicate one another," although in ways not always perspicuous to, or as quickly grasped by, the merely speculative individual.

Maimonides' prophet is therefore, no less than the philosopher, a conveyer of truths: moral truths intended to improve our characters, but also "speculative" metaphysical, theological, and scientific truths intended to improve us intellectually. He communicates both practical principles for our personal and social well-being and "correct opinions" that are philosophically demonstrable. The prophet can tell us how we ought to behave, but also what we ought to believe—about God, the universe, and ourselves.

Moreover, like the philosopher's wisdom, the prophet's visionary skill is a natural outgrowth of the development or perfection of his native faculties. Or, as Maimonides puts it, "prophecy is a certain perfection in the nature of man."[21] Maimonides thus naturalizes the phenomenon of prophecy. A person is not chosen arbitrarily or even deliberately by God to prophesize. There is no supernatural act, gratuitous or otherwise, by which God confers prophecy on an individual.[22] Maimonides explicitly rejects the view that "God, may He be exalted, chooses whom He wishes from among men, turns him into a prophet, and sends him with a mission," regardless of how well or ill prepared he may be for this vocation. For Maimonides, a person becomes a prophet through his own endeavors, working on whatever gifts in his material and spiritual faculties he may have from nature.

In the *Treatise*, Spinoza is deeply concerned to combat this notion of the prophet-philosopher. One of the goals of the work is to secure the separation of the domains of religion and philosophy so that philosophers might be free to pursue secular wisdom unimpeded by ecclesiastic authority. In Spinoza's view, philosophical truth and religious faith have nothing in common with one another, and one must not serve as the rule of the other. Philosophy should not have to answer to religion, no more than religion should have to be consistent with any philosophical system.

However, to the extent that Maimonides is correct in his account of prophecy—and his analysis of the role of the intellect and the imagination is found among other medieval philosophers[23]—the content of prophecy *is*, at least in part, philosophical. The philosopher and the prophet, in Maimonides's view, both convey truths—indeed, the *same* truths. And because one truth necessarily coheres with other truths, philosophy and prophecy must, when properly understood, always be consistent. For Maimonides, philosophical truth and revealed truth will never clash. Thus, prophetic texts must be read in such a way that they do not contradict a demonstrated philosophical principle. In turn, the philosopher must always respect the products of revelation, although the prophets' words may sometimes have to be read figuratively if a literal reading goes against an established philosophical truth.

To achieve his aim, then, Spinoza needs to show that there is a substantive (and not just presentational) difference between the information conveyed by revelation or prophecy and the knowledge which is the product of philosophy.

There is one very important point on which Spinoza agrees with Maimonides, and he uses it to his own polemical advantage. The prophets of the Hebrew Bible, Spinoza argues, were indeed, as Maimonides says, men of great imagination. They were not, however, philosophers, or even very learned. They did not have training in the speculative sciences; in fact, many of them were uneducated. For this reason, their pronouncements should not be regarded as sources of theological, philosophical, scientific, or historical truth. The goal of Spinoza's discussion of prophecy, then, is to downgrade its epistemological status, particularly in relationship to philosophy and science. Revelation, as portrayed in the Bible, while it has a very important social and political function to play, is not a source of truth.

Spinoza defines "prophecy or revelation" as "the sure knowledge of some matter revealed by God to man."[24] On the face of it, this seems perfectly traditional, although somewhat puzzling for anyone acquainted with Spinoza's philosophical and religious project. Spinoza's rigorous naturalism will not allow for any supernatural facts. Whatever happens, happens in and through Nature. Thus, any knowledge that comes to a person must come in an entirely natural way; there are and can be no exceptions to this. In Spinoza's system there is no transcendent God exercising supernatural, ad hoc communications. There is room for divine revelation, but only in a very particular sense. Because for Spinoza God is identical with Nature, and all human knowledge is natural, it follows that all human knowledge is also divine. If God is Nature understood as the active, substantial cause of all things, then whatever is brought about by Nature and its laws is, by definition, brought about by God. The human mind being as much a part of Nature as anything else is, its cognitive states all follow ultimately from "God or Nature." "Prophetic knowledge is usually taken to exclude natural knowledge. Nevertheless, the latter has as much right as any other kind of knowledge to be called divine, since it is dictated to us, as it were, by God's nature insofar as we participate therein, and by God's decrees."[25]

Moreover, the highest form of knowledge available to human beings is what Spinoza, in the *Ethics*, calls "the third kind of knowledge." This is an intuitive grasp of the essences of things, a deep causal understanding that situates them in their necessary relationships to each other and, more important, to higher, universal principles. "This kind of knowing proceeds from an adequate idea of the formal essence of certain attributes of God to the adequate knowledge of the essence of things."[26] In the third kind of knowledge, one grasps the nature of a thing or an event in such a way that one sees why it is as it is and could not possibly have been otherwise. But the universal causal principles of Nature just are God's (or Nature's) attributes of Extension (for physical things and their states) and Thought (for minds and their ideas). When a person connects the idea of a thing with the idea of the relevant attribute of God—when his idea of a body, for example, is properly cognitively situated with respect to the idea of the nature of extension and the laws of motion and rest—he has a thoroughly adequate knowledge of that thing. God's nature thus makes possible human knowledge because its concept serves as the foundation of our ultimate understanding of things. "Natural knowledge can be called prophecy"—that is, it can be called divine revelation—"for the knowledge that we acquire by the natural light of reason depends solely on knowledge of God and of his eternal decrees."[27] Only when we have knowledge of God or Nature do we truly have knowledge.

When "prophecy" or "divine revelation" is correctly understood in this broad sense, as whatever knowledge causally and cognitively depends on God, then it includes natural knowledge. More specifically, it includes philosophy and science, as well as other products of the intellect, and is therefore "common to all men." And while God is, in these ways, the ultimate cause of true knowledge, the proximate cause or the subject to which human knowledge immediately belongs is always a natural one: the human mind itself.

> Since, then, the human mind contains the nature of God within it-self in concept, and partakes thereof, and is thereby enabled to form certain basic ideas that explain natural phenomena and inculcate morality, we are justified in asserting that the nature of mind, insofar as it is thus conceived, is the primary cause of divine revelation. For as I have just pointed out, all that we clearly and distinctly understand is dictated to us by the idea and nature of God—not indeed in words, but in a far superior way and one that agrees excellently with the nature of mind, as everyone who has tasted intellectual certainty has doubtless experienced in his own case.[28]

As Spinoza says, however, his aim in the *Treatise* is not to examine the nature of prophecy properly understood—something that, it might be said, he does in the *Ethics*—but to consider prophecy as it is portrayed and proclaimed in Scripture, the primary source of latter-day ecclesiastic authority and, consequently, of religious meddling in political affairs. And in Scripture, a very different picture of prophecy emerges, one that represents it as an affair not of the intellect but of the imagination.

Spinoza notes that all prophecy in the Hebrew Bible occurs by way of words or images. The prophets hear voices and behold flashes of light; they confront talking animals and angels bearing swords; some even apprehend God in bodily form. Of course, not all the sights and sounds perceived by the prophets are real. According to tradition, only Moses heard real words from God. By contrast, Spinoza explains, the voice of God perceived by Samuel, Avimelech, Joshua, and others was illusory; it occurred either in a dream or in a vision. What he believes this shows, then, is that, according to Scripture, prophecy came not through the intellect but through the imagination, since that is the human faculty responsible for the visual and auditory phenomena in unreal dreams and visions. "Hence it was not a more perfect mind that was needed for the gift of prophecy, but a more lively imaginative faculty."[29]

The fact that biblical prophecy is a function of the prophet's imagination accounts for both the way in which the prophet apprehends the divine message and the narrative form in which he communicates it to others. Unlike the philosopher, whose material is intellectual and abstract and can be formulated in demonstrated propositions, the prophet receives and works with concrete appearances. "We shall no longer wonder why Scripture, or the prophets, speak so strangely or obscurely of the Spirit, or mind, of God . . . and again, why God was seen by Micaiah as seated, by Daniel as an old man clothed in white garments, by Ezekiel as fire."[30] What the prophet sees are visions, and the insights that he gleans from those visions are, in turn, passed on through parables and allegories. Such imaginative stories, while they may be an obstacle to intellectual understanding, are naturally suited for the products of the prophetic faculty and, just as important, for the prophet's audience.

Indeed, Spinoza insists, contrary to Maimonides, the intellect has nothing whatsoever to contribute to biblical prophecy. The prophets were not particularly learned individuals. They were usually simple men from common, even lowly backgrounds. They did not have philosophical wisdom, theological training, or scientific knowledge, and therefore they are not necessarily to be believed when they pronounce on such topics. Prophecy as Spinoza sees it is not a cognitive discipline. If, as Spinoza says, "the gift of prophecy did not render the prophets more learned,"[31] it is also true that listening to a prophet will not make one any more intelligent.

This is, in part, because prophecy is a highly subjective affair. It is an individualistic product shaped by both nature and nurture. What a prophet says on this or that matter, how the message is rendered by his imagination, and what kind of vision or dream he has are a function of the prophet's native faculties and his upbringing. It all depends on the life he leads, the ideas that occupy his mind, the social status he holds, even his manner of speaking, his temperament, and his emotional condition. The visions of a prophet who comes from the countryside will contain images of oxen and cows, while a more urbane individual will have a prophetic experience with very different content. And there is no reason why the preconceptions that inform and shape a prophet's revelation, like the beliefs acquired by anyone over the course of a lifetime, should necessarily be true. "I shall show . . . that prophecies or revelations also varied in accordance with the ingrained beliefs of the prophets, and that the prophets held various, even contrary beliefs, and various prejudices."[32] Since Joshua was no astronomer, he believed that the earth does not move and that the sun goes around the earth. Thus, when he saw the daylight lasting longer than usual during a battle, rather than attributing this to various meteorological phenomena he simply proclaimed that the sun stood still in the sky:

> If a prophet was of a cheerful disposition, then victories, peace and other joyful events were revealed to him; for it is on things of this kind that the imagination of such people dwells. If he was of a gloomy disposition, then wars, massacres and all kinds of calamities were revealed to him. And just as a prophet might be merciful, gentle, wrathful, stern and so forth, so he was more fitted for a particular kind of revelation.[33]

Spinoza admits that the fact that prophets were not learned does not mean that they were undistinguished from other individuals.

On the contrary, while they may not have had perfected intellects (as Maimonides had claimed), their supremely vivid imaginations were, as Maimonides said, rather extraordinary. Spinoza also shares Maimonides' view that the prophet's imaginative abilities give him something of an advantage over the philosopher. "Since the prophets perceived the revelations of God with the aid of the imaginative faculty, they may doubtless have perceived much that is beyond the limits of the intellect."[34] In the *Ethics*, Spinoza generally denigrates the epistemological value of the imagination in favor of the intellect. The ideas of the imagination, like those of the senses, are not a source of adequate knowledge, and serve mainly to foster the passions.[35] Nothing Spinoza says in the *Treatise* challenges this position. But he does grant that the strength of the prophet's imagination confers on him remarkable, if short-lived, perspicuity. The prophet has a certain quickness of insight, an intuitive ability to envision the ramifications of things that is not available to the person guided solely by the rational intellect and limited to only logical tools. "Many more ideas can be constructed from words and images than merely from the principles and axioms on which our entire natural knowledge is based." The prophet, because of the strength of his imagination, is a very perceptive person. He may not have the learning and deep metaphysical understanding of the philosophical sage, and he may never be able to achieve the condition of rational virtue and true *eudaimonia* of the intellectually perfected individual, but sometimes he can see things—practical things—that the latter cannot. Spinoza does not elaborate on this particular gift of the prophet, but what he appears to have in mind is the fact that sometimes people who work with images and concrete ideas have a quickness of mind and depth of insight into ethical situations that the more abstract thinker lacks. Perhaps the prophet, with his practical judgment enhanced by the imagination, is better able than an intellectual to size up a concrete situation, or to see how a general principle is to be applied in particular case.

More important—and Spinoza and Maimonides are in agreement about this as well—the prophets were ethically superior people. The prophets of Hebrew Scripture had a finely honed sense of right and wrong and a keen understanding of practical matters. "The minds of prophets were directed exclusively toward what was right and good . . . they won praise and repute not so much for sublimity and pre-eminence of intellect as for piety and faithfulness."[36] The prophets were better able than most people to resist the temptations of sensual pleasures and concerned above all with righteous action. They thus have important lessons to impart about charity and justice. If the parables of the prophets are of any value—and Spinoza agrees that they are—it is because of the moral message they convey so effectively. The prophets, with their virtuous characters and creative narrative gifts, were thus particularly good ethical teachers. As we shall see, Spinoza insists that if there is a common theme—a "divine message"—running throughout the Bible's prophetic writings, it is a very simple one: Love your neighbor. On this point, and this point alone, the prophets should be obeyed. The practical path to virtue provided by the prophetic writings may not be as exalted and transformative as the intellectual one offered by philosophy, but for most people it is the best one available.

The ancient Israelites recognized the imaginative talent and moral superiority of the prophets, and accordingly elevated them above ordinary human beings. But, according to Spinoza, because they could not find a way to explain through natural means how these individuals could be so virtuous and so perceptive, they attributed the prophets' powers to divine—that is, supernatural—inspiration. "Whatever the Jews did not understand, being at that time ignorant of its natural causes, was referred to God."[37] Like unusual works of nature ("called works of God") and unusually strong men ("called sons of God"), so the prophets, who surpassed other human beings in certain ways and whose powers "evoked wonder" among the people, were said to possess the spirit of God.

> The following Scriptural expressions are now quite clear: the Spirit of the Lord was upon a prophet, the Lord poured his Spirit into men, men were filled with the Spirit of God and with the Holy Spirit and so on. They mean merely this, that the prophets were endowed with

an extraordinary virtue exceeding the normal, and that they devoted themselves to piety with especial constancy.[38]

Although there is indeed something divine about their message, Spinoza wants to make it clear that the prophets did not literally receive some supernatural communication from an anthropomorphic deity such as the God that is portrayed in the Bible. This would be in keeping neither with the true nature of God nor with the true basis of prophecy. Prophecy is a perfectly natural, if unusual, phenomenon and arises from the excellence of certain human faculties. Again, here we find Spinoza in agreement with Maimonides.

As great as the prophets were, however, and as important a role as their writings may play in society and history—and, as Spinoza will explain, they do play a very important role—it remains the case that from an intellectual point of view they were inferior individuals. It is not just that they happened not to be as wise or as learned as philosophers. Rather, their prophesizing abilities rendered them constitutionally unsuited for the rational pursuit of knowledge. In this regard, they fell below the human norm. In a prophet, the overly strong imagination gets in the way of the intellect. Its images interfere with the clear and distinct apprehension of adequate ideas. This is precisely what, in Spinoza's view, Maimonides got wrong. You cannot perfect *both* the intellect and the imagination. The improvement of one necessarily entails the weakening of the other. A strong intellect is an obstacle to imagination, and vice versa. "Those with a more powerful imagination are less fitted for purely intellectual activity, while those who devote themselves to the cultivation of their more powerful intellect, keep their imagination under greater control and restraint, and they hold it in rein, as it were, so that it should not invade the province of intellect."[39]

As Spinoza sees it, the subjective, imaginative, variable, and non-cognitive character of prophecy has important consequences for

the prophet's audience. The prophet's domain is highly circumscribed. His authority extends only to moral matters, to the way
in which we pursue various goods, organize society, and treat other
human beings.

> [The prophets] may well have been ignorant of matters that have
> no bearing on charity and moral conduct but concern philosophic
> speculation, and were in fact ignorant of them, holding conflict-
> ing beliefs. Therefore knowledge of science and of matters spiritual
> should by no means be expected of them. So we conclude that we
> must believe the prophets only with regard to the purpose and sub-
> stance of the revelation; in all else one is free to believe as one will.[40]

When the prophet speaks about justice and charity, he knows
what he is talking about and should be heeded (although unlike
the philosopher, he is incapable of providing demonstrations for
these truths). On any other subject, he has no legitimate claim to
obedience at all.

The *Treatise*'s opening chapters on prophecy go far toward
achieving Spinoza's primary aim in the work: to demonstrate the
independence of intellectual matters from religious affairs, and to
defend the freedom to philosophize against political and religious
encroachment. They beautifully set up the remaining elements
of his case: the bold account of the origins of Scripture and the
proper way to interpret it, the distinction between "true religion" and mere ceremonial observance, his reading of the lessons
of Israelite history for the contemporary Dutch political scene,
and his argument for broad toleration and state control over public religious practices. The prophetic writings—including Moses'
Torah—are the core of Scripture and the source of its authority
throughout the ages. By showing that their insights are strictly
moral, and that their narratives are the product of the imagination and not the intellect, Spinoza has crafted an important tool
with which to undermine ecclesiastic control over people's public
and private lives.

It is true that prophecy points a way toward what Spinoza
understands as salvation—that is, toward virtue, happiness, and

well-being in this world. Thus, the lessons of the prophets are of significant value. But they are directed primarily toward the masses, who—unlike the philosophically educated—are not capable of the more difficult intellectual path toward human flourishing. The more accessible and colorful narratives of the prophets will indeed help inspire people toward at least an external conformity to the demands of justice and charity. In this way, their worth is strictly practical. The end of the prophetic writings, Spinoza insists, is obedience: getting people to observe proper ethical behavior. That same behavior can, to be sure, find a deeper and more stable foundation in rational knowledge, in a grasp of certain philosophical truths about God, nature, and human beings—above all, just those truths that are found in the ordered propositions of the *Ethics*. But while such deep understanding is not to be found in the Bible's prophetic texts, neither is it necessary for the success of those texts in motivating good behavior. Sometimes a few good fictional stories are more effective than a host of rigorously demonstrated philosophical truths.

Chapter 5

Miracles

In 1714, on the occasion of his inauguration as professor of natural and mathematical philosophy at the University of Altdorf, Johann Heinrich Müller gave a lecture with the title "On Miracles." Müller defined a miracle as "a certain unusual operation . . . producing such an effect, whose cause (*ratio*) cannot in any way be explained through the ordinary laws of nature, but rather is wholly contrary to them, and therefore requires that these necessarily be suspended for a time and that others be substituted in their place."[1] He then goes on to investigate whether miracles, so defined, are possible, and in particular how the laws of motion might be suspended. He concludes that since the laws of nature are themselves freely instituted by God, such a suspension is "not absolutely impossible," and is in fact required in the light of God's absolute power, not to mention his liberty and wisdom. "No one," he says, "can be dubious as to the possibility of miracles."[2] No one, that is, except Spinoza, "the most famous restorer and propagator of the myth whereby God is not distinct from the universe" and author of an "abominable hypothesis" on the topic of miracles.[3]

There are many things that Spinoza says in the *Theological-Political Treatise* that offended religious sensibilities of the time. But nothing appeared to his contemporaries to have as far-reaching and (from a religious perspective) pernicious consequences as his discussion of miracles in chapter six of the work. As the historian Jonathan Israel has noted, "no other element of Spinoza's philosophy provoked as much consternation and outrage in his own time as his sweeping denial of miracles and the supernatural."[4] If, as

Spinoza claimed, there was no such thing as miracles, understood as divine interventions in the course of nature and human history, then it would seem to follow that divine providence is fatally undermined and Scripture's narratives of miraculous happenings are nothing but fairy tales. When Hobbes said after reading the *Treatise* that the author of the work "had outthrown him a bar's length, for he durst not write so boldly," what most likely so astounded the usually unflappable Englishman was Spinoza's account of miracles.[5]

Philosophers of a progressive persuasion in the seventeenth century were committed to the new science of nature. For thinkers such as Galileo, Descartes, Huygens, Boyle, Newton, and others, explanations of natural phenomena in the physical realm were to be framed solely in terms of matter in motion. Gone were the "occult" powers of medieval Aristotelian Scholasticism, which explained phenomena by virtue of immaterial forms or qualities that inhabit and animate bodies and, like "little minds" (to quote Descartes, a harsh critic of the Scholastic system), were supposed to move them just as the human soul moves the human body. In the new philosophy, everything was explained in mechanistic terms, through the impact, conglomeration, and separation of material parts according to fixed laws of nature.

In the world of early modern mechanism, explanations of why things ordinarily come about make no appeal to an intelligent agent that, acting with a goal in mind, willfully directs them in a certain manner.[6] But this does not mean, on the other hand, that phenomena result from some spontaneous generation out of nothing. For the mechanist—at least insofar as he is engaged in science—there are neither purposes nor randomness in nature. Rather, whatever happens, happens because of antecedent causes that necessitate their effects. For the proponents of the new science, nature behaves in lawlike ways; its processes are reduced to causal chains, each link of which is nothing but matter in motion or at rest. They believed that this framework, which could be captured with mathematical precision, made possible perspicuous and informative theories of natural phenomena, theories with real explanatory power and predictive utility.

Still, this was the seventeenth century—a period in which Christian nations went to war with each other over religious differences, people were thrown into prison (and sometimes burned at the stake) for heresy, and books were placed on the Catholic Church's Index of Prohibited Books if they were deemed inconsistent with the dogmas of the faith. No philosophy of nature, no matter how progressive, could dispense entirely with the divine. Nature may operate through uniform material causes behaving with nomological necessity, but it was still God's creation. The world was not an independent, self-subsisting system of mechanistic agents devoid of providential oversight. There may not be mindlike forms or qualities intelligently directing the course of events from within nature—heavy bodies no longer "seek" their natural resting place at the earth's center—but early modern philosophers and scientists were not about to adopt the Epicurean model of a world generated and governed only by blind necessity.

Thus, Descartes, in his *Discourse on Method* of 1637, claimed that the most general laws of physics that govern all bodily phenomena were themselves instituted by God when he created the world. We may not be able fully to penetrate the divine wisdom and understand in all cases why God has arranged things as he did. But Descartes was not willing to deny that such arrangements testify to divine providence and benevolence.[7] Likewise, the German polymath Gottfried Wilhelm Leibniz, one of the most brilliant minds of his time and a leading physicist in the mechanistic tradition, argued that the existence itself of the world can be explained only by God's wise and determinate choice of it as the best of all possible worlds, while Newton insisted that the way in which bodies behave according to natural laws is the best evidence of God's dominion. Indeed, Newton claimed, there is no better example of supernatural providence than the mathematically describable operation of the force of gravity. In the Age of Reason, God had as great a role to play in the regular course of nature as ever.

Still, God's creation of the world and ordinary concourse with its operations is one thing; his miraculous intervention is, at least to most philosophers of the period, quite another. Considerations about the divine will and providence need not make any significant difference in the way science is done.[8] As Leibniz insisted, such metaphysical questions, while important for establishing the foundations of physics, were not a part of physics proper. But once the possibility of miracles is allowed, the necessity of nature is threatened and its lawlike regularity open (at least in principle) to exceptions. Conversely, the alleged necessity of nature threatens the possibility of any miraculous exceptions to its operations. There was a serious tension at the heart of early modern mechanism for its more pious proponents.

A miracle is typically understood to be a divinely caused event that contravenes or at least surpasses the natural order. Such a supernatural occurrence might be an explicit violation of the laws of nature, such as a body being moved by God contrary to the laws of physics or suddenly transmogrified into another substance altogether. Thus, Scripture relates that God caused the waters of the Red Sea to part for the Israelites on the exodus from Egypt, Aaron's rod to turn into a serpent (Exodus 7.8–11), and the sun to cease its motion across the sky so that Joshua might have more time to take vengeance upon Israel's enemies (Joshua 10.12–15: "The sun stayed in mid-heaven and made no haste to set for almost a whole day"). Or, to use a distinction employed by some medieval thinkers, a miracle might be an event that, while itself not inconsistent with nature's laws, either occurs displaced from the natural order of things (the example given by Thomas Aquinas is a human being living again *after* having died), or is an extraordinary and statistically unusual event that nature *could* possibly explain but is in fact brought about not by the operation of natural causes but by God (for example, Daniel's emerging from the lions' den unscathed), or is a perfectly ordinary event that nature *does* usually do (such as healing the sick) but that in this rare case is explained by the divine power alone.[9]

Philosophical discussions of miracles in the Middle Ages focused not only on the definition of what a miracle is but also on God's modus operandi in generating miracles. Few thinkers believed that God's causal role here consisted in multiple, ad hoc interventions tailored to particular occasions, with God acting at the proper moment to introduce a temporary change in nature's order. This might be the conception of miracles that best captures the popular imagination. However, to many medieval philosophers it seemed too fanciful and anthropomorphic (and perhaps insufficiently prescient) a conception of divine agency, one that was inconsistent with divine simplicity, omniscience, and wisdom. Rather, Jewish, Christian, and Muslim philosophers of this extended period were more likely to see miracles as having been embedded in the course of events at creation. God, operating with a preconceived plan, knows exactly what must happen and when, both according to and notwithstanding the laws of nature. He then so orders things from the start that miracles or exceptions to those laws arise on the appropriate occasion. This might happen either through God so crafting the nature of a thing (such as Aaron's rod) that at a certain point in time it will, through that nature, take on a new and unusual form (a serpent); or with God introducing into the planned course of nature, and *despite* the natures of things, temporary exceptions to those natures and suspensions of nature's laws and operations. In either case, the implanted miracle occurs as an ordained item in the series of events as this unfolds over time. As one medieval philosopher described this position,

> all miracles which deviate from the natural course of events, whether they have already occurred or, according to promise, are to take place in the future, were foreordained by the Divine Will during the six days of creation, nature being then so constituted that those miracles which were to happen really did afterward take place. Then, when such an occurrence happens at its proper time, it may have been regarded as an absolute innovation, where in reality it was not.[10]

Because the miracle has been decreed by God, it occurs of necessity; but the necessity of nature itself, as represented by its laws, is thereby disrupted.

This debate over the nature of God's activity and the generation of miracles carried over into the seventeenth century and engaged many of Spinoza's contemporaries. The French intellectual Pierre Bayle, a Calvinist refugee who would eventually settle in Rotterdam, may be one of the few in this period who believed that *if* there were miracles (and he seems to have wanted to minimize their occurrence), they were ad hoc divine interventions designed to subvert the operations of nature in a particular case.[11] Leibniz, on the other hand, insisted that a world in which God needs continuously to introduce miracles is a rather imperfect world needing constant upkeep, and is hardly worthy of God's choice.[12] Miracles, he believed, are a divinely instituted and pre-programmed part of nature's general order, not a disruption of it, although such extraordinary events surpass the natural powers of created beings.[13]

The devotion of the most progressive thinkers to mechanistic explanations in science and a nature governed by laws and causal necessity did not diminish their commitment to finding room for miracles. Indeed, since antiquity, philosophers working in Hebrew, Arabic, and Latin generally regarded it as a serious shortcoming of any philosophy of nature if it rendered miracles impossible. There is necessity, and then there is *necessity*. Aristotle's system of nature is governed by causal necessity, but it seemed to his later critics to be a necessity so extreme that miracles were impossible. The unchanging, eternal Unmoved Mover does not, cannot, intervene in nature.[14] Many religious thinkers, even those partial to Aristotelianism in general, thus reject this particular feature of the Peripatetic philosophy. They complain that Aristotle's doctrine of the uncreated eternity of the world and the consequent necessity of its existence and all its contents leaves no room for miraculous changes in things and thereby threatens God's governance of his creation.

For nearly all medieval and early modern philosophers, then, the metaphysical possibility of miracles is nonnegotiable.

Whether out of sincere piety or from a desire not to run afoul of the theological faculties, Spinoza's predecessors and contemporaries were not willing to rule out, at least in principle, divinely caused suspensions of the regular course of nature. God may not be able to do what is logically impossible—he cannot make a square circle—but he can surely do what is naturally impossible. This is because the limits of what is naturally possible—that is, the laws of nature—are established by God.

Equally important as the issue of what miracles are and how they occur is the question of what purpose they serve. And here, too, there is broad consensus across the religious and philosophical traditions. Christian, Jewish, and Muslim thinkers; Aristotelians, Platonists, and Cartesians; rationalists, empiricists, and voluntarists—they all believed that miracles do indeed serve a purpose, although not necessarily a purpose whose rationale is accessible to human understanding. Regardless of how one understood the nature of miracles—whether as on-the-spot supernatural interventions or divinely preplanted disruptions of nature's regularity—it was agreed that God does not act capriciously. Miracles are providential events and have religious and moral significance.

Thinkers may differ on the details of how exactly miracles fit into God's providential purposes. For some, miracles serve to attest to God's presence and power; for others, they are used by God to convey important messages or warnings. Miracles are often said to provide certainty for prophetic claims (anyone can pretend to be a prophet, but a true prophet establishes his credentials with a miracle), and they are sometimes seen as aiding the historical progress of God's plan when human obstinacy stands in its way. Of course, the Bible's miracles do all of these things, and the disagreement is often only about how the narrative of the miracle is to be interpreted: Is it to be read literally or metaphorically? Is the miracle to be seen as the communication of some truth or merely as a practical expedient for moving things along?

Even the most rationalistic philosophers took these questions very seriously. It may be, as one scholar notes, that the clash between religious tradition and philosophical speculation is most acute on the question of miracles, particularly as these represent a threat to the rational understanding of the world.[15] Depending on the ancient sources a later philosopher favored and the religious tradition to which he belonged (nominally or with a deep faith), he was partial to one or another solution. But any disagreements on the nature and extent of God's miraculous and supernatural involvement in the world were strictly intramural and took place against the background of general agreement that such involvement could occur and, at least at a certain period in history, did.

In one of Spinoza's early writings, the "Metaphysical Thoughts" appended to his geometric exposition of Descartes's *Principles of Philosophy* and published in 1663 under his own name, he provides a glimpse of his mature view of miracles, although he is somewhat cautious about stating things too explicitly:

> There is the ordinary power of God, and his extraordinary power. The ordinary is that by which he preserves the world in a certain order; the extraordinary is exercised when he does something beyond the order of nature, e.g., all miracles, such as the speaking of an ass, the appearance of angels, and the like.
>
> Concerning this last there could, not without reason, be considerable doubt. For it seems a greater miracle if God always governs the world with one and the same fixed and immutable order, than if, on account of human folly, he abrogates the laws which (as only one thoroughly blinded could deny) he himself has most excellently decreed in nature, from sheer freedom. But we leave this for the theologians to settle.[16]

Miracles are dubious at best, an inferior testimony to God's power, but it remains unsaid whether or not they are at least possible.

Several years later, in the *Treatise*, the caution has disappeared. Miracles in the traditional sense, Spinoza now boldly says, are an "absurdity" and the belief in them sheer "folly." Not only are they unnecessary for, even contrary to, real piety, but they are inconsistent with the true nature of God and the proper metaphysical account of the universe. Miracle stories are convenient tools long used by ecclesiastics to manipulate the credulity of the masses. Holding up Scripture—with its tales of parting seas, talking donkeys, and the dead being brought back to life—to bolster their authority, preachers are thereby able to exercise control over people's spiritual lives and even civil society. Spinoza's attack on the belief in miracles thus represents an important element in his overall theological-political project.

According to the "multitudes" (*vulgi*), Spinoza says, a miracle occurs when "nature for that time suspended her action, or her order was temporarily interrupted." It is an event that occurs not through natural causes but through supernatural intervention. It represents the action of a transcendent God who is "lawgiver and ruler" and who is endowed with the psychological and moral characteristics of will, wisdom, justice, and mercy. According to this confused and imaginative conception, such a divinity, having created nature out of nothing, will on occasion suspend its operations for a providential purpose.

> Thus they imagine that there are two powers quite distinct from each other, the power of God and the power of Nature, though the latter is determined in a definite way by God, or—as is the prevailing opinion nowadays—created by God. What they mean by the two powers, and what by God and Nature, they have no idea, except that they imagine God's power to be like the rule of some royal potentate, and Nature's power to be a kind of force and energy. Therefore unusual works of Nature are termed miracles, or works of God, by the common people; and partly from piety, partly for the sake of opposing those who cultivate the natural sciences, they prefer to remain in ignorance of natural causes, and are eager to hear only of what is least comprehensible to them and consequently evokes their greatest wonder.

This attitude is commonly held to be the properly devout one and the most conducive to the true awe of God.

Naturally so, since it is only by abolishing natural causes and imagining supernatural events that they are able to worship God and refer all things to God's governance and God's will; and it is when they imagine Nature's power subdued, as it were, by God that they most admire God's power.

In fact, Spinoza insists, those who think this way "have no sound conception either of God or of nature. They confuse God's decisions with human decisions, and they imagine nature to be so limited that they believe man to be its chief part."[17] Anyone with true understanding knows that it is absolutely impossible for an event to occur that is a violation of nature's laws and processes—not because God, standing apart from nature, is impotent to transgress its order, but because that order just *is* the unique expression of God's power.

Spinoza's main argument against miracles in the *Treatise* does not presume that one accepts his own philosophical conception of *Deus sive Natura*. He begins with the claim that whatever God, by definition an eternal and necessary being, understands through the divine wisdom involves "eternal necessity and truth." But since in God will and intellect are one and the same thing—there can be no multiplicity of faculties in God—to say that God understands something is thereby to say that God wills it. Therefore, whatever God wills also must involve eternal necessity and truth. God's will, just like God's wisdom, is eternal and immutable. It cannot change. "The necessity whereby it follows from the divine nature and perfection that God understands some thing as it is, is the same necessity from which it follows that God wills that thing as it is." Since whatever is true is true only because of divine decree, "the universal laws of Nature are merely God's decrees, following from the necessity and perfection of the divine nature." Therefore, if anything were to happen contrary to Nature's laws, it would happen contrary to God's decrees. That is, God, in causing a supernatural miracle, would be acting in opposition to himself. "If anyone were to maintain that God performs some act contrary to the laws of Nature, he would at the same time have to maintain that God acts contrary to His own nature—than which nothing could be more absurd."[18]

Moreover, if miracles did in fact occur, Spinoza insists, they would testify not to God's infinite and eternal power but, on the contrary, to his limitations and even impotence. For a system that requires outside interventions must be a rather imperfect system, and thus reflect the incapacities or lack of foresight of its creator. The belief in miracles implies that

> God created Nature so ineffective and prescribed for her laws and rules so barren that he is often constrained to come once more to her rescue if he wants her to be preserved, and the course of events to be as he desires. This I consider to be utterly divorced from reason.[19]

Nature, as Spinoza describes it in the *Treatise*, observes a "fixed and immutable order"; its laws involve "eternal necessity and truth," and thus they are inviolable. Whatever happens, happens with necessity, even if that necessity is not always manifest to us and we are therefore occasionally tempted to see contingency in nature.

While Spinoza speaks in the *Treatise* of the "virtue and power of Nature" being identical with "the very virtue and power of God," and of the "laws and rules of Nature" being "God's eternal decrees and volitions," he stops short of explaining exactly what this is supposed to mean. His argument here against miracles, because it refers to God's "will," "decrees," and "wisdom," seems perfectly compatible with the traditional picture of God. Spinoza is trying to show that even those who are wedded to such a conception of God, as anthropomorphic as it might be, must deny the possibility of miracles. Still, *Deus sive Natura* is never far away. It is not too difficult to see behind these claims in the *Treatise*, barely concealed, the metaphysical theology and necessitarian conception of natural phenomena more extensively presented and argued for in the *Ethics*.

As we have seen, for Spinoza, God or Nature—being one and the same thing—just is the whole, infinite, eternal, necessarily existing, active system of the universe within which absolutely everything exists. This is the fundamental principle of the *Ethics* that one might see in the *Treatise*'s claim that "the power of Nature is the divine power." In the *Ethics*, the first necessary and eternal effects of this substance's power—in particular, the first effects of its most general "attributes" or ways of being (Thought, Extension, etc.)—are the principles and laws that govern all things; for example, within the attribute of Extension, the laws of physics governing the motion of bodies. Following from these first effects, with equal necessity from God or Nature, is the world itself, an eternal and infinite series of durationally existing finite things (that is, a series populated by the familiar items around us).[20] Because the laws of nature and the world of existing things follow with absolute necessity from an eternal and absolutely necessary being (that is, God or Nature itself), the world and its particular train of events could not have been otherwise than as it is.

Spinoza's cosmos is, in other words, a strictly deterministic, even necessitarian one. Everything, without exception, is causally determined to be such as it is; and, given its causes, no thing could possibly have been otherwise. Moreover, because the ultimate and most general causes themselves (the attributes of God or Nature and the laws that derive from them) from which all other causes follow exist with absolute metaphysical or logical necessity, Spinoza concludes there is no contingency whatsoever in the universe: not for the universe itself, and not for anything within it: "In nature there is nothing contingent, but all things have been determined from the necessity of the divine nature to exist and produce an effect in a certain way."[21]

In short, for Spinoza the actual world is the *only* possible world. If it is absolutely impossible for God to exist but the particular series of finite individuals and states of affairs that makes up this world not to exist; and if God's (Nature's) existence is, as Spinoza argues, absolutely necessary in itself, then this world is the only possible world.[22] This extraordinary claim is something that Spinoza seems to embrace. "Things could have been produced by God in no other way, and in no other order than they have been produced."[23] The only way there could be a different world, for "the order of nature" to be different, is if God's nature, from which that order necessarily follows, could be different. But since God's nature is absolutely

necessary in itself, that nature could not possibly have been different. Therefore, the world of things—including the unfolding of
events over time—no less than the universal features of the cosmos,
has to be what it is and could not have been otherwise.

It should be clear from all this, as well, that in the *Ethics*,
Spinoza is denying that there is any such thing as the *creation* of
the world, if what is meant by that is that God exists before voluntarily bringing the world into being ex nihilo, from a prior state
of nonbeing, and that God could also have *not* brought the world
into being. If, as Spinoza claims, the world of existing things is
a necessary and co-eternal effect of God's (Nature's) being, it is
absolutely impossible for God to exist but the world not to exist.
Spinoza thereby rejects the opening chapters of the Bible as an
imaginative fiction. But, as many philosophers have recognized,
where creation goes, so goes miracles. A world co-eternal with
God is not open to divine interventions.

In Spinoza's metaphysics, the necessity that governs the
universe—in its origins and in its inner workings—is nothing
less than the absolute necessity found among the truths of mathematics. This is a conclusion that he is not shy about publicly proclaiming. In the early publication "Metaphysical Thoughts," he
asserts that "if men understood clearly the whole order of Nature,
they would find all things just as necessary as are all those treated
in Mathematics."[24] Mathematical necessity allows for no exceptions. And without exceptions, there are no miracles.

Spinoza knows the dangerous path he is treading in the *Ethics*.
After demonstrating that "all things proceed by a certain eternal
necessity of nature" and are never brought about by anything except purely natural causes, Spinoza lambasts those who resort to
the will of God to explain things whose natural causes they do not
understand. He complains that they thereby take refuge in "the
sanctuary of ignorance" but are lauded for their piety. By contrast,

one who seeks the true causes of miracles, and is eager, like an educated man, to understand natural things, not to wonder at them, like
a fool, is generally considered and denounced as an impious heretic

by those whom the people honor as interpreters of nature and the Gods. For they know that if ignorance is taken away, then foolish wonder, the only means they have of arguing and defending their authority is also taken away.[25]

There are serious religious, even political matters at stake in the realm of miracles.[26]

The first readers of the *Treatise* would have known nothing of Spinoza's necessitarianism and the philosophical theology on which it rests (aside from what they may have gleaned, with sufficient care, from the "Metaphysical Thoughts"). But neither did Spinoza want the message of the *Treatise* to be dependent on the more radical theological theses of the *Ethics*. Most of his audience was not sufficiently prepared for those deeper and more difficult (and possibly more disturbing) insights, and the success of the theological-political appeal being made by the *Treatise* must not be made to rest on them. Thus, Spinoza had to accommodate these readers by not revealing too much of his views on God and Nature.[27]

Still, the conclusion that Spinoza draws in the *Treatise* captures well, if in nongeometric format, the important metaphysical lessons of the *Ethics*: "Nothing happens in Nature that does not follow from her laws . . . her laws cover everything that is conceived even by the divine intellect, and . . . Nature observes a fixed and immutable order."[28] The belief in miracles is an expression not of pious insight but of ignorance. Or, as Spinoza puts it in a letter to Oldenburg, "miracles and ignorance are the same."[29]

In fact, it is precisely this perspective that allows Spinoza to concede that there is a meaningful sense in which we *can* speak of miracles. Rather than supernatural violations of nature, however, a miracle should properly be understood simply as an event whose natural causal explanation remains unknown. "The word *miracle* can be understood only with respect to men's beliefs, and means simply an event whose natural cause we—or at any rate the writer or narrator of the miracle—cannot explain by comparison with any other normal event."[30] It may be that the event can indeed be explained in accordance with the current state of scientific knowledge, in which case the label "miracle" is relative only to the narrator's own ignorance of science and nature and to his aims in writing his narrative. The biblical writers—"men of old [*antiqui*]," Spinoza calls them—being generally unlearned in science but also desirous of instilling awe among their audience, were thus given to ascribing wonderful and unusual events to the will of God. When the rainbow appears to Noah as the flood waters recede, which Spinoza notes is "nothing other than the refraction and reflection of the sun's rays which they undergo in droplets of water," this is described by the writer of the passage as "God setting the rainbow in the cloud":

> There can be no doubt that all the events narrated in Scripture occurred naturally; yet they are referred to God because . . . it is not the part of Scripture to explain events through their natural causes; it only relates to those events that strike the imagination, employing such method and style as best serves to excite wonder, and consequently to instill piety in the minds of the masses.[31]

Because the biblical writer and his audience, "the common people," are generally unfamiliar with the physics behind the phenomenon of the rainbow, they readily refer all such phenomena that cannot be assimilated to "a similar happening [in the past] which is ordinarily regarded without wonder" to divine intervention.

Or perhaps the ignorance belongs not only to the narrator of the miracle but also to the scientific and philosophical community at-large, which has yet to fully understand the particular laws governing such phenomena or to discover the antecedent natural causes that, according to those laws, would sufficiently explain the event. Even in this case, where an event truly does "surpass human understanding," it remains the case that, in principle, there is a natural explanation for it.[32]

Spinoza's position on miracles is much more radical than the famous skepticism of David Hume half a century later. Hume, the great philosopher of the Scottish Enlightenment and generally given to doubts about grand metaphysical knowledge claims, would argue that it is exceedingly hard, even impossible, to justify the belief in a miracle. By definition, a miracle is a violation of the laws of nature, and thus something that goes against "a firm and unalterable experience."[33] The testimony on which the belief in a miracle is based is to be judged like all testimony, according to its probability. And with an overwhelming preponderance of instances to the contrary ("there must, therefore, be a uniform experience against every miraculous event, otherwise the event would not merit that appellation"), there is a high degree of improbability, even "a direct and full proof" against the event in question. Thus, all reports of miracles must remain unbelievable: the grounds for believing in a miracle are never sufficient to make its occurrence more credible than the belief either that its report was an innocent mistake or that there is deliberate deception among its witnesses.[34]

But Hume is making only an epistemological point, about what a person does or does not have good reasons to believe. Spinoza, by contrast, is making a stronger, metaphysical point, about reality. His view is not just that miracles are highly improbable and their stories implausible. Rather, he is claiming that they are absolutely impossible. "No event can occur to contravene Nature, which preserves an eternal fixed and immutable order. . . . Nothing can happen in Nature to contravene her own universal laws, nor yet anything that is not in agreement with these laws or that does not follow from them."[35] For Hume, a miracle is highly unlikely, to the point of incredibility; for Spinoza, "a miracle, either contrary to Nature or above Nature, is mere absurdity."[36]

Spinoza was not the only seventeenth-century thinker to deny the possibility of miracles. Two years before the publication of the *Treatise*, the unfortunate Koerbagh had published his "dictionary" of the Dutch language, *Een Bloemhof*. As we have seen, he used this excursion into linguistic history and usage to make subversive theological and political points. Among the terms "defined" in the book is *Mirakel*: "A work of wonder, deed of wonder. The theologians insist that a work of wonder should be something that happens contrary to or above nature, which is false, since nothing can happen contrary to or above nature."[37] Koerbagh, however, was by this point already familiar with and converted to his friend Spinoza's philosophical principles; indeed, he elsewhere argues against miracles on the basis of his identification of God and Nature and the eternity, necessity, and immutability of God's (Nature's) infinite power.[38] That is, Koerbagh's denial of miracles stands directly on Spinozistic foundations, and so his radical position represents not so much an interesting precedent for Spinoza's view but rather a kind of foretaste of Spinoza's more thorough metaphysical articulation of it in the *Treatise* and the *Ethics*.

A more illuminating comparison in this connection involves two philosophers who *did* have a significant influence on Spinoza, and on the *Treatise* in particular: Maimonides and Hobbes.

Maimonides' attitude toward miracles is notoriously complicated. Scholars have had a good deal of difficulty deciding what exactly he believed regarding both the possibility of miracles and their actual occurrence in history.[39] Part of the problem is that, as Maimonides explicitly tells readers of the *Guide of the Perplexed*, for their own good (lest the "ignoramuses" among them be confused by its doctrines and fall into disbelief), he is intentionally hiding some of his real views amid contradictions in the text. Certain deep truths are to be revealed only to those who are sufficiently prepared (by moral, logical, philosophical, and theological training) to grasp them without risk to their faith. Apparently among these truths are those concerning miracles.

Maimonides does not include the belief in miracles among the thirteen essential principles of the Jewish faith. He also appears throughout the *Guide* to maintain a belief in natural causal determinism. At the same time, he is not willing to abandon miracles altogether. His conclusion seems to be that miracles are, in fact, "something that is, in a certain respect, in nature." They are simply events that, when judged by the regularities that generally characterize nature and the ordinary behavior of things, are anomalous. But such anomalies are still produced by perfectly natural means. Maimonides suggests that miracles so understood are implanted in nature by God. Quoting approvingly the rabbinic sages, he notes that "they say that when God created that which exists and stamped upon it the existing natures, He put it into these natures that all the miracles that occurred would be produced in them at the time when they occurred." It was "put into the nature of water to be continuous and always to flow from above downwards except at the time of the drowning of the Egyptians." The parting of the Red Sea is thus explained by the nature of the sea's water itself. "All the other miracles can be explained in an analogous manner."[40]

Of course, it should make no difference whether an event contrary to nature's regularities is inserted ad hoc into nature at a given moment in history or planted therein at the beginning of time; it is presumably still a divine intervention bringing about an exception to the constancies that characterize nature's usual ways. But Maimonides can be read as saying that these anomalies should be regarded as events that, while rare, are just as natural as those that belong to the ordinary course of nature. They arise from the laws of nature, but not in as perspicuous a manner as other things. The parting of a sea, like an earthquake or a tsunami, is brought about through natural causes and is, at least in principle, explicable in rational, scientific terms.[41]

Maimonides does downplay the value of miracles as evidence of God's providence and wisdom, which are better seen in the ordinary working of nature than in any anomalous exceptions to it. "What is the way to love and fear God? When a person contemplates God's wondrous and great works and creatures, and sees through them God's infinite wisdom, he or she immediately loves and extols and experiences a great desire to know the great God."[42] God's perfection is most evident in nature itself, in the unexceptional order of the cosmos. "The works of the deity," which Maimonides identifies with the ordinary course of nature, "are most perfect, and with regard to them there is no possibility of any excess or deficiency. Accordingly they are of necessity permanently established as they are, for there is no possibility of something calling for a change in them."[43] Spinoza's explicit denial of miracles in the *Treatise* may represent the ultimate terminus of the naturalism that seems to undergird Maimonides' discussion in the *Guide* and elsewhere.

Given his position as rabbi and religious leader, Maimonides was understandably cautious about coming right out and denying that miracles, traditionally understood, are possible. Hobbes, with his hostility to religious authority and mocking attitude toward superstition, was willing to go further. He knows the importance granted to miracles in Scripture, including their role in determining whether or not a self-proclaimed prophet is indeed truly prophesying (although he concludes that, since the age of miracles is over, there is no longer any sure way to distinguish a prophet from a delusional madman).[44] But if the question concerns not what Scripture thinks about miracles but rather what it is reasonable to believe about them, Hobbes takes a fairly radical stance.

He describes miracles as "admirable works of God . . . therefore, they are also called *wonders*," and distinguishes two essential features of such wonders: first, they are events that are "strange," or occur very rarely, and second, those who witness them "cannot imagine [them] . . . to have been done by natural means, but only by the immediate hand of God." Thus, "if a horse or a cow should speak, it were a miracle, because both the thing is strange, and the natural cause difficult to imagine."[45] Such wonder is dispelled, however, along with the ignorance that grounds it. As soon as we determine a natural cause for the event, or, if no precise cause is discovered, when we realize that the event is not as uncommon as we originally thought, we no longer regard the phenomenon as miraculous.

> The first rainbow that was seen in the world was a miracle, because the first, and consequently strange; and served for a sign from God, placed in heaven, to assure his people there should be no more an universal destruction of the world by water. But at this day, because they are frequent, they are not miracles, neither to them that know their natural causes, nor to them that know them not.[46]

Hobbes is being careful here. He is not explicitly denying the possibility of miracles, understood as events actually brought about
not through natural causes but "by the immediate hand of God."
Indeed, he does at least say that there was a period in the past when
miracles did occur, although there is reason to doubt that he means
this seriously.[47] Some event is *called* a miracle if *we cannot imagine*
how nature brings it about or if it is unusual from our perspective.
That is, he makes the reports of miracles relative to the experience and knowledge of observers. "Seeing admiration and wonder
is consequent to the knowledge and experience wherewith men are
endued, some more, some less, it followeth that the same thing
may be a miracle to one and not to another." Thus, those who are
either ignorant or superstitious "make great wonders of those works
which other men, knowing to proceed from nature (which is not
the immediate, but the ordinary work of God) admire not at all."[48]

Does Hobbes nonetheless believe that miracles have actually
occurred, or are at least possible?[49] He does not say that the rainbow
that Noah saw in the sky, the "first" rainbow, was truly miraculous
in the sense that it was something brought about directly and immediately by God, but only that, because of its strangeness (relative to human experience), it was regarded as a miracle. On the
other hand, when Hobbes formally defines what a miracle is, he
calls it "a work of God (besides his operation by the way of nature,
ordained in the creation), done for the making manifest to his
elect the mission of an extraordinary minister for their salvation"
(for example, a prophet).[50] But, again, this seems to be his reading of the nature and role of miracles according to the narratives
of Scripture, not a recognition that such events "wrought by the
immediate hand of God" have indeed taken place.

Although his considered view about miracles may be no less
extreme than Spinoza's, Hobbes seems be playing it a little safer
in writing. Unlike Spinoza, he seems less interested in making
a metaphysical point about the possibility of miracles and more
concerned with showing how people are too easily enchanted and
abused by those who, through performing "tricks," take advantage of their credulity. "Two men conspiring, one to seem lame,

another so to cure him with a charm, will deceive many; but many conspiring, one to seem lame, another so to cure him, and all the rest to bear witness, will deceive many more."[51] If there is a warning here, it is to put us on our guard against ecclesiastics who would take advantage of "the aptitude of mankind to give too hasty belief to pretended miracles."[52] Hobbes's official position on miracles in *Leviathan* is best described as a very strong skepticism, along with hostility toward those who use reports of miracles for the aggrandizement of their own power. This is still a radical position to take, one that no doubt explains the attacks on the work by religious authorities. But Hobbes does not adopt—or, at least, does not publicly express—the thoroughgoing, dogmatic, and more radical naturalism of Spinoza's *Treatise*; after all, he "durst not write so boldly."[53]

Maimonides and Hobbes recognized the important providential role granted to miracles in Scripture, particularly as they serve to validate a prophetic mission or move along the accomplishment of God's plan.[54] But such a conception of providential activity requires that distinction between the regular course of nature and its interruption by divine fiat that Spinoza so vigorously rejects. For him, divine providence is immediately manifest in nature's normal and mundane routine, not in any alleged supernatural exceptions to it.

It was a medieval and early modern philosophical commonplace that the existence and design of the world may be used to demonstrate God's existence. God as first cause of a contingent universe, God as intelligent designer of a well-ordered cosmos—these conclusions are supposed to follow from readily available and perfectly natural empirical premises. Some thinkers also thought that the regular order of nature might serve as a guide to understanding God's attributes—Descartes, for example, believed that the laws of nature follow from and therefore testify to the perfection, simplicity, and goodness of their author. An equally common but more powerful belief, however, was that it is the extraordinary (rather

than the ordinary) that offers the best and most striking evidence of
God's power, and that it is the supernatural (rather than the natural) that most directly reveals God's providence. Nature may take
its course, but God shows his providential hand when he intervenes
within it. Spinoza insists that this is above all the view of "the common people," as he describes it in the *Treatise*.

> They suppose that God's power and providence are most clearly dis-
> played when some unusual event occurs in Nature contrary to their
> habitual beliefs concerning Nature, particularly if such an event is
> to their profit or advantage. They consider that the clearest possible
> evidence of God's existence is provided when Nature deviates—as
> they think—from her proper order. Therefore they believe that all
> those who explain phenomena and miracles through natural causes,
> or who strive to understand them so, are doing away with God, or
> at least God's providence. They consider that God is inactive all the
> while that Nature pursues her normal course, and, conversely, that
> Nature's power and natural causes are suspended as long as God is
> acting.

It is those who think this way who "imagine that there are two
powers quite distinct from each other, the power of God and the
power of Nature." However, this is grounded on that false, even
opaque conception of an anthropomorphic God that informs sectarian religions. "What they mean by the two powers, and what
by God and Nature, they have no idea, except that they imagine
God's power to be like the rule of some royal potentate."[55]

For Spinoza, as we have seen, the power of God *is* the power of
Nature. It follows, then, that God's providence cannot be mani-
fested or furthered along by the exercise of extraordinary supernatural actions, by miracles. If what is meant by "divine providence" is a
plan being carried out by a transcendent, intelligent, and purposive
agent, then there is and can be no such thing in Spinoza's universe.

Spinoza does not categorically reject the idea (or, at least, the
language) of providence. But his understanding of it is so different
from the vulgar one that it would be all but unrecognizable to his
contemporary readers. Providence, in Spinoza's sense, cannot possibly perform its traditional (and scriptural) function.

Since God is nothing but Nature and its lawlike, exceptionless operations, divine providence is manifest exclusively in the natural order itself. All things come about in and by Nature. To put it in the terms of the *Ethics*, all bodily things and their states follow from the attribute of Extension and its infinite modes; all mental things and their states follow from the attribute of Thought and its infinite modes. But this means that God's providence just *is* the universal causal efficacy of Nature. Providence thereby extends to *all* things, just because there is nothing that is outside Nature's dominion. Everything that happens, whether it is beneficial or harmful to an individual, is the effect of divine providence. The phrase is thereby rendered morally neutral and, from a Spinozistic perspective, theologically harmless. As Spinoza, continuing his discussion of miracles, explains,

> God's decrees and commandments, and consequently God's providence, are in truth nothing but Nature's order; that is to say, when Scripture tells us that this or that was accomplished by God or by God's will, nothing more is intended than that it came about by accordance with Nature's law and order, and not, as the common people believe, that Nature for some period has ceased to act, or that for some time its order has been interrupted.[56]

This approach allows Spinoza to at least employ the language of divine providence with little cost. As long as one is aware that such language is really only talk about Nature's necessary ways, it is empty and does not commit one to any superstitious claims about God providing rewards to the virtuous and punishments to the wicked or taking any special care for individuals. It is a reductive view of providence with no moral implications.

It also means that the surest path to the knowledge of God lies not in the cataloguing of miraculous and exceptional events but solely in the investigation of Nature's regularities.

> Knowing that all things are determined and ordained by God and that the workings of Nature follow from God's essence, while the laws of Nature are God's eternal decrees and volitions, we must

unreservedly conclude that we get to know God and God's will all
the better as we gain better knowledge of natural phenomena and
understand more clearly how they depend on their first cause, and
how they operate in accordance with Nature's eternal laws.

Spinoza does not believe that one must accept his metaphysical theology in order to find a valuable lesson here. He is clearly
speaking not only to those who (perhaps in the light of the *Ethics*)
have been persuaded by his own concept of God or Nature, but
also to those who may still cling to traditional religious ideas.
Even the latter, while they remain wedded to a false, anthropomorphic conception of God, need to understand at least that
"God's will and decrees" (notions that, strictly speaking, Spinoza
rejects) are best seen in the ordered ways of the world he causes.
Events whose natural causes remain hidden, while they "appeal
strongly to the imagination and evoke wonder," are less suited to
providing "a higher knowledge of God" than the works of Nature
that we clearly and distinctly conceive. Spinoza concludes that
"from miracles we cannot gain knowledge of God, his existence
and providence, and that these can be far better inferred from Nature's fixed and immutable order."[57]

Spinoza's naturalistic understanding of divine providence in
the *Treatise* can also accommodate, in some sense, an important
feature of the common religious view of providence, namely, that
which sees God as managing a system of rewards and punishments. The providential God of the Abrahamic traditions ensures
that, at least in the very long run, human virtue and vice receive
their just deserts. This is the moral dimension of providence directed at individuals that earlier Jewish philosophers called "special providence," to distinguish it from the "general providence"
that runs through the laws of nature and endows each species with
characteristics essential for survival (for example, rationality in
human beings or speed in gazelles).[58] What Spinoza cannot allow,
however, is that there is a distribution of rewards for virtue carried out by an intelligent moral agent, a kind of person, freely and
actively dispensing them from on high.

In the *Ethics*, Spinoza shows that the virtuous person pursues and acquires true and adequate ideas, a deep rational understanding of Nature and its ways. As we have seen, this intellectual knowledge, unlike information that comes by way of the senses or the imagination, provides insight into the essences of things and especially the ways in which they depend necessarily on their highest causes in Nature. Spinoza insists that this knowledge of God or Nature and how things relate to it is of the greatest benefit to a human being in two ways.

First, he suggests that an understanding of Nature's essences and laws provides the virtuous individual with the tools needed to navigate life's obstacle course. The ways of Nature are transparent to the intellectually perfected person. His capacity to manipulate things and avoid dangers is greater than that of the person who is governed by the senses and imagination and thus subject to chance and whatever may happen. The virtuous person has greater control over events; others are more at the mercy of luck. A deep knowledge of things benefits one in this very practical manner.

Second, and more important, true knowledge is, for the virtuous person, the source of an abiding happiness and peace of mind that is resistant to the vicissitudes of fortune. When a person understands Nature, he sees the necessity of all things, and especially the fact that the objects that he values are, in their comings and goings, not under his control. More precisely, he sees, for example, that all bodies and their states and relationships—including the condition of his own body—follow necessarily from the essence of matter (Extension) and the universal laws of physics; and he sees that all ideas, including all the properties of minds, follow necessarily from the essence of Thought and its universal laws.

Such insight can only weaken the power that the irrational passions have over an individual. Herein lie the natural benefits or rewards of virtue. When a person achieves a high level of understanding of Nature and realizes that he cannot control what it brings his way or takes from him, he becomes less anxious over things, less governed by the affects of hope and fear over what may or may not come to pass. No longer obsessed with or despondent over the loss of his possessions, he is less likely to be overwhelmed with emotions at their arrival and passing away. Such a person will regard all things with an even temper and will not be inordinately and irrationally affected in different ways by past, present, or future events. His life will be tranquil and not given to sudden disturbances of the passions. The result is self-control and a calmness of mind.

> The more this knowledge that things are necessary is concerned with singular things, which we imagine more distinctly and vividly, the greater is this power of the Mind over the affects, as experience itself also testifies. For we see that Sadness over some good which has perished is lessened as soon as the man who has lost it realizes that this good could not, in any way, have been kept. Similarly, we see that [because we regard infancy as a natural and necessary thing], no one pities infants because of their inability to speak, to walk, or to reason, or because they live so many years, as it were, unconscious of themselves.[59]

What Spinoza calls the "free person"—the virtuous individual who "lives according to the dictate of reason alone"[60]—bears the gifts and losses of fortune with equanimity, does only those things that he believes to be "the most important in life," refuses to chase after or be anxious about ephemeral goods, and is not overly concerned with death. His understanding of his place in the natural scheme of things brings him happiness and true peace of mind.

Virtue, then, has its rewards. The natural consequence of the striving for and acquisition of understanding and knowledge is well-being.[61] Our freedom, our physical and psychological flourishing are directly dependent on our knowledge of Nature, including our understanding both of the necessity of all things and of our place in the world. Virtue is a source of an abiding happiness that is free from chance. Such is the true but entirely natural benefit of virtue. This, if anything, constitutes a special kind providence within Spinoza's system, one that is available only to rational beings.

Of course, for Spinoza there is an important sense in which *everything* is the result of divine providence. There is nothing that happens in Nature—and whatever happens must happen in Nature, for there is nothing that is outside Nature—that is not brought about by God or Nature. Therefore, *all* benefits and *all* harms that come to a person, indeed, all the benefits and all the harms that come to anything, and not just the happiness that is the natural byproduct of virtue, are the result of divine providence. When a virtuous person suffers or a vicious person prospers, this too is providence at work.

But from the point of view of human agents, it makes all the difference in the world whether benefits come haphazardly (as judged from the agent's perspective and convenience) and according to the various but all-natural ways in which he is buffeted back and forth by external things, on the one hand, or, on the other hand, are possessed in a deliberate and controlled manner.

This is the distinction that appears in the *Treatise* between God's "external help" (*auxilium externum*) and God's "internal help" (*auxilium internum*).

> Whatever human nature can effect solely by its own power to preserve its own being can rightly be called God's internal help, and whatever falls to a man's advantage from the power of external causes can rightly be called God's external help.[62]

The external help is simply the circumstances in which we find ourselves through the operation of external causes; it is, Spinoza says, often a matter of "fortune" and causes beyond our control, of providence working in a very general way. But the internal help is grounded in the God- or Nature-given power that constitutes the essential being of any individual (what Spinoza in the *Ethics* calls *conatus*, or striving to persevere). The internal help consists in a person, moved by this power under the guidance of reason, acquiring knowledge through his own resources and thereby increasing his well-being and gaining an advantage in the world.

Spinoza, then, can agree that providence has within its scope rewards or benefits for the righteous. But no supernatural interventions or violations of the laws of nature are required for this "special" providence. It is, on the contrary, a perfectly natural process whereby, just because of the laws of nature, certain effects follow necessarily from certain causes. Any verbal concessions made in the *Treatise* to God's "will and decrees" or to divine providence are consistent with Spinoza's general naturalistic project. They are also in keeping with the absolute denial of miracles.

Chapter 6

Scripture

When Spinoza died, in February 1677, he had been living on the Paviljoensgracht in The Hague. The house was owned by Hendrik van der Spyck, a master painter, and the philosopher occupied a single room on the first floor. To pay off some of Spinoza's creditors, as well as to recoup his own expenses, Van der Spyck planned to auction off Spinoza's clothes, furniture, and other belongings. In preparation for the sale, an inventory was taken in March by the notary Willem van den Hove. Among Spinoza's possessions was a relatively large library containing works of philosophy, science, mathematics, religion, politics, and literature (including poetry). He was an eclectic and multilingual reader. There are Torah commentaries in Hebrew, classical histories and dramas in Latin, Dutch medical and political treatises, and Spanish comedies. Spinoza owned the *Observationes medicae* by Nicholas Tulp, whose anatomy lesson was immortalized by Rembrandt; a book of poems by the Spanish Golden Age writer Francisco Gómez de Quevedo; and the complete works of Machiavelli. There is even a Passover haggadah, a guide to ancient Greek, and an Italian vocabulary.

Spinoza also owned five Bibles. There are two Latin editions, one of which dates to 1541, and two Hebrew Bibles: Buxtorf's 1618 *Biblia Sacra Hebraica*, and a Venetian text published in 1639. And, like most of the members of Amsterdam's Talmud Torah congregation, Spinoza frequently read the Bible in Spanish; the translation in his library was published in Amsterdam in 1646. Among the Dutch Sephardim in the seventeenth century, domestic and business affairs were conducted in Portuguese; in their kitchens and on the street, they spoke the language of what was, for most of them, their ancestral homeland. Even those in the community not of Iberian background—such as Rabbi Mortera, an Ashkenazic Jew originally from Venice—had to learn Portuguese if they were going to get along in this cosmopolitan but close-knit world. When it was time for sacred literature or works of high culture, however, whether Torah study or literary drama, the pages turned by Amsterdam's "Hebrews of the Portuguese Nation" (many of whom had at best only a rudimentary grasp of Hebrew) were usually in Spanish.

Whether they read the Bible in Spanish, Hebrew, Latin or Dutch, Spinoza's contemporaries, like the generations before them, all made a categorical assumption about the origin of the work. Amsterdam's Calvinists, Lutherans, and Jews, as well as the Catholics who (to avoid harassment) continued to worship in private homes, believed that the Bible had a divine source. Its author, literally, was God, and its sentences faithfully (if sometimes metaphorically) conveyed his thoughts and commands and described his actions.

There is a sense, even with this assumption, in which the Bible is a human and historical document. God's message was revealed to and transcribed by human beings at certain moments in time. The words now appearing in print before early modern readers were first written down by the ancient prophets. According to tradition, Moses wrote the Pentateuch, the first five books of the Hebrew Bible, while successive individuals (Joshua, Samuel, David, Jeremiah, and so on) composed the books that bear their names or the historical chronicles in which they play a major role. But in the grand scheme of things, this is a rather trivial kind of historicity. The mortal writers were merely the privileged recipients of an eternal content, *amanuenses* charged with accurately recording God's word and with relating the history of God's chosen people. Their ephemeral manuscripts conveyed a story and laid down laws that were, without exception, divine and timeless. Scripture is certainly not, in the traditional view, the product of or response to any historical contingencies.

It is precisely this view about the divine origin of Scripture that Spinoza attacks in chapters seven through ten of the *Treatise*. He will conclude that the Hebrew Bible does *not* have its source in some supernatural revelation. Rather, it is simply a work of human literature that arose from the political circumstances of the ancient Israelites. His argument is grounded in a variety of philosophical, linguistic, and historical considerations, including his own metaphysics of God or Nature (still only subtly present in the *Treatise*) and his views on prophecy and miracles.

Spinoza was not the first to insist on the historicity of the Bible. There was already a long tradition, especially after the Reformation, of critical approaches to biblical texts. Mainstream Catholic and Protestant theologians before him had urged a philological and historical study of Hebrew Scripture, particularly as they regarded the written and, later, printed document (but not the divine content it communicated) as a work of human hands subject to all the vagaries of transmission. While Reformation principles called for a return to "Scripture itself," a direct acquaintance by faithful (but not necessarily learned) readers with the pages of the Bible for the purpose of grasping its clear and accessible lessons, late Renaissance and early modern humanists pursued their philological and linguistic studies in order to determine its less obvious, more "genuine" historical meanings. By the seventeenth century there was a well-developed tradition of scholarly interest in the origin and provenance of biblical manuscripts leading up to contemporary printed editions.[1]

The sixteenth-century Dutch Catholic humanist Desiderius Erasmus, for example, insisted on using original language (Greek and Hebrew) sources, classical authors, and the writings of the Church fathers to evaluate and even revise Jerome's Vulgate (Latin) edition of the Gospels, as well as to compose his own commentary on the Psalms and other books. While such scholarship was not wholly to the liking of ecclesiastic authorities, especially when it was put to polemical purposes—Erasmus was strongly condemned by the Church theologians for his audacity—it certainly was not uncommon, especially within the universities. But Spinoza took the historical study of Scripture, and especially the question of its mundane authorship, much further than earlier thinkers. More than anyone else, Spinoza, with his willingness to go wherever the textual and historical evidence led, regardless of religious ramifications, ushered in modern biblical source scholarship. To many latter-day readers of the Bible, the notion that its authors were mere humans addressing social and political contingencies of their day may seem perfectly commonplace.[2] But Spinoza's conclusions on the origins of Scripture and the history and implications of its transmission scandalized his contemporaries as much as his view on miracles.

Moses is supposed to have written every single word of the Torah. At least, as Hobbes contemptuously notes, this is a nonnegotiable principle within the Abrahamic traditions, especially among the orthodox and outside scholarly circles. It is believed, he says in *Leviathan*, "on all hands that the first and original author of [Scripture] is God."[3] More precisely, God communicated all the commandments to Moses on Mount Sinai, as well as the story of the Creation, the account of the generations that lived before Moses, and the narrative of the subsequent tribulations of the Israelites. Moses alone is said to have combined all of this legal, historical, political, religious, and metaphysical material into one single work that was handed down unchanged and uncorrupted through the ages. This guarantees the divine authority, and thus eternal validity, of these books: they came directly from God to the prophet Moses, and then to the people, with no break in the transmission and thus no concerns about whether they truly represented the word of God.

It was evident to more reflective readers of various religious (and antireligious) persuasions throughout history that such a position runs up against some serious problems. A number of Jewish and Christian commentators, arguing on the basis of the text, known historical facts, and undeniable empirical principles

("Dead men tell no tales"), suggested, ever so carefully (and sometimes only implicitly), that Moses could not have written everything found in the Pentateuch. In fact, by Spinoza's time, there was nothing new about raising the question of Moses' authorship of every sentence of the Pentateuch, and even in claiming positively that he did not write absolutely all that is therein.

The most glaring problem concerns the account of the death of Moses himself. It is obviously impossible for someone to write about his own death and burial. Even the sages of the Talmud, committed as they are to the principle that all of the Torah was written by Moses, concede that the last eight verses were added by Joshua.[4]

The twelfth-century exegete Abraham Ibn Ezra took things a little further, although he was very careful not to state his opinion too boldly. In his commentary on the Pentateuch, he suggests that a number of elements in the text lead to the conclusion that there are several verses that could not have been written by Moses. In his remarks on Genesis 12.6 ("And the Canaanite was then in the land"), Ibn Ezra says that "there is a secret meaning to this text. Let the one who understands it remain silent." The "secret meaning," derived from the grammar of the sentence, seems to be that when the verse was written the Canaanite was no longer in the land, having been expelled by the Israelites (which occurred only under the leadership of Joshua); thus the verse was written at least a generation after Moses. Commenting on Deuteronomy 1.1 ("These are the words that Moses addressed to all Israel beyond the Jordan River, in the wilderness, in the desert, across the Red Sea, between Paran and Tofel, and Lavan, and Hasherot, and Di-Zahav"), Ibn Ezra speculates what the meaning of this verse might be, since Moses did not get to cross over the Jordan River. He concludes his interpretation of the passage by mysteriously noting that "if you understand the secret of the twelve and also that of 'So Moses wrote' (Deut. 31.22); 'And the Canaanite was then in the land' (Gen. 12.6); 'In the mount where the lord is seen' (Gen. 22.14); and 'behold, his [Og's] bedstead was a bedstead of iron' (Deut 3.11), then you will recognize the truth."[5] Commentators are generally agreed that what Ibn Ezra means is that just as the last twelve verses of Deuteronomy were not written by Moses (this is "the secret of the twelve"), so neither were the other cited verses. Moses would not have referred to himself in the third person ("So Moses wrote . . ."), and he would have had no need to give evidence of the height of Og, the giant king of Bashan, by mentioning his bed, since his extraordinary size would have been known to his contemporaries. Moreover, when Moses was still alive, the Temple ("the mount where the Lord is seen") had not yet been built. The "truth," then, is that there are a number of sentences in the Torah that were not composed by Moses but were added by others coming after him.

It is a very limited claim that Ibn Ezra is hinting at (and it is something that he dare not proclaim openly, lest some readers conclude that there are many other verses, perhaps entire chapters, not written by Moses). He still believes that Moses was the author of almost all of the Pentateuch; he is certainly *not* saying what Spinoza, in the *Treatise*, takes him to be saying, namely, "that it was not Moses who wrote the Pentateuch but someone else who lived long after him."[6]

Ibn Ezra's commentary was well known to Jewish and Christian exegetes, and many thought the questions he raised were reasonable ones. A number of prominent theologians, in fact, turned his veiled hints into unambiguous conclusions. Luther, for one, did not believe it was a big deal if a few lines of the Pentateuch were not by Moses' own hand. Foreshadowing Spinoza's radical claim about the Pentateuch as a whole, some of these commentators even focused on Ezra the Scribe, in the Second Temple period, as the likely author of those verses not written by Joshua.[7]

By the seventeenth century, then, it was well within the bounds of respectability to suggest that there were passages of the Pentateuch not written by Moses himself. Not everyone subscribed to this idea, but even its critics took it seriously. Somewhat less respectable, but still apparently within the realm of legitimate debate, was the notion that all of Hebrew Scripture as we have it received its current redacted form long after Moses and the other prophets, organized by a later editor or team of editors, although the sources they were working with were authentically Mosaic. The Catholic theologian Andreas Masius, for example, argued in his book on Joshua, *Iosuae imperatoris historia illustrata atque explicata* (Antwerp, 1574), that the Mosaic and Joshuan raw materials were "collected, arranged and united, as it were, into one volume" by Ezra, assisted perhaps by colleagues in the Great Synagogue.[8]

It was Spinoza, however, who took things to an unprecedented extreme and, in the eyes of his contemporaries, crossed the line. He was not alone in doing so. As we shall see, his view of the Bible as an all-too-human document was shared by one or two others in the period. But such company was cold comfort, and did nothing to deflect the attacks on the *Treatise*—indeed, it only inflamed them.

Spinoza is well aware of the risky stand he is taking in the *Treatise*. "The author [of the Pentateuch] is almost universally believed to be Moses, a view so obstinately defended by the Pharisees[9] that they have regarded any other view as a heresy."[10] It is important to his theological-political project, however, that he address this dogma. Troubled by the expansion of ecclesiastic power in the Dutch Republic, and especially the meddling of Calvinist preachers in public affairs and in the lives of private citizens, Spinoza recognized that one of their most effective tools for justifying their usurpations was the Bible.[11] They proclaimed their actions to be backed by the word of God and held up the Bible as the source of their moral, social, and even political authority. Moreover, they set themselves up as the sole qualified interpreters of Scripture and read it to suit their purposes. Thus Spinoza:

> On every side we hear men saying that the Bible is the Word of God, teaching mankind true blessedness, or the path to salvation. . . . We see that nearly all men parade their own ideas as God's word, their chief aim being to compel others to think as they do, while using

religion as a pretext. We see, I say, that the chief concern of theologians on the whole has been to extort from Holy Scripture their own arbitrarily invented ideas, for which they claim divine authority.[12]

Waving the Bible was (and still is) a powerful means of persuading the masses, not to mention the ruling elites, that the way of the *predikanten*—sectarian, intolerant, and (in terms of Dutch politics) conservative as it is—is God's way.

By showing that the Bible is not, in fact, the work of a supernatural God—"a message for mankind sent down by God from heaven," as Spinoza mockingly puts it—but a perfectly natural human document; that the author of the Pentateuch is not Moses; that Hebrew Scripture as a whole is but a compilation of writings composed by fallible and not particularly learned individuals under various historical and political circumstances; that most of these writings were transmitted over generations, to be finally redacted by a latter-day political and religious leader—in short, by naturalizing the Torah and the other books of the Bible and reducing them to ordinary (though morally valuable) works of literature, Spinoza hopes to undercut ecclesiastic influence in politics and other domains and weaken the sectarian dangers facing his beloved Republic: "In order to escape from this scene of confusion, to free our minds from the prejudices of theologians and to avoid the hasty acceptance of human fabrications as divine teachings," he insists, it is necessary to see what exactly Scripture is and the "true method" by which it should be read. "For unless we understand this we cannot know with any certainty what the Bible or the Holy Spirit intends to teach."[13]

Spinoza begins where he believes his illustrious medieval predecessor left off. Building on Ibn Ezra's subtle message, Spinoza marshals additional evidence to show that the author of the first five books of the Hebrew Bible was not Moses but "someone who lived many generations later." He cites the fact that the writer of those books refers consistently to Moses in the third person, compares Moses to the prophets that came after him ("declaring that he excelled them all"), narrates events that occurred after the death of Moses ("the children of Israel did eat manna forty years until they came to a land inhabited, until they came unto the borders of the land of Canaan" [Exodus 16.35]—that is, Spinoza notes, "until the time referred to in Joshua 5.12"), and uses the names of places that they did not bear in Moses time but acquired much later (for example, where the Bible says that Abraham "pursued the enemy even unto Dan" [Genesis 14.14], Spinoza notes that the city did not have that name "until long after the death of Joshua"). Spinoza's conclusion is (despite what he says) much stronger than anything Ibn Ezra, or anyone else up to that time, explicitly says or even envisions: "From the foregoing it is clear beyond a shadow of doubt that the Pentateuch was not written by Moses, but by someone who lived many generations after Moses."[14]

There is, Spinoza says, an authentic Mosaic core to the text of the Pentateuch. He believes, on the basis of the Bible's own testimony, that Moses himself wrote three items: an account of the war against Amalek and of the journeying of the Israelites (called the "Book of the Wars of God"), an abbreviated rendering of God's "utterances and laws" (called "Book of the Covenant"), and a more extensive explanation of God's commandments and of the covenant between God and his chosen people ("Book of the Law of God"). None of these books, of course, is extant, and none can be identified with the Pentateuch itself. Rather, the true author of the Pentateuch had access to at least the "Book of the Law of God" and "inserted [it] in proper order in his own work."[15]

In similar fashion, Spinoza argues that Joshua was not himself the author of the book that bears his name ("some events are narrated that happened after Joshua's death") but that it was "written many generations after Joshua"; that "nobody of sound judgment can believe that [the book of Judges] was written by the judges themselves"; and that, "inasmuch as the history is continued long after his lifetime," neither were the books of Samuel composed by Samuel, nor the book of Kings composed by the monarchs that appear in it, but all of these were in fact drawn from a number of ancient chronicles. "We may therefore conclude that all the books [of the Hebrew Bible] that we have so far considered are the works of other hands, and that their contents are narrated as ancient history."[16]

Who, then, did write (or at least did the bulk of the editorial work) on Hebrew Scripture? Spinoza is convinced that it was "a single historian who set out to write the antiquities of the Jews from their first beginnings until the first destruction of the city." The books of the Torah and other writings, despite their distinct and varied sources, are so thematically connected with each other and so skillfully constructed into one well-ordered and continuous (but not seamless) narrative—with relatively smooth transitions from one historical period or political regime to the next—that, he concludes, "there was only one historian," working many generations after the events he narrates, "with a fixed aim in view." And from the narrative itself it is quite clear what that historian's aim was: "To set forth the words and commandments of Moses," the first and most important leader of the Israelites, "and to demonstrate their truth by the course of history."[17]

Spinoza concedes that it cannot be determined with absolute certainty who the historian was. But in his view, as others before him had suggested, all the evidence points to Ezra. The text makes it clear that the writer could not have lived before the mid-sixth century BCE, since he tells of the liberation of Jehoiachim, the king of Judah, from Babylonian captivity, an event that occurred ca. 560 BCE. Moreover, Spinoza notes, Scripture itself says that Ezra, "alone of all men of his time," was devoted to establishing and setting forth the law of God (Ezra 7.10) and was a scribe learned in the law of Moses (Ezra 7.6). "Therefore," he concludes, "I cannot imagine anyone but Ezra was the writer of these books."[18] Ezra called the first five books of his work after Moses because the life of Moses is their main subject. For the same reason, he called other books after Joshua, the Judges of Israel, Ruth, Samuel, and Kings.

Ezra obviously did not compose all of these works from scratch. Neither was he able to complete his project. Rather, he collected histories written by various ancient Hebrew authors, sometimes simply copying their accounts word for word, with the intention of ultimately revising them and weaving them into a single polished narrative. Material from Moses, Joshua, Isaiah, and others were "collected indiscriminately and stored together with a view to examining them and arranging them more conveniently at some later time."[19] Spinoza speculates that Ezra may have died before he had a chance to put the finishing touches on his book. The selection of certain writings for canonization into Scripture, and the rejection of other, equally ancient works, was, in Spinoza's view, done many generations after Ezra, and certainly no earlier than the Maccabean period (ca. second century BCE), but probably even later. The Pharisees are the most likely candidates, and Spinoza suggests that their decisions were grounded in defending their tradition and their position on the law against their opponents, the Sadducees. "Men learned in the Law summoned a council to decide what books should be received as sacred and what books should be excluded."[20] It was, in other words, a very human, and politically motivated, process.

The result—as is clear from the present state of the text of Hebrew Scripture, with its many repetitions, omissions, fragmentary stories, chronological discrepancies, and outright inconsistencies—is a "mutilated" (*truncatum*), incomplete, insufficiently edited anthology. There are two accounts of the creation of the world that differ in important and irreconcilable respects; Philistine armies that, in one chapter (1 Samuel 7), are so defeated by the Israelites that they are said to be incapable of ever invading again, only to reappear shortly thereafter (1 Samuel 13), launching yet another attack; kings with indeterminate but occasionally overlapping reigns; and implausible chronologies. "In 1 Kings 6 we are told that Solomon built his temple 480 years after the exodus from Egypt, but the narratives themselves require a much greater number of years."[21] Even the most casual reader of the Bible cannot help but be struck by the apparently haphazard way in which it is organized. "It must be admitted that these narratives were compiled from different sources, without any proper arrangement or scrutiny."[22]

Making things even more difficult are numerous scribal errors and variant readings that, Spinoza insists, have crept into the text as the original manuscript was copied again and again and handed down through the generations. Spinoza, like most of the young men of his generation born into the Amsterdam Portuguese Jewish community (but not necessarily their Iberian-born fathers), knew Hebrew well—he composed a grammar of that language for his gentile friends in the late 1660s—and he was a careful reader of the Hebrew Bible. His conclusions are based on close analysis of that text and technical linguistic considerations, including "doubtful readings" due to missing or mistaken words, copying errors made between similarly formed letters (the *resh* and the *dalet*, for example, might be taken for each other), and changes in vocalization.

> That the text is mutilated cannot be doubted by anyone who has the slightest acquaintance with the Hebrew language, for it [1 Samuel 13.1] begins thus, "Saul was in his __ year when he began to reign, and he reigned for two years over Israel." Who can fail to see, I repeat, that the number of years of Saul's age when he began to reign has been omitted? And I do not think that anyone can doubt too that the narrative itself requires a greater number for the years of his reign. For chapter 27 v. 7 of the same book tells us that David sojourned among the Philistines, to whom he had fled for refuge from Saul, a year and four months. By this calculation the other events of his [Saul's] reign must have occupied eight months, a conclusion which I imagine no one will accept.[23]

Spinoza was not alone among his contemporaries in using textual evidence and historical considerations, including the works of ancient writers such as Josephus, to draw radical conclusions—ones that went well beyond what earlier scholars had been willing to claim—about the human origins of the Bible. But neither did he have much company. And those few who, some years before, had published similar views certainly did not prepare a more receptive environment for Spinoza's theses; on the contrary, they probably put the authorities on greater alert against such blasphemies against Scripture, although it is unlikely that there could be any circumstances in the seventeenth century under which the claim that the Pentateuch is not at all the work of Moses might get an unbiased hearing.

In *Leviathan*, Hobbes had argued that Scripture as we have it is not uniformly and literally the word of God—that it is, in important respects, a very human and historical document. He grants that "God is the first and original author" of Scripture. Through supernatural revelation, God conveyed his word to the prophets. But it follows from this that those prophets are the only individuals who can be certain as to what exactly the word of God is. Only the direct recipient of a revelation has a chance of truly knowing both *what* was revealed and *that* it was revealed by God. Since the writings now canonized as Scripture are many times removed from those original revelations and from whatever was immediately written down by the prophets who received them, the firsthand knowledge of revelation is lost.

Working, like Spinoza (and Ibn Ezra),[24] from the obvious problems raised by a Mosaic authorship ("It were a strange interpretation to say *Moses* spake of his own sepulcher . . . that it was not found to that day wherein he was yet living"), Hobbes concludes that Moses did not write all or even most of the Pentateuch, although he did write everything in it that he is explicitly said to have written, particularly the Mosaic law (for example, Hobbes believes that Deuteronomy 11–26 are by Moses' own hand). Neither did Joshua write the book of Joshua; it was composed "after his own time," just as Judges, Ruth, Samuel, and other books were written much later than the events they narrate. In fact, Hobbes concludes, the "Old Testament" is a compilation of writings "by divers men," though "all endued with one and the same spirit, in that they conspire to one and the same end, which is the setting forth of the rights of the kingdom of *God*, the *Father*, *Son* and *Holy Ghost*." These inspired writings were put together "long after the Captivity," and Hobbes's opinion as to its author-editor is the same as Spinoza's: "Scripture was set forth in the form we have it in by Ezra."[25]

What has come down through the generations as the Hebrew Bible, then, is, as Spinoza would assert in the *Treatise*, a work of human literature that carries a divine message.[26] However, in no way can this natural product justifiably be identified with the supernatural word of God as this was originally revealed to the prophets. Too much time has gone by since that act of divine communication, and the post-exilic documents that are "the true registers of those things which were done and said by the prophets" have subsequently passed through too many scribal hands under various regimes, for us to be able to say with any confidence that what we have is, in all of its particulars, the word of God.

This is where Hobbes puts his analysis of the Bible—including the Christian Gospels—to political use. For he concludes that whatever authority the text of Scripture has must come not from any sure knowledge about its divine origin (which, absent a special revelation to confirm this, cannot be had) but solely from the sovereign who governs the land (or, more precisely, its official church) and proclaims the text of Scripture to be God's word.

> None can know they [Scriptures] are God's word (though all true Christians believe it) but those to whom God himself hath revealed it supernaturally. . . . He, therefore, to whom God hath not supernaturally revealed that they are his, nor that those that published them were sent by him, is not obliged to obey them by any authority but his whose commands have already the force of laws (that is to say, by any other authority than that of the commonwealth, residing in the sovereign, who only has the legislative power).[27]

Hobbes first published *Leviathan* in English in 1651. His discussion of the problem of biblical authorship in that work is relatively brief, and, while it anticipates the arguments of the *Treatise*, does not match the scope and detail of Spinoza's discussion. Four years later, a book published in Amsterdam in Latin (but probably written in the 1640s), reviewed the case in somewhat more extensive terms than Hobbes. It was quickly condemned as a "blasphemous" and "Godless" work, as *Leviathan* and the *Treatise* themselves would be in the 1670s.

The author of the *Prae-Adamitae* (Pre-Adamites) was one of those peripatetic figures who populate the landscape of the early modern Republic of Letters. Isaac La Peyrère went wherever his work as secretary to the Prince of Condé took him: Bordeaux, Paris, Amsterdam, London, Spain, even Scandinavia. In the process, he expanded not only his official business contacts but his intellectual acquaintances as well, and it is possible that he met both Spinoza and Hobbes.[28]

The primary thesis of La Peyrère's work was that Adam was not the first man. Rather, there was a lineage of human beings existing before Adam. The evidence that La Peyrère marshals for this thesis includes contemporary scientific developments, such as the discovery of new lands with heretofore unknown peoples who "did not descend from Adam," and recently uncovered ancient histories describing civilizations not accounted for in the Bible. La Peyrère also points to evidence internal to Scripture. Where, he asks, would Cain's wife have come from if there were not other people besides Adam's own progeny? The book of Genesis, he concludes, is the history of the origin not of all humankind but only of the Jewish people, and the creation of Adam was simply the creation of the first *Jewish* man.

In the course of pursuing this theory, La Peyrère argues that the text of the Hebrew Bible as we have it is not by the hand of Moses—again, Moses could not have written about his own death or about events that took place after he died—or by the prophets themselves, but is an edited document that draws on a variety of ancient writings. "I need not trouble the Reader much further to prove a thing in itself sufficiently evident, that the first five books of the Bible were not written by Moses, as is thought."[29] In fact, "these things were diversely written, being taken out of several authors."[30] The final author-editor did not do a very skilled job, in La Peyrère's estimation, and the extant product is an inconsistent collection that varies in quality among its parts and whose manuscript tradition—involving numerous "careless transcribers"— exhibits an inordinate number of variant readings. "Nor need anyone wonder after this, when he reads many things confused

and out of order, obscure, deficient, many things omitted and mis-
placed, when they shall consider with themselves that they are a
heap of copie confusedly taken."[31] La Peyrère doubts that this corrupt text, what he disparagingly calls a "heap of copie of copie,"
is an accurate source for what is to be found in the original, "real"
Bible and a reliable record of what God revealed to the prophets.

Despite embedding his account of the Bible's origins in the
context of his "shocking" pre-Adamite theory, La Peyrère, as one
scholar puts it, "was not just a nut-case." His book was widely
read, and "he was known to many of the leading Bible scholars
of the time."[32] Spinoza owned a copy of the *Prae-Adamitae*. He
also had in his library Hobbes's *De Cive* (*The Citizen*), in which
the Englishman's views regarding Scripture's origin and Mosaic
authorship are only hinted at—he notes in *De Cive*, for example,
that the Bible is "that which God hath spoken" not completely
but only in "innumerable places."[33] It cannot be doubted, however, that Spinoza also read *Leviathan* while composing the *Treatise*,
either in his friend Abraham van Berckel's 1667 Dutch translation
or in the 1668 Latin translation published in Amsterdam. It is
impossible to say whether Hobbes or La Peyrère exercised any influence on Spinoza.[34] Spinoza was well acquainted with Ibn Ezra
and other medieval Jewish commentators on Torah and the rest of
Hebrew Scripture, and probably needed no help from Hobbes or
La Peyrère (neither of whom knew Hebrew[35]), or any other contemporary thinker, for that matter, in forming his views on biblical authorship.[36]

For Spinoza (and for Hobbes and La Peyrère), then, the Hebrew Bible is a jumble of texts by different hands, from different periods and for different audiences. Just as significant—and
this seems to be a point original with Spinoza—there was much
contingency and even some arbitrariness to the inclusion of some
sources but not others. The original, Second Temple–era author-
editor of the texts was able only partially to synthesize his sources
and create a single work out of them. Moreover, this imperfectly
composed collection was then subject to the changes that naturally creep into writings during the transmission process as they

are copied and recopied again and again, over many generations. It is a "faulty, mutilated, adulterated and inconsistent" piece of work, a mixed breed by its birth and corrupted by its descent and preservation. The Hebrew Bible is full of passages that are, as Spinoza is fond of saying, clearly *truncata*, and it shows its less obvious fault lines to someone who knows how to look for them. "That the text is mutilated cannot be doubted by anyone who has the slightest acquaintance with the Hebrew language."[37]

What is not *truncatum*, however, is the ultimate teaching of Scripture, whether the Hebrew Bible or the Christian Gospels. It is, in fact, a rather simple one: Practice justice and loving kindness to your fellow human beings. The point of all the commandments and the lesson of all the stories, surviving whole and unadulterated throughout the divergencies, errors, ambiguities, and corruptions of the text, is that basic moral message. It is, Spinoza insists, there in the Hebrew prophets ("Do not seek revenge or bear a grudge against one of your people, but love your neighbor as yourself" [Leviticus 19.18]) and it is in the Gospels ("He who loves his neighbor has satisfied every claim of the law" [Romans 13.8]). "I can say with certainty, that in the matter of moral doctrine I have never observed a fault of variant reading that could give rise to obscurity or doubt in such teaching."[38] The moral doctrine is the clear and universal message of the Bible, at least for those who know how to read it properly. But the question is, what is the proper way to read it?

When Spinoza's exposition of Descartes's philosophy, *René Descartes' Principles of Philosophy, Parts I and II, Demonstrated According to the Geometric Method*, appeared in 1663, it was accompanied by a preface by one of his good friends, Lodewijk Meijer. Meijer, slightly older than Spinoza, was a Lutheran, although probably not a very pious one. Most of his energies were devoted to intellectual and artistic matters. He had degrees in philosophy and medicine from the University of Leiden, and by the early 1660s had published some poetry and drama of his own. He would go on to become the director of the Amsterdam Municipal Theater, from 1665 to 1669, and the founder of the dramatic and literary society Nil Volentibus Arduum (Nothing Is Difficult to Those Who Are Willing).

In 1663, however, Meijer was just another medical doctor in Amsterdam who also happened to have a deep interest in philosophy. He wrote the preface to Spinoza's first publication to alert its audience to the precise nature of his friend's goal in setting forth the basic metaphysical and epistemological principles of Cartesian thought, and to warn the reader not to confuse the contents of this work with the author's own philosophy. "I should like it to be particularly noted that in all these writings . . . our Author has only set out the opinions of Descartes and their demonstrations, insofar as these are found in his writings, or are such as ought to be deduced validly from the foundations he laid. . . . So let no one think that he is teaching here either his own opinions, or only those which he approves of."[39] Spinoza's exposition of his own principles would be reserved for the *Ethics*, which he was working on at the same time as he composed this Cartesian manifesto but which would not be published until after his death, and (although Meijer could not yet have known this) the *Treatise*.

Meijer was interested in more than just shepherding Spinoza's ideas into print. He had philosophical views of his own, ones that his many contemporary critics found rather objectionable. Three years after introducing Spinoza's book to the public, Meijer published in Amsterdam his *Philosophy, Interpreter of Scripture* (*Philosophia S. Scripturae Interpres*; a Dutch edition appeared a year later) in which he makes the radical proposal that philosophy, or reason, is to be the touchstone in interpreting the Bible. Philosophy, according to Meijer, was not the handmaiden of religion, forced to conform its conclusions to theological dogma and the literal word of the Bible; on the contrary, Scripture had to answer to philosophy. Indeed, the exact same truths proclaimed by Scripture were accessible to human reason alone, without the need of any special acts of divine revelation.

In his book, Meijer distinguishes between the simple meaning of a sentence (what it literally and strictly means when the words are read according to common usage), the "true meaning" of that sentence (what the author of the sentence intends to convey by it), and the truth (the correspondence of the meaning of the sentence with reality). Authors often express their thoughts using words in metaphorical ways, and in such cases the literal meaning will differ from the true meaning, "the ideas and concepts in the mind of the one who has produced the sentence." And just because an author says (and means to say) that something is the case, it does not follow that it truly is the case, that it is "in agreement with the facts as they exist in actuality independent of the speaker's understanding."[40] The literal meaning of the sentence "God is king of nations" may be quite different from the meaning that its speaker intends to convey by it (God is all-powerful). And it is a yet further question as to whether or not the sentence, so understood, is true.

This tripartite distinction holds for all human utterances and almost all works of literature . . . except one, the Bible. In the case of the Bible, the true meaning of any sentence is necessarily identical with the truth. This is because the author of Scripture is an omniscient, omnipotent, wise, and essentially veracious being— God, "who can neither deceive nor be deceived." And it is inconceivable that the proposition intended by God to be conveyed by a sentence is not also the absolute truth.

> The Holy Writings have for their author God himself who, in making use of scribes, led them by the hand, as it were, on the road of truth; and in these scribes was ever present the Spirit of Truth, on whom not even a shadow of falsity or error could fall. It is therefore quite certain that whatever is inscribed in Scripture contains nothing but the purest truth, completely free from any taint of falsity and error. Thus the true meanings of the divine utterances are always in accord with truth.[41]

In the case of Scripture, every true meaning will be a truth. Moreover, since God is infinite in intellect and power and incapable of deceit, there is no reason why each of the sentences of Scripture needs to be univocal and have only one true meaning. All the truths successfully expressed by any passage in the Bible are to count among its true and intended meanings. God can pack as many truths into a sentence as he wants, and all of them will be true and legitimate ways to interpret that sentence. "Since the reader or listener encounters no truths in Scripture which the Spirit of God has not foreseen he will encounter—indeed, has provided for this—and since the reader or listener may encounter all these, it follows that all these truths in that passage were deliberately intended by him, and that they are therefore also true meanings."[42]

Meijer concludes from this account of the author and nature of Scripture that philosophy is "the norm and rule for interpreting and judging [Scripture]."[43] Deciding what the true meaning of a scriptural passage is, is a matter of determining which of the possible candidates is true and demonstrable; and determining what is true and demonstrable is precisely the task of philosophy. By "philosophy" Meijer does not mean the particular philosophical system of this or that thinker—whether it be Plato, Aristotle, or even Descartes—but reason itself, our rational faculty for discovering, through rigorous demonstrations, what is true and what is false. God is the author of both Scripture *and* human reason; therefore, the pronouncements of both must be true and mutually consistent. As Meijer, like many philosophers before him, insists, "truth cannot be contrary to itself."

For Meijer, then, "philosophy is the sure and infallible norm both for interpreting the Holy Writings and for examining interpretations."[44] Any proposed interpretation of Scripture must pass the test of objective, independent reason. If an interpretation, no matter how well grounded in the text it may be, is inconsistent with what reason tells us with certainty to believe—that is, with philosophical truth—then that interpretation must be rejected. For example, reason tells us that God cannot be "agitated" by human emotions; that would be inconsistent with a perfect and infinite Being. Therefore, any sentence in the Bible that describes God as being angry or sad or disappointed cannot be read literally;

the "simple meaning" cannot be the true meaning of the passage. In this case, only a figurative or metaphorical interpretation will do, one that reads the sentence in such a way that it ascribes to God only properties that reason agrees are consistent with the divine nature. Similarly, philosophy has proven that "nothing comes from nothing"; therefore, the scriptural account of God's ex nihilo creation of the world cannot be taken at face value. In this way, Meijer says, "the more difficult texts of Scripture are explained with the help of philosophy."

In fact, Meijer goes further and says that, strictly speaking, Scripture is not necessary for discovering religious truths. Because Scripture's true meanings are truths plain and simple, a rational person could, in principle, discover all of them for himself, without ever reading Scripture. Scripture does indeed teach the truth, but there are other means to it as well. The function of Scripture is "only to rouse its readers and to impel them to think about the matters set out therein, to look into them and consider whether the facts are as there set out. . . . Its function is to provide occasion and material for our thinking, thinking about things on which perhaps we would never otherwise have reflected."[45] The Bible may be an effective means for stimulating us to think true thoughts about God, but philosophy can do just as good a job on its own.

Unsurprisingly, Meijer was widely condemned for the "innovations" and "heresies" in his "atheistic" and "licentious" book. In 1666, immediately after publication, the Haarlem *classis* of the Reformed Church proclaimed the work to be filled with "godlessness and blasphemy," while among the propositions explicitly condemned by the curator of the University of Leiden in 1676 is that *philosophiam esse S. Scripturae interpretem* (philosophy is the interpreter of Holy Scripture).[46] Meijer was clearly aware of the reaction his book would provoke, since he had taken the precaution of publishing it anonymously. A 1674 edition would be printed in a single volume with Spinoza's *Treatise*, and for a long time some believed Spinoza to be the author of both works. In fact, the true identity of the author would remain a mystery until after Meijer's death in 1681.

The leadership of the Reformed Church in particular, with its devotion to Scripture as the foundation of its own interpretation (*sola Scriptura*), was incensed by Meijer's arguments that their position was incoherent and easily refutable. To these clerics, the idea that we need to go *outside* Scripture to some independent standard of truth, and especially philosophy or secular reason, was intolerable. So was the idea that a scriptural passage might have many legitimate and equally justified readings, some of which are literal but others figurative or allegorical. The standard position among Reformation theologians of the time was that Scripture has only one meaning, and it is the literal one (Meijer's "simple meaning"). Luther himself had insisted that "only the true principal meaning that is provided by the letters can produce good theologians." It may take some significant textual, linguistic, and historical work to discover what that "principal" meaning is; or, as Calvin claimed, the proper, literal interpretation of Scripture might require special illumination by the "Divine Spirit"—a view equally ridiculed by Meijer. But Luther, at least, is clear that "even though the things described in Scripture mean something further, Scripture should not therefore have a twofold meaning. Instead, it should retain the one meaning to which the words refer. . . . It is much more certain and much safer to stay with the words and the simple meaning."[47]

It was hardly an innovative or novel thesis that Meijer was propounding. Galileo, for one, insisted on it when defending the claim that Copernicanism is not inconsistent with Scripture.[48] Indeed, it was a view that Spinoza himself may have held at one point—in a book for which Meijer had written the preface! In the "Metaphysical Thoughts" that appeared just a few years before Meijer's treatise and in some elements of which Spinoza offers glimpses of his own views on metaphysical and theological matters, he notes that "Scripture teaches nothing which contradicts the natural light." He then uses this principle as a basis for the interpretation of Scripture.

> It suffices that we demonstrate those things [that we can grasp most certainly by natural reason] for us to know that Sacred Scripture

must also teach the same things. For the truth does not contradict the truth, nor can Scripture teach such nonsense as is commonly supposed. For if we were to discover in it anything that would be contrary to the natural light, we could refute it with the same freedom which we employ when we refute the Koran and the Talmud. But let us not think for a moment that anything could be found in Sacred Scripture that would contradict the natural light.[49]

If Spinoza is indeed presenting his own "thoughts" here, it is tempting to conclude that Meijer learned his lessons on scriptural interpretation from Spinoza, before his friend completely changed his mind on this topic.

Meijer's book certainly made an impression on his contemporaries. But perhaps the most important defender of this kind of rationalist approach to the interpretation of Scripture was Maimonides, although even the great philosopher came in for harsh attacks from medieval rabbis and gentile critics on just this point.

In the *Guide of the Perplexed*, Maimonides is concerned to combat the anthropomorphization of God to which common people, and even the learned, are prone. An infinite, eternal being cannot have anything in common with finite creatures; there can be no analogy drawn between human beings and God, and nothing about the divine nature can be known by considering human nature. This is obviously true in the case of body, and many chapters of the *Guide* are devoted to dispelling the notion that God has any physical features (fingers, face, feet, etc.). But Maimonides also believes that the true understanding of God, such as we can obtain it, must exclude attributing to God features of human psychology as well: anger, jealousy, envy, and other mental states familiar to us from introspection.

However, the Bible repeatedly refers to God in both psychological and physical terms. The reader is told of God's wrath, regret, and forgiveness, as well as his sitting down and rising up, his coming and going, even his looking and hearing. Read literally, these passages encourage, even demand, an anthropomorphizing of God. It is just this kind of "perplexity" generated by an apparent inconsistency between reason and faith that the *Guide* is intended to cure.

Maimonides believes that a literal reading of the writings of the Hebrew prophets is the primary or default reading. Unless there are compelling reasons not to, one should opt for a straightforward, simple interpretation of the text. However, if such an interpretation yields a meaning that is inconsistent with a demonstrable philosophical truth, then a figurative or metaphorical interpretation *must* be adopted. Thus, reason tells us that God cannot possibly have a body. The principle "God is one" is the most important principle in all of Judaism—indeed, a fundamental theological truth for any monotheistic faith. And it can be rationally demonstrated with absolute certainty that a being that is essentially one, a simple unity, cannot possibly be corporeal. "There is no profession of unity unless the doctrine of God's corporeality is denied. For a body cannot be one, but is composed of matter and form, which by definition are two; it is also divisible, subject to partition."[50] Thus, a reading of a scriptural passage that involves attributing corporeal parts to God runs up against a demonstrated philosophical truth and, for that reason, must be rejected. Any mention of God's "eye" is to be read as referring to his watchfulness, his providence, or his intellectual apprehension; while prophetic talk of God's "heart" is to be understood as referring to his thought or his opinion (although what God's thought or opinion is like cannot be inferred from what our human thoughts or opinions are like).

On the other hand, when a literal reading of a passage, however odd it may seem, does not contradict any demonstrated truth, it should be adopted. Thus, Maimonides insists that although some philosophers (including Aristotle) firmly believe that the world is eternal and necessary, no one—including, he insists, Aristotle—has yet offered a conclusive proof of this. Therefore, there is no justification for reading the Bible's account of creation figuratively.

> That the deity is not a body has been demonstrated; from this it follows necessarily that everything that in its external meaning disagrees with this demonstration must be interpreted figuratively. . . .

However, the eternity of the world has not been demonstrated. Consequently in this case the texts ought not to be rejected and figuratively interpreted in order to make prevail an opinion whose contrary can be made to prevail by means of various sorts of arguments.[51]

Maimonides is committed to this rationalist principle of interpretation because, as we have seen, he believes that prophecy, biblical or otherwise, is essentially the communication of scientific, metaphysical, and moral truths in concrete and imaginative form. The prophet is like the philosopher in that the content of what he proclaims comes to him as an "intellectual overflow" or emanation from God. Thus, there is a sense in which prophetic utterances are of the same nature, derive from the same source, and have the same cognitive stature as philosophical or rational statements. The prophet, like the philosopher, has achieved perfection in his speculative or rational faculties (the difference between the two is that the prophet has also achieved perfection in his imaginative faculty). It follows that what the prophet communicates is, in its substance, rational knowledge, and reason will therefore be the key to interpreting true prophetic writings.[52]

In his mature philosophical writings, Spinoza rarely names other philosophers, either those with whom he agrees (such as Descartes) or those with whom he differs (also, on occasion, Descartes). Such personal touches would not be in keeping with the geometric format of the *Ethics*. In the *Treatise*, there is the occasional mention of Plato or Aristotle, and his admiring review of Ibn Ezra's discussion of Mosaic authorship. However, such exceptions tend to prove the rule about Spinoza's normal reserve in referring to the thought of others. In his discussion in the *Treatise* of the interpretation of Scripture, however, he makes a major exception to this general policy.

Spinoza's theory of biblical hermeneutic is presented in explicit and highly critical contrast with that of Maimonides (and, by implication, that of his friend Meijer as well). Unlike the more subtle engagement with Maimonides in his discussion of prophecy, where Spinoza exhibits Maimonidean tendencies of his own, in his examination of "the views of those who disagree with me" on the matter of scriptural interpretation he goes to great lengths to show that "the method of Maimonides is plainly of no value [*inutilis*]."[53] Among other things, that method twists the meanings of biblical passages to make them fit independent philosophical doctrines. "[Maimonides] assumes that it is legitimate for us to explain away and distort the words of Scripture to accord with our preconceived opinions, to deny its literal meaning and change it into something else even when it is perfectly plain and absolutely clear."[54] This is especially inappropriate in the case of the prophetic writings, whose authors were not philosophically learned and who were more concerned with encouraging moral obedience than with communicating intellectual truths.

Moreover, Spinoza insists, Maimonides' hyper-rationalist method, which demands that one know the truth value of a proposition in order to determine whether or not it is being expressed by a biblical passage, makes the meaning of the Bible inaccessible to ordinary people without philosophical training and absolutely certain knowledge of highly speculative doctrines. "For as long as we are not convinced of the truth of a statement, we cannot know whether it is in conformity with reason or contrary to it, and consequently neither can we know whether the literal meaning [of a biblical passage] is true or false." The interpretation of Scripture would need "a light other than the natural light," and only philosophers would be qualified to determine what the Bible is trying to say.

> If this view were correct, it would follow that the common people, for the most part knowing nothing of logical reasoning or without leisure for it, would have to rely solely on the authority and testimony of philosophers for their understanding of Scripture, and would therefore have to assume that philosophers are infallible in their interpretations of Scripture. This would indeed be a novel form

of ecclesiastical authority, with very strange priests or pontiffs, more likely to excite men's ridicule than veneration.[55]

For these reasons, Spinoza concludes, "we can dismiss Maimonides' view as harmful, unprofitable and absurd."

A proper method of interpreting Scripture—one that is accessible to all who are endowed simply with the natural light of reason—is, for Spinoza, of the utmost importance, particularly because of contemporary tendencies to manipulate the meanings of biblical passages for political and social ends. Seventeenth-century Dutch theologians and religious leaders in particular are given to finding in Scripture exactly what will suit their purposes. They justify their convenient but unwarranted readings by appealing to "the inspiration of the Holy Spirit." This, for certain Calvinists, is the supernatural illumination that is supposed to be the true guide for understanding what the prophets are saying; it is, however, like divine grace, available only to the favored few.[56]

> We see that nearly all men parade their own ideas as God's Word, their chief aim being to compel others to think as they do, while using religion as a pretext. We see, I say, that the chief concern of theologians on the whole has been to extort from Holy Scripture their own arbitrarily invented ideas, for which they claim divine authority. . . . They imagine that the most profound mysteries lie hidden in the Bible, and they exhaust themselves in unraveling these absurdities while ignoring other things of value. They ascribe to the Holy Spirit whatever their wild fantasies have invented, and devote their utmost strength and enthusiasm to defending it.[57]

So pursued, the interpretation of Scripture is without an anchor. These theologians, guided only by their mysterious faculty, try to pass off "human fabrications as divine teachings." The results are ungrounded in any objective method and, thus, unverifiable. Their readings reflect nothing but the prejudices they hold and the superstitions they hope to encourage in others. The inevitable consequence, as history has shown again and again, is religious feuding and the disruption of civil peace.

The true way to interpret Scripture and discover what exactly it teaches and what it does not teach—and Spinoza believes this to be practically a trivial claim—is to seek the meanings intended by its authors. Lodewijk Meijer was absolutely right to distinguish the meaning of a passage from the question of its truth. Where he went wrong was in identifying the two in the case of the Bible. He and many others

> suppose, as a foundation for understanding Scripture and unearthing its true meaning, that it is everywhere true and divine. So what we ought to establish by understanding Scripture, and subjecting it to a strict examination, and what we would be far better taught by Scripture itself, which needs no human inventions, they maintain at the outset as a rule for the interpretation of Scripture.[58]

The goal of the interpreter of Scripture, like the goal of a sincere interpreter of any work of human literature, is to discover what the work means, and this—for Spinoza, at least—is simply what message the author wants to convey through his writing. "The point at issue is merely the meaning of the texts, not their truth."[59] It is one thing to ask whether it is true that God is subject to emotions such as anger and jealousy; this is an inquiry best left to philosophers. It is quite another thing to determine whether Moses believed (and wanted others to believe) that God can be angry or jealous, and this is the task of the interpreter. His goal is to know "what was, or could have been, the author's intention . . . concentrating [his] attention on what the author could have had in mind."[60]

Spinoza, with astonishing boldness, compares the proper procedure for interpreting Scripture (and, presumably, any literary work) with the methods of natural science. "I hold that the method of interpreting Scripture is no different from the method of interpreting Nature, and is in fact in complete accord with it."[61] And just as a scientific knowledge of nature must be sought "from Nature itself," without presupposing any substantive, a priori metaphysical or theological principles, so "all the contents of Scripture . . . must be sought from Scripture alone [*ab ipsa Scriptura sola*]."[62]

What Spinoza has in mind, in particular, are the elements of an empirical scientific method, such as those described in Francis Bacon's *New Organon* (1620).[63] The scientist's initial step is "a detailed study of Nature" that involves gathering all the relevant facts through raw and, more important, controlled observation—the compilation of what Bacon called "natural and experimental histories" and what Spinoza labels "assured data." From this collection of data, which are the phenomena that the scientist hopes to understand, he will ultimately derive (presumably by induction and the experimental testing of hypotheses) "definitions of the things of Nature". By "definitions," Spinoza means essences or natures, or the basic properties constitutive of kinds of things. A very specific example of such a definition is Spinoza's explanation of the homogeneous particulate composition of niter (potassium nitrate, or saltpeter), found in his letters to Oldenburg in which he disputes Robert Boyle's claim that niter is composed of heterogeneous particles.[64]

The discovery of these essences proceeds by first formulating (on the basis of the controlled observational data) the universal principles that govern natural phenomena, such as the laws of motion that cover all bodies. These are the primary "teachings" that the natural philosopher discovers from his critical study of nature. From such universal principles it is possible to move to less global laws of nature, those that explain only certain kinds of phenomena.

> In examining natural phenomena, we first of all try to discover those features that are most universal and common to the whole of Nature, to wit, motion-and-rest and the rules and laws governing them which Nature always observes and through which she constantly acts; and then we advance gradually from these to other less universal features.[65]

Individual phenomena are then subsumed under these principles, generating clear causal conceptions of them. Like the adequate knowledge that the *Ethics* holds out as our highest intellectual achievement, the essences of natural phenomena discovered by the scientist provide a perspicuous understanding of the constitution of things and why they are as they are.[66] Such essences are the equivalent within natural science of what meanings are for hermeneutic science. And as Spinoza sees it, at no point in this process does the natural scientist go *outside* nature itself—for example, to theological principles about God, such as Descartes had done in formulating the most general laws of nature in his *Principles of Philosophy*.[67]

Similarly, the interpreter of Scripture must not go outside Scripture itself in order to discover its "principles," that is, the teachings its authors intended to convey. Whatever religious lessons and ethical maxims the prophets wanted their readers to learn from their writings must be sought from those writings alone, with the aid of "the natural light."

> The task of Scriptural interpretation requires us to make a straightforward study of Scripture, and from this, as the source of our fixed data and principles, to deduce by logical inference the meaning of the authors of Scripture . . . allowing no other principles or data for the interpretation of Scripture and study of its contents except those that can be gathered only from Scripture itself and from a historical study of Scripture.[68]

The moral principles propounded by Scripture can indeed be known independently of Scripture, by reason alone, much as Spinoza shows in the *Ethics*. They are, after all, purely rational principles that "can be demonstrated from accepted axioms."[69] However, *that* Scripture teaches this or that principle cannot be discovered except by looking at Scripture itself in a critical manner.

By "Scripture alone" (*sola Scriptura*), Spinoza certainly means to exclude both the Maimonidean-rationalist recourse to an external philosophical canon and Calvin's appeal to special divine illumination (the Holy Spirit). On the other hand, he also wants to avoid the individualistic, highly subjective approach to the reading of Scripture favored by certain dissident Reformed sects. Quakers and Collegiants, for example, among whom Spinoza counted many friends, leave it up to the individual to interpret Scripture as his conscience or "inner light" leads. For Spinoza, there is an objective method for interpreting Scripture, one that should guide its practitioner, despite the many difficulties standing in his way, to at least an approximate understanding of its authors' intended meanings in many—and among them, the most important—of its passages.

To be sure, Spinoza has a rather extended understanding of *sola Scriptura*. The proper approach to the Bible will require examining not only the text itself and the language in which it was written but also factors such as the social and political circumstances of its composition and the biographies of its authors. Examining Scripture "from Scripture alone" apparently means studying it from exclusively, but *all*, relevant scriptural considerations. It is as if to say that by "Bible" is meant the *world* of the Bible. What Spinoza is demanding is a historical approach to Scripture, and it involves looking at the diverse contexts within which the writings were originally created.

Moreover, while Spinoza's Bible hermeneutics is not a rationalism in the Maimonidean (or Meijerian) sense, reason nonetheless has an important role to play in it. The interpretation of Scripture does require the use of one's rational faculties working methodically on textual and historical material. Again, like the science of nature, which requires no supernatural insight,

> it is now obvious to all that this method [of interpreting Scripture] demands no other light than the natural light of reason. For the nature and virtue of that light consists essentially in this, that by a process of logical deduction that which is hidden is inferred and concluded from what is known, or given as known.[70]

In *Philosophy, Interpreter of Holy Scripture*, Meijer distinguishes two ways in which reason might play a role in the interpretation of the Bible. According to one approach, which he (and Maimonides) adopts, reason is "the norm and rule for interpreting and judging"; any proposed interpretation that is inconsistent with "true and indubitably certain knowledge which reason . . . draws forth and arranges under the most certain light of truth"—that is, with true philosophy—is to be rejected.[71] In this view, reason provides the *content* against which proposed readings are to be assessed.

On the other hand, Meijer notes, reason may be only "the means and instrument for tracing and eliciting the meaning of the Holy Writings," and not "the norm according to which all interpretation must be directed and decided."[72] Spinoza is sensitive to this distinction between reason as a body of doctrine and reason as a tool of discovery. He knows that, subtle as it may be, it is essential to grasping the difference between his rationalism with respect to Scripture and the kind of rationalism characteristic of Maimonides' and Meijer's account. Above all, it is what allows him to claim that anyone endowed with reason—that is, anyone—has what it takes (at least in principle) to understand Scripture's most important messages.

> Since the supreme authority for the interpretation of Scripture is vested in each individual, the rule that governs interpretation must be nothing other than the natural light that is common to all, and not any supernatural light, nor eternal authority. Nor must this rule be so difficult as not to be available to any but skilled philosophers; it must be suited to the natural and universal ability and capacity of mankind.[73]

Like the science of nature, the "science" of interpreting the Bible begins with the gathering of data. In the case of Scripture, the main relevant data are the various pronouncements themselves: what one biblical writer says about God, as these statements may be found in the books he is said to have composed; what another writer says about divine providence; and, most important of all, what different writers have to say about ethical matters, about what is right and good. Once collected, all of this material should be properly organized by author and subject matter. "The pronouncements made in each book should be assembled and listed under headings, so that we thus have to hand all the texts that treat of the same subject."[74] At the same time, the interpreter, who needs to be well-versed in ancient Hebrew—since "all the writers of both the Old and the New Testaments were Hebrews"—should note any ambiguities or obscurities (defined as "the degree of difficulty with which the meaning can be elicited from the context, and not . . . the degree of difficulty with which its truth can be perceived by reason") among the passages he has collected, as well as any inconsistencies or contradictions that are found in material both by the same writer and among different writers.

In addition to this textual data, the interpreter needs to gather everything that can be known about the writers of the Bible. He needs to inquire into the biographical, historical, political, even psychological background of each book's author.

> Our historical study should set forth the circumstances relevant to all the extant books of the prophets, giving the life, character and pursuits of the author of every book, detailing who he was, on what occasion and at what time and for whom and in what language he wrote . . . for in order to know which pronouncements were set forth as laws and which as moral teaching, it is important to be acquainted with the life, character and interests of the author. Furthermore, as we have a better understanding of a person's character and temperament, so we can more easily explain his words.[75]

Spinoza is saying that in many cases you cannot know what a person is trying to say unless you know who that person is, what he cares about, why he is writing, and to whom he is communicating. "It is essential for us to have some knowledge of the authors if we seek to interpret their writings."[76] This applies as much to the biblical prophets as it does to the author of *Oliver Twist*, all of whom are engaged in creating imaginative literature with a moral and social message, though of different literary genres and for different kinds of audiences. Indeed, it is a particularly important rule for understanding the prophets, who lived many centuries ago and in historical and cultural circumstances far removed from those of a seventeenth-century Dutch burgher.

The final set of crucial data involves the history of the transmission of the biblical texts. This is essential for determining their authenticity and for discovering, when possible, any corruptions or "mutilations" they may have suffered over generations. The interpreter will need to know "whether or not [the books] have been contaminated by spurious insertions, whether errors have crept in, and whether these have been corrected by experienced and trustworthy scholars."[77]

With all this at hand, the interpreter, like the scientist, can now proceed to discover the general principles that govern the phenomena. Or, in this case, he is ready, on the basis of the literary data, to discern the doctrines that are proclaimed throughout all the prophetic writings by their authors. If the natural scientist is seeking the laws of nature, the Bible scholar is after "that which is most universal and forms the basis and foundation of all Scripture; in short, that which is commended in Scripture by all the prophets as doctrine eternal and most profitable for all mankind."[78]

Spinoza believes that there are such universal principles expressed everywhere by Scripture, regardless of a book's author: that God exists, that God is one, that God should be worshipped, and that God cares for everyone and loves above all those who worship him and love their neighbors as themselves. This is the simple message of all of Scripture. In fact, Spinoza believes—somewhat incredibly—that these propositions are so clearly the meaning of many of Scripture's passages that very little interpretive work is needed to find them. "These and similar doctrines . . . are taught everywhere in Scripture so clearly and explicitly that no one has ever been in any doubt as to its meaning on these points."[79]

Not everything in Scripture is so explicit and unambiguous, however. Spinoza rejects the view held by many of his Protestant contemporaries that Scripture's entire meaning is fairly obvious and needs practically no interpretation. (The French-Dutch Reformed theologian Samuel Desmarets [or Maresius], for example, believed that the Bible's passages are so perspicuous that a literal reading, according to the common usage of the words and "their public and ordinary sense," will yield its one true meaning.)[80] A good deal of serious hermeneutic work on the data is required for determining, as far as we can, precisely what each author thinks on such metaphysical and theological matters as what God is, how God exercises providence, and the nature of miracles. These are the more restricted principles that correspond to the more particular laws formulated by the natural scientist. They differ from the universal laws in that there is no agreement among the biblical authors on these questions. Moreover, when it comes to principles that are "of less universal import but affect our ordinary daily life"—namely, the particularities of moral conduct and the different sorts of actions recommended by each prophet as constituting justice and charity—many obscurities, contradictions, and ambiguities will be found. While these are supposed to "flow from the universal doctrine like rivulets from their source," their derivation may not come easy. Among other things, the interpreter must consider the occasion on which the passage was written and to whom its content was directed.

Spinoza provides the example of Moses, who is reported in the Torah as saying that God is fire and that God is jealous. How to interpret such statements, and especially determining whether to read them literally or figuratively, is not a matter of deciding whether or not a literal reading is consistent with demonstrated philosophical truths about God. Rather, it involves looking at the relevant passages in the light of the basic principles of Scripture already derived from the data, along with other things that Moses says and the circumstances in which he is saying them. Since Moses does clearly and consistently state elsewhere that God has no resemblance to visible things, the sentence in which he says that God is fire must be read metaphorically. "The question as to whether Moses did or did not believe that God is fire must in no wise be decided by the rationality or irrationality of the belief, but solely from other pronouncements of Moses."[81] The Hebrew word for "fire" can be used to refer to anger, and because a leader would find such imagistic language to be more effective for motivating others to obey God, it can be concluded that Moses did not mean to assert that God is literally flamelike. As Spinoza says to van Blijenburgh some years earlier, in a letter from early 1665, sometimes the authors of Scripture tailored their language to the understanding of the masses. "Scripture, being particularly adapted to the needs of the common people, continually speaks in merely human fashion, for the common people are incapable of understanding higher things."[82]

On the other hand, because Moses is nowhere reported as saying that God does not have emotions, the sentence in which he says that God is jealous can be read literally. Although such a reading is opposed to reason—at least, so Spinoza argues in the *Ethics*—it is not inconsistent either with the universal proclamations of Scripture ("God is one," etc.) or with any more particular principles espoused by Moses himself.[83]

Similarly, Jesus is reported in the Gospel of Matthew to have said, "If a man strike you on the right cheek, turn to him the left also." If this is understood to be a literal direction to judges and lawgivers, such toleration of injustice and submission to wrongdoing would, Spinoza argues, be inconsistent with the law of Moses, which demands that every crime deserves a corresponding and just punishment ("an eye for an eye").

> Therefore we should consider who said this, to whom, and at what time. This was said by Christ, who was not ordaining laws as a lawgiver, but was expounding his teachings as a teacher, because . . . he was intent on improving men's minds rather than their external actions. Further, he spoke these words to men suffering under oppression, living in a corrupt commonwealth where justice was utterly disregarded, a commonwealth whose ruin he saw to be imminent.[84]

The result of Spinoza's interpretive method is not a subjective or even relativistic reading of Scripture; there is an objective meaning to be gotten out of the text by using the proper tools. Rather, what Spinoza offers is a contextual reading, one that looks at Scripture for what it is: a very human document composed at a particular time for very human purposes.

There are, Spinoza admits, many obstacles to deciphering the Bible's true meaning. While it is relatively easy to grasp the work's general moral message—"we can understand the meaning of Scripture with confidence in matters relating to salvation and necessary to blessedness"—grasping its less universal principles and exhortations and revealing many of the beliefs of the prophets proves to be more difficult. In many instances, we can in fact only conjecture what a prophetic author is trying to say.

This is due to a number of factors. First, there is the poverty of our understanding of the biblical languages, or what Spinoza calls "our inability to present a complete account of Hebrew." So much linguistic information has been lost over the millennia, including certain grammatical rules and common vocabulary, that we now have at best a fragmentary knowledge of Hebrew. "The men of old who used the Hebrew language have left to posterity no information concerning the basic principles and study of this language. At any rate, we possess nothing at all from them, neither dictionary nor grammar nor textbook on rhetoric." With the disappearance of native speakers of ancient Hebrew and Aramaic, much information ordinarily possessed by the daily users of a language has disappeared. "Nearly all the words for fruits, birds, fishes have perished with the passage of time, together with numerous other words."[85] Moreover, even when the meanings of particular words are known, what is lacking is an idiomatic and colloquial knowledge that would allow us to make sense of an obscure passage.

There are also, Spinoza insists, ambiguities in the Bible that are due to certain peculiarities of ancient Hebrew. These include the multiple meanings of words, especially particles and adverbs (the *vav*, for example, can be conjunctive or disjunctive); letters that look the same (such as the *resh* and *dalet*); and the lack of a clear and precise tense system among the verbs. More significant is the absence of vowels and punctuation in the original Hebrew text (the vocalization marks were added in the Middle Ages by the Masoretes, whom Spinoza calls "men of a later age whose authority should carry no weight with us," since their insertions reflect their own interpretations of Scripture).

Finally, there is the sheer difficulty of accurately reconstructing the history surrounding such ancient writings. About most of

Scripture's authors we either have no knowledge whatsoever, or only partial and dubious information. Their social stature, political persuasion, and audience must be inferred on the basis of very slim evidence. Their psychological lives are hidden from us, and we can only speculate on their motives in writing.

All of these difficulties, Spinoza concludes, are "so grave that I have no hesitation in affirming that in many instances we either do not know the true meaning of Scripture or we can do no more than make conjecture."[86]

Spinoza's naturalization of Scripture and his historical approach to its interpretation, while deflationary to some degree, is not meant to rob the Bible of all of its authority. On the contrary, Spinoza believes that it is those who focus too much on the words of Scripture and not its message that have betrayed it. By promoting myths about the supernatural origin of the Bible, sectarian religions have fostered the worship of letters on a page rather than the ethical doctrines that its authors hoped to spread. And this, Spinoza contends, is idolatry. "Instead of God's Word, they are beginning to worship likenesses and images, that is, paper and ink."[87]

In fact, it is the moral content alone in which the true authority—indeed, the *divinity*—of Scripture consists.

> If we want to testify, without any prejudgment, to the divinity of Scripture, it must be made evident to us from Scripture alone that it teaches true moral doctrine; for it is on this basis alone that its divinity can be proved.[88]

What makes something divine is not that it has its origin in an alleged act by God. (This is especially the case for Spinoza, whose identification of God and Nature means that everything is caused by God.) Rather, something is divine if and only if it moves people to act according to justice and charity, if it leads them to love God and their fellow human beings. "A thing is called sacred and divine only for as long as men use it in a religious way"—that is, insofar as it is associated with pious behavior.[89] Thus, "the divinity of Scripture must be established solely from the fact that it teaches true virtue." And Spinoza does believe that there really is something special about the Bible in this regard. Because of the ethical superiority and imaginative gifts of its prophetic authors, the Bible, when properly read, truly is an excellent teacher of virtue and piety.

Spinoza thereby self-consciously relativizes what is sacred about the Bible. Nothing is sacred or divine in itself, "in an absolute sense," but "only in relation to the mind."[90] A book, considered alone, is just a book. Were Scripture to lose its moral efficacy, its power of bringing people toward devotion to God and love of their neighbors, then it would be, like any book, "nothing more than paper and ink . . . their neglect [would] render it completely profane."[91] (Conversely, just as the mere acquaintance with Scripture, without any understanding of its true moral message, is not *sufficient* for bringing people to blessedness, so a reading of Scripture is not *necessary* for piety and religious virtue—these can be achieved by someone who has never even heard of the Bible. "He who is totally unacquainted with the Biblical narratives, but nevertheless holds salutary beliefs and pursues the true way of life, is absolutely blessed.")[92]

For this reason, Spinoza insists—in yet another audacious statement that must have incited the rage of his critics—that any book can be called divine, as long as its message is the proper one and it is effective in conveying it. "Books that teach and tell of the highest things are equally sacred, in whatever language and by whatever nation they were written."[93] Thus, it is still true, in a sense, that God is "the author of the Bible—not because God willed to confer on men a set number of books, but because of the true religion that is taught therein."[94] But the Word of God can, at least in principle, be found in many books. There is no reason why one particular work of human literature, written by the Hebrews several millennia ago, should have a monopoly on the teaching of true religion.

Chapter 7

Judaism, Christianity, and True Religion

Sometime in early 1671, Spinoza received a letter from Jacob Ostens. An acquaintance of Spinoza's probably from the late 1650s, Ostens was a surgeon and Mennonite pastor in Rotterdam. He was also a friend of Lambert van Velthuysen, a physician in Utrecht, sometime intellectual and relatively liberal thinker. In his writings, Van Velthuysen promoted both Cartesian philosophy and Copernicanism, bringing him into trouble with religious authorities. Van Velthuysen was not so progressive, however, that he was able to read Spinoza's *Treatise* with equanimity. In January 1671, in response to Ostens's query as to what he thought of the recently published book, Van Velthuysen replied with a severely negative review. His fear was that the *Treatise*—with its view of miracles, prophecy, and God—is a real threat to revealed religion. After his critical summary of Spinoza's views, he closed by noting that "I think I have not strayed far from the truth, nor am I unfair to the author, if I denounce him as teaching sheer atheism with furtive and disguised arguments."[1] Ostens thought that Spinoza should see Van Velthuysen's remarks, so he forwarded them to him.

Spinoza was not pleased to read the harsh things that a Cartesian, from whom he would have expected more, had to say about the *Treatise*. It took him some time to send a reply to Ostens. "You are doubtless surprised that I have kept you waiting so long, but I can hardly bring myself to answer that man's letter."[2] He accuses Van Velthuysen of writing either from malice or ignorance, and of distorting his views. While defending his doctrines against the particular criticisms leveled by Van Velthuysen, Spinoza also addresses the general charge that he is an atheist. "He [Van Velthuysen] then continues, 'to avoid the accusation of superstition, I think [Spinoza] has renounced all religion.' But what he understands by religion and what by superstition, I do not know."[3]

In other words, Spinoza is saying, it all depends on what you mean by "religion."

There are religions, and then there is religion. There are organized religions, essentially sectarian cults united by dogma, bound by specific rites and ceremonies, and governed by authoritative hierarchies. And then there is true piety, the simple love of God and of one's fellow human beings.

Judaism, Christianity, and Islam are, naturally, Spinoza's paradigmatic organized religions. As the major Abrahamic traditions, they obviously share common patriarchal origins. But what distinguishes them from one another and provides their exclusivity is that they recognize different individuals as the supreme prophet (Moses, Jesus, and Mohammed) and different texts as canonical, and that they demand different beliefs and rituals of their adherents. Spinoza is certain, however, that none of this matters when it comes to true religion.

To take the case of Judaism, with which Spinoza is primarily concerned in chapters three through five of the *Treatise*, Moses instituted the laws of the Torah—and Spinoza reminds his reader that it was Moses, and not some transcendent deity, who made those laws—for a very mundane purpose: to create a viable political society and compel obedience among its members. Having led the Israelites out of slavery in Egypt, Moses had to work practically from scratch to unify the people into a commonwealth. At the time, the liberated Hebrews were basically in what Spinoza and other political philosophers of the period called a "state of nature." They were not the citizens of any domain or subject to any political authority. "Unbound by the laws of any nation," they were free to organize themselves in any way they wanted.

When they first left Egypt, they were not longer bound by the legislation of any other nation, so they were permitted, as they wished,
to enact new laws or to ordain new legislation, and to have a state
wherever they wished, and to occupy what lands they wished. Nevertheless, they were quite incapable of ordaining legislation wisely and
retaining the sovereignty in their own hands, as a body. Almost all
of them were crude in their mentality and weakened by wretched
bondage. Therefore, the sovereignty had to remain in the hands of
one person only, who would command the others and compel them by
force, and who would prescribe laws and afterwards interpret them.[4]

Sovereignty was placed in the hands of Moses, who was perceived
"to surpass all others in divine power," and he proceeded to lay
down a set of laws that would confer order and unity upon the
masses he led. These are the six hundred and thirteen *mitzvot*, or
commandments, of the Torah. They were necessary because "no
society can subsist without government and coercion, and consequently without laws to control and restrain men's lusts and
their unbridled urges."[5] So as to leave nothing to chance or individual choice, the laws covered not only major aspects of the
community—including liturgical, social, moral, and economic
affairs—but also the most minute details of daily life, such as the
clothes they wore, the foods they ate, and even the cutting of hair.

Moreover, Moses realized that a society whose members obey
the law willingly, out of piety and devotion rather than out of
fear, is a more stable and powerful one. Thus, he persuaded the
people that the laws he was laying down were in fact from God
and that the state itself had divine sanction. He identified the
laws of the Hebrew commonwealth as God's commandments and
thereby created a state religion. To obey the state was to obey God,
and even the most ordinary action became infused with religious
significance.

Thus the historical origins of the regulations and ritual observances of Judaism. The ceremonial laws of Moses, Spinoza concludes, "contribute nothing to blessedness" but have to do only
with the political and economic well-being of the ancient Israelite

commonwealth. "The observance of ceremonies has regard only to the temporal prosperity of the state and in no way contributes to blessedness. . . . Scripture promises for ceremonial observance nothing but material advantages and pleasures, while blessedness is promised only for observance of the universal Divine Law."[6]

Similar considerations apply to the ceremonies of Christianity, such as baptism, prayers, and the celebration of holy days.

> If [these ceremonies] were ever instituted by Christ or the Apostles (of which I am not yet convinced), they were instituted only as external symbols of a universal Church, not as conducing to blessedness or as containing an intrinsic holiness. Therefore, although it was not to support a sovereign state that these ceremonies were instituted, yet their only purpose was the unification of a particular society, and thus he who lives in solitude is by no means bound by them.[7]

Spinoza is taking some serious risks here. He is questioning the Gospel accounts of the Last Supper and denying the relevance of the sacraments, which could certainly upset many of his Christian readers (Reformed or otherwise), for whom the Eucharist was of the utmost importance.[8] Spinoza's point is that the rituals of Judaism and Christianity (and Islam, for that matter) are neither necessary nor sufficient for the achievement of the highest human good and salvation. They are not sufficient because one may know and follow every single one of the Torah's commandments and still have nothing of true religion; one can be a rigorously observant Christian and still not enjoy true piety. They are not necessary because one can be a paragon of true religious devotion and know or care nothing at all for Jewish law or Christian ritual. "He who, while unacquainted with [the writings of Scripture], nevertheless knows by the natural light that there is a God having the attributes [of wisdom and righteousness], and who also pursues a true way of life, is altogether blessed—indeed, more blessed than the multitude."[9]

The core of true religion, for Spinoza, is obedience not to manmade ceremonial laws but to divine law. While human law is meant to prescribe what one should do to "safeguard life and the commonwealth," protect oneself and one's property from others, and ensure the well-being of the state, divine law prescribes what one should do to obtain the "supreme good," that is, what is most to one's advantage not as a physical, social, or political being but as a rational and moral being. And what that law commands is, at least on the face of it, quite simple: to know and love God and to love one's neighbor as oneself.

The command to know and love God is an ambiguous one for Spinoza. Its meaning depends on whether it is addressed to someone who is philosophically sophisticated and intellectually superior to the masses or to someone who, belonging to the multitude (*vulgus*), is unlikely to achieve cognition of higher speculative truths.

In its truest form, the knowledge of God is a highly abstract, metaphysical achievement. Spinoza explains, in both the *Treatise* and (at greater length) in the *Ethics*, that what is most advantageous to a rational being is the perfection of its proper and "better" part, that is, the rational faculty or intellect. And what perfects the intellect, bringing it to its ideal condition, is knowledge. Accordingly, what provides for the *highest* perfection of one's intellectual nature is the highest kind of knowledge, one that offers a consummate understanding of things. This would be a knowledge of God itself, understood as the universal principle of all that there is. But since for Spinoza it is also the case that, in all metaphysical truth, God just *is* Nature, to know God is ultimately to have an adequate causal understanding of natural phenomena.

> Our supreme good and perfection depends solely on the knowledge of God. Again, since nothing can be or be conceived without God, it is clear that everything in Nature involves and expresses the conception of God in proportion to its essence and perfection; and therefore we acquire a greater and more perfect knowledge of God as we gain more knowledge of natural phenomena . . . the greater our knowledge of natural phenomena, the more perfect is our knowledge of God's essence, which is the cause of all things. So the whole of our

knowledge, that is, our supreme good, not merely depends on the
knowledge of God but consists entirely therein.[10]

In Spinoza's system, the command to "know God" is, in its philosophically proper form, a command to know and understand Nature, to grasp things from the perspective of their eternal causes
and thus to see their necessity.

This knowledge of God or Nature, as the *Ethics* demonstrates
and the *Treatise* reiterates, is what constitutes "man's highest happiness and blessedness, and the final end and aim of all human action." Such knowledge secures human flourishing and well-being
through the peace of mind that it brings. It also constitutes the
sum of divine law, insofar as that law demands the pursuit of this
supreme end. The more particular and practical elements of divine
law are made up of specific imperatives to seek the means that
further this end and "the rules for living a life" in accordance with
it. These include "the love of one's neighbors," that is, behaving
in certain ethical ways toward others and helping them flourish
and achieve virtue. This is because the virtuous person will know
that his own pursuit of perfection and virtue is supported, even
enhanced, by being surrounded by others who are also virtuous,
and so he will act with generosity, honesty, and love—"justice and
charity"—in his dealings with them.[11]

The divine law in this form, as well as its subordinate maxims,
comes not from some transcendent lawgiver but are deducible
from human nature itself. These are "God's commands, for they
are ordained for us by God himself, as it were, insofar as he exists
in our minds . . . it is merely a consideration of human nature
that leads us to this natural Divine Law."[12] In the *Ethics*, Spinoza
argues for these conclusions on the basis of metaphysical and epistemological propositions about the human mind and its place in
Nature. The command to know God (or Nature) and to do what
is required for that is, thus, an eternal and rational principle, "of
universal application . . . to all mankind"; it is knowable a priori
and follows from the essence of what we are. "By the natural light
of reason, all can clearly understand the power and eternal divinity

of God, from which they can know and infer what they should seek and what they should avoid."[13] It is a command that is, in fact, innate in the human mind.

The individual who achieves this intellectual cognition of God will naturally, even necessarily experience a love of God. "The love of God," Spinoza says in the *Treatise*, "arises from the knowledge of God."[14] This love will not be the emotional kind of love that is a response to the way external things affect us; such a passion is unstable and not a good foundation for happiness. Rather, the "intellectual love of God" possessed by the sage will consist in his consciousness that God, as the ultimate source of his deep knowledge of things, is thereby the cause of his perfection and well-being. He will therefore love God, in accordance with Spinoza's definition of love in the *Ethics* as nothing but joy accompanied by a conception of the object that is the cause of the joy. One loves the thing that brings about an improvement in one's condition or the person who benefits one.[15]

Spinoza explains in the *Ethics* that when a person acquires an adequate understanding of nature—and especially of his own mind and body as parts of nature—he achieves a kind of divine perspective on things. He sees an eternal truth about his relationship to God or Nature. "Insofar as our mind knows itself and the body through the perspective of eternity, it necessarily has knowledge of God, and knows that it is in God and is conceived through God."[16] This is the highest knowledge possible for a rational agent and the supreme achievement for a human being. "He who knows things by this kind of knowledge passes to the greatest human perfection."[17] He also, therefore, experiences the greatest joy or "satisfaction of mind" possible. Because this highest joy consists in understanding (primarily of oneself and of God), and because God is recognized as the cause of this understanding, one also knows that the true cause of this joy is God. Thus, one loves God.

> From [this] kind of knowledge, there necessarily arises an intellectual love of God. For from this kind of knowledge there arises joy, accompanied by the idea of God as its cause, i.e., love of God, not

insofar as we imagine him as present but insofar as we understand God to be eternal. And this is what I call intellectual love of God.[18]

While the intellectual love of God is a prominent feature of much Jewish and Christian medieval philosophy, the most important precedent for Spinoza's conception of *amor Dei intellectualis* is, without question, Maimonides. The love of God (*ahavat ha-kadosh-baruch-hu*) appears in both Maimonides' philosophical works and his legal writings. In the *Mishneh Torah*, Maimonides insists that one should serve God not to receive any blessings or avoid any punishment for doing so—that is, not out of self-interest or the desire for some benefit—but out of a pure dedication to observing the divine commandments for their own sake. The wise person does what is right solely for the sake of wisdom and righteousness. His motivation is not fear (of evil consequences) or hope (for reward) but love. Moreover, it is an obsessive love, one that occupies the entire mind of the wise person.

> What is the proper [degree] of love? That a person should love God with a very great and exceeding love until his soul is bound up in the love of God. Thus, he will always be obsessed with this love as if he is lovesick. [A lovesick person's] thoughts are never diverted from the love of that woman. He is always obsessed with her; when he sits down, when he gets up, when he eats and drinks. With an even greater [love], the love of God should be [implanted] in the hearts of those who love Him and are obsessed with Him at all times as we are commanded [Deuteronomy 6.5: "Love God . . .] with all your heart and with all your soul."[19]

Maimonides insists, however, that such a love of God can arise only on the foundation of knowledge. Indeed, the degree of one's love of God is proportionate to one's intellectual achievement. And what one is supposed to have knowledge of is God himself.

> One can only love God [as an outgrowth] of the knowledge with which he knows Him. The nature of one's love depends on the nature of one's knowledge. A small [amount of knowledge arouses] a lesser love. A greater amount of knowledge arouses a greater love.[20]

This same view informs the *Guide of the Perplexed*, where (as it is for Spinoza) the love that constitutes a human being's supreme perfection is an intellectual condition, a state of knowing. The great knowledge possessed by those with superior intellects is, as we have seen in Maimonides' discussion of prophecy, a result of the wisdom in the divine overflow that is received by properly prepared minds in this terrestrial realm—primarily philosophers and prophets. One who is connected to the overflow and has reached this supreme level of understanding enjoys a formidable cognitive union with God, a union that, under the best circumstances, occupies the whole mind and leads to proper worship and the enjoyment of divine providence.[21] Maimonides speaks of the "bond" that such a person enjoys with God. It is clear, though, that this bond is primarily an intellectual one. "If you have apprehended God and His acts in accordance with what is required by the intellect, you should afterwards engage in totally devoting yourself to Him, endeavor to come closer to Him, and strengthen the bond between you and Him—that is, the intellect."[22] To unite oneself intellectually to God, Maimonides continues, is the true meaning of one of Judaism's central commands: "To love the Lord your God with all your heart and all your soul and all your might."

There is, however, an important difference between Spinoza and Maimonides on this matter. For Maimonides, the intellectual love of God is accompanied by fear, dread, and awe. This is because these represent the natural response for someone who is in such close and constant proximity to God. When one is conscious of being in God's presence —as the perfected individual is—one cannot but feel that God is standing in judgment.

> Just as we apprehend Him by means of that light which he caused to overflow toward us . . . so does He by means of this selfsame light examine us; and because of it, He, may He be exalted, is constantly with us, examining from on high. . . . Understand this well. Know that when perfect men understand this, they achieve such humility, such awe and fear of God, such reverence and such shame before Him, may he be exalted—and this in ways that pertain to true

reality, not to imagination—that their secret conduct with their wives and in latrines is like their public conduct with other people.[23]

This fear and awe before God are not the result of conceiving God through the imagination—which ordinarily gives rise to illusory and superstitious beliefs about God, such as the idea that God has a body—but belong to someone who has perfected his intellectual understanding, and thus they are not grounded in any misconceptions about God. "Some excellent men obtain such training that they achieve human perfection, so that they fear, and are in dread and awe, of God."[24]

For Spinoza, by contrast, fear, dread, and awe of God result only from conceiving God inadequately, through the ideas of the imagination, which lend support to an anthropomorphic notion of God. Since Spinoza's God is no judge and does not possess the personal psychological life or moral characteristics with which traditional religious conceptions endow him, he is not properly an object of fear or other passions. In fact, Spinoza's intellectual love of God is the key to dispelling fear and hope, not generating them. Such love is certainly not the kind of religious feeling, mixed with awe, encouraged by traditional religious faiths.[25] It involves not passivity but activity and an appreciation of one's own powers and their cause. It is, in Spinoza's view, the proper accompaniment of virtue.

Spinoza's claim that the divine law is innate in the human mind is a rather strong one:

> God's eternal word and covenant and true religion are divinely inscribed in men's hearts—that is, in men's minds—and this is the true handwriting of God which he has sealed with his own seal, this seal being the idea of himself, the image of his own divinity, as it were.[26]

In principle, anyone should be able to discover for himself, through self-directed reasoning, what the supreme end is and how to achieve it.

Still, that divine word may be not evident to those unaccustomed to or incapable of reflection on such matters. The capacity
of the philosopher to deduce and obey the law in its true form, and
thus the knowledge and love of God available to him, is not really
within the reach of most people.

Fortunately, the divine law and true religion—"to know and
love God"—are also taught by Scripture in a manner that is more
accessible for the masses, "who lack the ability to perceive things
clearly and distinctly." For the majority of people, the knowledge
of God consists not in deep metaphysical truths about *Deus sive
Natura* but in grasping the principles about God unanimously expressed by the prophets. "Scriptural doctrine contains not abstruse
speculation or philosophic reasoning, but very simple matters able
to be understood by the most sluggish mind."[27]

The prophets, Spinoza notes, did not perceive God adequately.
They believed all sorts of things about him that are, in fact, false.
They tended to think of God in anthropomorphic terms, and thus
with a variety of psychological and moral attributes. Moses, for
example, "imagined God as a ruler, lawgiver, king, merciful, just
and so forth; whereas these are all merely attributes of human nature, and not at all applicable to the divine nature."[28] The prophets depicted God as issuing commandments and as rewarding
those who obey and punishing those who disobey. They conceived
a providential God who acts with justice, charity, and mercy, and
who is "an exemplar of true life." For Jeremiah, God is "the Lord
who exercises loving-kindness, judgment and righteousness in the
earth, for in these things I delight" (9.23), while John in his Gospel
emphasizes God's justice and charity. Neither prophet, however,
enjoyed "the intellectual knowledge of God which contemplates
his nature as it really is in itself."[29]

And yet, despite—or probably because of—the inadequate
ways in which the prophets thought of God, Scripture succeeds in
communicating the core of the divine law. "From Scripture itself
we learn that its message, unclouded by any doubt or any ambi-
guity, is in essence this, to love God above all, and one's neighbor
as oneself."[30] For the multitude, this is a command not to pursue

intellectual cognition of God but both to accept what the prophets say about his (moral) attributes and to imitate those attributes in their own actions. "God through his prophets asks no other knowledge of himself than the knowledge of his divine justice and charity, that is, such attributes of God as men find it possible to imitate by a definite rule of conduct."[31] What Moses, Jeremiah, and the others express is "the knowledge of God which it is the duty of every man to have . . . that God is supremely just and supremely merciful, that is, the one perfect pattern of the true life."[32]

While such a conception of God does not constitute true understanding of God and thus does not bring about true virtuous behavior grounded in intellectual knowledge, it is highly effective in leading untutored minds to just and charitable behavior toward others, that is, to the love of their neighbors. Indeed, it may be generally more effective in this regard than the intellectual knowledge of God, which, because of its philosophical abstractness, is "a nature which men cannot imitate by a set rule of conduct nor take as their example—[and] has no bearing on the practice of a true way of life."[33] The more accessible and colorful narratives of the prophets are intended to inspire people toward at least an external conformity to the demands of justice and charity. In this way, the value of those narratives is strictly practical. The end of the prophetic writings, Spinoza insists, is obedience: getting people to observe proper ethical behavior. That same behavior can, to be sure, find a deeper and more stable foundation in a rational understanding of certain truths about God, nature, and human beings—above all, just those truths that are found in the ordered propositions of the *Ethics*.[34] Coming to virtue by reason, however, is a difficult enterprise and not for the masses. This is where the Bible comes in.

I wish to emphasize in express terms . . . the importance and necessity of the role that I assign to Scripture, or revelation. For since we cannot perceive by the natural light that simple obedience is a way to salvation, and since only revelation teaches us that this comes about by God's singular grace which we cannot attain by reason, it follows that Scripture has brought very great comfort to mankind. For all men without exception are capable of obedience, while there are only a few—in proportion to the whole of humanity—who acquire a virtuous disposition under the guidance of reason alone. Thus, did we not have this testimony of Scripture, the salvation of nearly all men would be in doubt.[35]

While the Bible's prophetic texts do not offer a profound, or even a true, understanding of God and nature, their model of a deity who governs his creation with justice and charity motivates good behavior. "If by believing what is false [a person] becomes obedient to the moral law, he has a faith which is pious."[36]

Not all of Scripture's narratives are relevant to teaching piety; many are stories of merely historical interest, and some inform us more about their authors' beliefs and prejudices than about anything having to do with authentic obedience to God's word. And then there are the many brutal and abhorrent things performed by God and human beings in Hebrew Scripture, actions that one would have a hard time describing as "just" or "charitable." Still, Spinoza believes, many of the Bible's passages really do encourage moral behavior and thus convey a true religious message. As we have seen, this is, in fact, the clear and consistent universal message of all the prophetic writings, one that comes down to us "uncorrupted and unmutilated." "The common people, then, need to be acquainted only with those narratives that are most effective in instilling obedience and devotion."[37]

Of course, if they can get that same message without Scripture, either through some other book or simply through philosophy and rational contemplation, it does not matter.

> He who abounds in these fruits—charity, joy, peace, patience, kindness, goodness, faithfulness, gentleness and self-control, against which (as Paul says in Galatians 5.22) the law is not laid down, he, whether he be taught by reason or by Scripture alone, is in truth taught by God, and is altogether blessed.[38]

This is, Spinoza insists, the opposite of what Judaism expects. "The Jews take a completely contrary view. They maintain that

true beliefs and a true way of life contribute nothing to blessedness as long as men embrace them only from the natural light
of reason, and not as teachings revealed to Moses by prophetic
inspiration."[39] In fact, Judaism defines "the true way of life" not in
terms of moral virtue but as obedience to the ceremonial laws, and
for this reason mistakes for the word of God what are really superstitious rituals that have only historical and political significance.

On Spinoza's view, then, the divine law includes no historical
content, no metaphysical doctrines, and no prescriptions of ceremonies. It does not require the belief in any narratives of events
in the past, the assent to any philosophical claims about God's nature or about the cosmos and its origins, or the performance of any
devotional rituals ("acts which are in themselves of no significance
and are termed good merely by tradition"). The divine law does
command certain actions, because it includes directives for how
one should behave with justice and charity toward other human
beings. "[We are] to uphold justice, help the helpless, do no mur-
der, covet no man's goods, and so on."[40] For the philosophically
superior individual, these practical imperatives are recognized as
ultimately in the service of one's own flourishing, insofar as the
pursuit of virtue and intellectual perfection demands that one
contribute to the virtue and intellectual perfection of others. For
the multitude, the command to love others is observed because
that is how one is to imitate God's action (as this is described by
the prophets) in one's own life. None of these concrete practical
imperatives, however, has anything to do with sectarian rituals.
The commandments regarding ceremonies "do not contribute to
blessedness and virtue."

True religion, then—as opposed to sectarian religion—is about
nothing more than moral behavior. It is not what you believe but
what you do that matters. Writing to Oldenburg in 1675, Spinoza
says that "the chief distinction I make between religion and superstition is that the latter is founded on ignorance, the former on
wisdom."[41] Religion demands that we do what is to our greatest
advantage and constitutive of human flourishing. This is to know
and love God by pursuing the knowledge of nature and to love

our fellow human beings as ourselves, by acting toward them with charity and justice and doing what we can to bring them to a condition of flourishing. In short, the divine law commands only virtue. "Religion stands in no need of the trappings of superstition. On the contrary, its glory is diminished when it is embellished with such fancies."[42]

Spinoza's relationship to Judaism is, to say the least, a complicated one.[43] He was well educated in an openly observant community in Amsterdam by a diverse and learned cadre of rabbis. But he had clearly lost his faith and commitment to normative Jewish life as a young man. While he seems to have continued his study of Jewish sources even after his expulsion from the Talmud Torah congregation, he maintained a highly critical, even hostile attitude toward Jewish traditions throughout the rest of his life.

Spinoza certainly had a great deal of contempt for all organized religions, insofar as they fail to meet the standards of "true religion" and end up fostering division in society. He has some very severe things to say about Catholicism in his private correspondence.[44] And he did not believe Judaism to be any worse than Christianity in terms of its superstitious elements and pernicious effects—indeed, he no doubt believed Christianity, as the majority religion and because of its influence with the secular powers, to be the greater threat to social peace and personal well-being (although in the *Treatise* Spinoza had to be careful what he said lest he alienate and anger his Christian audience). Even so, he seems to have maintained an especially harsh animus toward his own native faith.[45] He admired the great Jewish thinkers of the past, and earlier Jewish philosophy strongly influenced Spinoza's views in metaphysics, ethics, and other domains; both the *Ethics* and, as we have seen, the *Treatise* show traces of Maimonideanism. But he was also a highly unorthodox, even revolutionary disciple of his Jewish intellectual forbearers. He was above all an unforgiving critic of their religion.

Nowhere is this more clear than in his discussion of Judaism in the *Treatise*. While in the *Ethics* he engages in a subtle and implicit dialogue with earlier Jewish philosophy, in the *Treatise* Spinoza directly examines a number of essential features of rabbinic Judaism. In particular, he argues against the continued validity of Torah—understood in its broad sense to include not just the Pentateuch but also later rabbinic legal literature, such as the Talmud—and the obligation of latter-day Jews to observe most of its commandments; and he reduces the alleged "divine chosenness" of the Jewish people to a set of natural but now extinct facts about their ancient government.

A couple of years after Spinoza's *herem*, he is said by some contemporaries to have confessed that he was expelled because he was insisting that "the Law is false."[46] The witnesses do not tell us what exactly he meant by that. However, his discussion of Jewish law in the *Treatise*, begun less than ten years later, fills in some of the details.

Insofar as many of the commandments found in the Torah relate only to ceremonial practices and sectarian religious rites, instituted by Moses under unique historical circumstances and for specific political purposes, they are only of limited scope and validity. Unlike the true divine law, which is universally valid for all human beings, the ceremonial laws of Judaism are particularistic and directed only to a given people—the ancient Hebrews—and adapted to their condition at a certain extended period in time. These include laws about the priesthood, ritual purity, sacrifice, worship, and other liturgical matters, as well as the laws that gave the Hebrew commonwealth its unity, identity, strength, and stability (especially the regulations about diet, agriculture, clothing, and so forth that distinguished it from surrounding nations).

Consequently, with the end of the Hebrew commonwealth and, especially, the final destruction of the Temple in Jerusalem in 70 CE, Moses' laws have lost their raison d'être and, thus, their obligatory force. In exile, without a state of their own, the Jews have no obligation or even reason to obey Jewish law; the only laws to which they are justifiably subject are the laws of the state in which they live, and the law of nature which prescribes the

path to true blessedness.[47] "The Hebrews are not bound to practice their ceremonial rites since the destruction of their state. . . .
Since the fall of their independent state, Jews are no more bound
by the Mosaic Law than they were before their political state came
into being," that is, before Moses issued the law in the form of the
commandments.[48] In Spinoza's view, Jewish law, for a seventeenth-
century Jew (indeed, for all Jews after 70 CE), is anachronistic and
obsolete.

There can be no more serious offense within rabbinic Judaism than denying the continued validity of Jewish law. To deny
Torah—written and oral—especially before the late nineteenth
century and the development of alternative, less orthodox branches
of Judaism (such as Reform Judaism), is to deny Judaism itself.
Spinoza, as we shall see, is perfectly aware of this.

Another, somewhat less dogmatic tenet of Judaism is the notion that the Jews are God's chosen people. The divine "election" of
the Jewish people is said to have begun with the unique covenant
that God first established with Abraham and renewed over the
course of subsequent generations. As Moses reports God's words in
Deuteronomy (7:6), "you are a people holy to the Lord your God;
the Lord your God chose you out of all nations on earth to be his
special possession." Even when a disobedient nation turns away
from God, transgresses the Mosaic law, and, worse, worships other
gods, they remain God's elect, distinct from all other peoples.

Jewish chosenness informs the prophetic writings, rabbinic
commentaries, and, in one form or another, later philosophical
thought.[49] (It also informs the daily liturgy: the ritual blessing
of the Torah scroll, repeated multiple times during worship, proclaims that God "has chosen us from among all peoples.") This
election is ordinarily understood not simply as a matter of the Israelites enjoying divine favor and (with Moses) being given the
law, but as the bestowal of a distinctive kind of holiness (*kedushah*)
upon them.[50] As several Jewish prayers proclaim, God has "sancti-
fied" the Jewish nation and provided it with a specific destiny. God
does indeed care about other peoples as well; *all* human beings
are, according to Hebrew Scripture, made "in the image of God."
But Jewish chosenness implies that the Jewish nation stands in a

special relationship to God and that this confers a special quality on it (which in turn creates particular obligations among Jews with respect to God). One strain of Jewish thought even goes so far as to claim that there is also something metaphysically distinctive about Jewish souls, making members of Israel essentially different from and inherently superior to other nations. The medieval philosopher-poet Judah Halevi, for example, insists that even if someone were to convert to Judaism, while he would share in the good fortune that Jews enjoy, he would still "not be equal to us."[51]

To Spinoza, the idea of Jewish specialness is both irrational and, insofar as it divides people and prevents them from working together for the common good, dangerous. To combat it, he provides in his an analysis of "the vocation of the Hebrews" in chapter three of the *Treatise* a naturalistic and rather deflationary account of God's election. It is "childish," he insists, for people to base their happiness on the uniqueness of their gifts. The fact that someone else possesses the same benefit that I possess does not take away my privilege in having it, nor should it lessen my enjoyment of it. In the case of the Jews, what is infantile is their insistence on the uniqueness of their being chosen by God from among all nations and all peoples.

In fact, Spinoza argues, the ancient Hebrews did not, as a group, surpass other nations in their wisdom, their character, or (which amounts to the same thing) their proximity to God. They are not—nor is *any* religious group—intellectually or morally superior to other peoples. This principle is dictated by Spinoza's universal naturalism, according to which all things (and thus all people) belong to nature in the same way and are governed by the same laws. Reason and the capacity for virtue are distributed by nature equally among all individual human beings, and there is no reason why the achievement of the supreme good might not be found among all nations. "The Hebrews surpassed other nations not in knowledge nor in piety . . . the Hebrews [were] chosen by God above all others not for the true life nor for any higher understanding."[52]

There is, then, no cognitive or moral sense in which the Jews are a special people. And, contrary to Halevi, they cannot be metaphysically different from other human beings. As Spinoza demonstrates in the *Ethics*, all individual human beings are equally a part of Nature, finite modes of Thought and Extension. No group is more or less endowed with gifts or favor by God or Nature than any other group. All human beings have the same share in "God's external help," the goods (and evils) that come our way by the regular course of nature. As we have seen, given Spinoza's identification of God with Nature, divine providence in this general sense is identical with the laws of nature.

> By God's direction I mean the fixed and immutable order of Nature, or chain of natural events. . . . It is the same thing whether we say that all things happen according to Nature's laws or that they are regulated by God's decree and direction.[53]

Whatever fortuitously happens to a person or group for good, "whatever falls to a man's advantage from the power of external causes," Spinoza says, "can rightly be called God's external help." We can certainly try to direct these causes to work for our benefit, but there will always remain a degree of luck involved in whether or not things go our way. "In this matter the fool and the wise man have about an equal chance of happiness or unhappiness."[54]

Fortunately, there is that more secure path to happiness accessible to all rational beings. Any individual human being, no matter what his religious affiliation, is also free to avail himself of the more special kind of providence, or "God's internal help." A person can, through his own God-given (i.e., natural) powers, take advantage of means for preserving himself individually and even maximizing his flourishing.[55] This is what happens when an individual actively pursues knowledge and virtue because he recognizes their importance for his security and well-being. Jews, Christians, Muslims, presumably even atheists all naturally have God's internal help within reach. All are equally at the mercy of the forces of nature, but all are also endowed with rational faculties through which they can successfully navigate their way to happiness.

A group or nation may also take advantage of God's internal help by doing what it can to preserve itself and increase its power. There are natural means, through "human contrivance and vigilance," by which a people can organize itself "to achieve security and to avoid injuries from other men and from beasts." There is, Spinoza insists, no better way to do this than by organizing their society with good and fixed laws within a settled territory. The wiser the lawmakers and the more widespread the obedience to them, the more effective the laws will be for maintaining a stable polity that can resist its enemies and survive the vicissitudes of fortune.

With this distinction between God's external and internal aid, Spinoza can conclude there is some meaning to the notion of the election of the Jewish people. They *were* chosen by God (or Nature). But Spinoza reduces this to a set of purely historical claims, devoid of any moral or theological import and without any willful and deliberate activity by a providential deity.

The ancient Israelites did indeed surpass other nations and enjoy God's favor in two very mundane respects: their geopolitical good fortune and their social organization. On the one hand, they were simply lucky. For a long time the Jewish people benefited, through no particular virtue of their own, from God or Nature's general providence.

> A merely casual perusal [of Scripture] clearly reveals that the Hebrews surpassed other nations in this alone, that they were successful in achieving security for themselves and overcame great dangers, and this chiefly by God's external help alone. In other respects, they were no different from other nations, and God was equally gracious to all.[56]

The Israelites were "chosen" by God, then, because fortune (Nature) smiled upon them. Things happened to go their way. Perhaps their opponents were generally weaker than they were, or the climate was right for their agriculture. Because of these and other favorable circumstances, Israelite society flourished; it enjoyed prosperity and repulsed its enemies. But apparently Spinoza believes that, to a certain degree, things could just as well have gone the other way.

On the other hand, the Israelites do bear some responsibility for their success, as they were also able to take advantage of God's internal help. They tended to obey the laws that had been set for them by their lawgivers, with the natural consequence that their society was well-ordered and their autonomous government long-lived. The process of "election" requires no supernatural intervention—just competent political and ethical leaders and widespread observance of the rules. If a group is provided with wise and pragmatic laws and lives by them, then the result will (naturally) be an independent, secure, and prosperous polity.

> The Hebrew nation was chosen by God before all others not by reason of its understanding nor of its spiritual qualities, but by reason of its social organization and the good fortune whereby it achieved supremacy and retained it for so many years. . . . Therefore their election and vocation consisted only in the material success and prosperity of their state. . . . In return for their obedience the Law promises them nothing other than the continuing prosperity of their state and material advantages, whereas disobedience and the breaking of the Covenant would bring about the downfall of their state and the severest hardships.[57]

The election of the Jews was thus a temporal and conditional one. It applied only to the group and was valid only for a limited time. "The individual Jew, considered alone apart from his social organization and his government, possesses no gift of God above other men, and there is no difference between him and a Gentile."[58] With the Israelites' kingdom now long gone, their distinction has come to an end. The circumstantial good fortune and self-created political thriving in which their chosenness consisted is over. "At the present time there is nothing whatsoever that the Jews can arrogate to themselves above other nations."[59] With respect to understanding, virtue, and true happiness, with respect to blessedness, there is not, never has been, and never will be anything peculiar to the Jews.[60]

Spinoza's dismissive attitude toward Jewish law in the *Treatise* has given rise to the idea that he played an important role in the secularization of Judaism, and even that he was himself the first secular Jew. However, to believe that Spinoza envisioned a Judaism unencumbered by the prescriptions of Torah and the strict observance of Jewish ritual is to misunderstand much of what Spinoza says about both Judaism in particular and religion in general.

The secularization of Judaism can mean a number of things, but is most often understood to be the opportunity for a non-religiously observant or cultural Judaism. A secular Jew, in this view, would be an individual who is (by birth or by conversion) Jewish and who expressly self-identifies as Jewish, but who does not follow Jewish law or order his life by Jewish ritual. It is a person for whom Jewishness lies outside regular observance or even membership in a community. Such a person must still maintain a Jewish identity, a sense of belonging to a certain culturally or ethnically circumscribed group and to a certain history, and this must make some practical difference in his or her life. This person may also have a conscious commitment to what might be called secularized Jewish beliefs and values, that is, certain moral and social principles that, while divorced from religious, theological, and ceremonial foundations, nonetheless derive in some way from Torah and Jewish history.

The claim that Spinoza played a role in the development of secular Judaism is also ambiguous. On the one hand, it could mean that Spinoza explicitly conceived the possibility of living and thinking as a secular Jew outside any organized Jewish community and observance, and perhaps even that he himself led such a life. On the other hand, it could simply mean that Spinoza, while not envisioning such a thorough secularization of one's Jewish identity or complete break from Jewish belief and observance, nonetheless argued for what one scholar has called "the individuation of belief within the traditional context of revealed religion."[61] According to this somewhat weaker reading of Spinoza's contribution to the secularization of Judaism, his role was to defend a kind of freedom of conscience *within* Judaism, such that one could, perhaps in order to make certain accommodations to modern secular society, pursue individualistic or heterodox forms of observance while nonetheless remaining *within* traditional Jewish communal life. On either reading, what Spinoza is supposed to have seen is that one could be an unorthodox, even unobservant Jew but, nonetheless, still a Jew.

It is hard to defend the idea that Spinoza was *himself* the first secular Jew. After his *herem*, not only did he cut off all formal relations with any congregation; and not only did he undoubtedly cease to practice any of the rituals and observances of Jewish life; but the mature Spinoza seems to have had practically no residual sense of Jewish identity. Being Jewish evidently played no role whatsoever in his self-image (although it did continue to play a role in the image that others had of him, as we can see by Huygens's reference to him as "the Jew of Voorburg"[62]). There is no reason to believe that, throughout the remainder of his life, Spinoza regarded himself as Jewish. One is struck, for example, not only by the contempt he shows for Jewish traditions in the *Treatise* but also by the way he uses the third person to refer to the Jewish people. "They" are the ones who lack any kind of theological or moral chosenness; "they" are the ones who have emasculated themselves through their laws.

More generally, Spinoza seems in his writings, including his extant correspondence, to lack all identification or sympathy with Jewish religion and history, and even to go out of his way to distance himself from them. But to be even a secular Jew—as opposed to being a secular individual whose background happens to be Jewish—demands some continued sense of Jewish identity, even if the source of that identity lies not in any specific religious beliefs or practices but rather in distinguishing oneself from others by one's belonging to a certain historical, ethnic, or social community. Thus, from a biographical perspective, there is no reason to think that Spinoza was the *first* secular Jew, for he was not a secular Jew at all. If anything, he was the most prominent early modern model of the secular individual, someone for whom religious affiliation or heritage played no role whatsoever in his self-identity.

But even if Spinoza did not see himself as Jewish and thus cannot be said to have lived the life of a secular Jew, does not his dismissal of Jewish law and ceremony as irrelevant to contemporary life, as well as his reduction of the "true religion" to a basic ethical principle, without any theological-metaphysical dogma, in fact lay the groundwork for a secular Judaism? Do the arguments of the *Treatise* at least make it possible to be a secular Jew, one who, while remaining a Jew, nonetheless makes certain essential accommodations to modern society, and even leads a completely secular life—a Jew for whom the demands of civil citizenship and social assimilation take precedence over the requirements of a strictly Jewish life?

There are a number of reasons why Spinoza might be thought to allow for the possibility of Judaism in the absence of Jewish law. First, he believes that the hatred directed at the Jews has, over the generations, and even in the absence of ritual observance, helped to preserve them as a separate people. Spinoza insists that even after Jews have left Judaism behind and converted to some other religion, as happened in Spain and Portugal in the fifteenth and sixteenth centuries, anti-Semitism served to maintain Jewish identity.

> As to their continued existence for so many years when scattered and stateless, this is in no way surprising, since they have separated themselves from other nations to such a degree as to incur the hatred of all. . . . That they are preserved largely through the hatred of other nations is demonstrated from historical fact.[63]

Then there is Spinoza's remark, one that perhaps should not be taken seriously, that "I consider the mark of circumcision to be such an important factor in this matter that I am convinced that this by itself will preserve their nation forever"[64]—just as, he unfortunately adds, the Chinese have been able to maintain their identity solely through the pigtail.

More significant, if Jewish ceremonial law is no longer valid because it has lost its legitimizing context, what would happen to Judaism if the observance of its commandments withered away? Would the Jewish people disappear as well? Or, on the contrary, would they continue in the absence of their laws, only now as a more secular group? When Spinoza says that Mosaic law is no longer binding on latter-day Jews, one might take him to be recommending that they should pursue their Jewishness without the laws of the Torah, and thus as foreseeing a kind of secular Judaism.

This would, however, be a mistake. Spinoza clearly believes that without the law, the Jewish people have no sustaining source of difference and identity. For him, the notion of a secular Jew— even in the face of hatred and even with his circumcision—would be incoherent. This is particularly evident in the light of his argument that there is no theological or metaphysical or moral sense in which the Jews are chosen by God from all other nations. If there are no intrinsic differences among peoples and no natural kinds to distinguish them one from another, then what *does* separate the Jew from the gentile? Especially now that there is no longer an Israelite commonwealth and the Jews are scattered over all the nations of the world, what provides their distinctiveness as a people? What makes a Jew?

The answer, according to Spinoza, is: the ceremonial law. "They have separated themselves from other nations . . . through external rites."[65] He notes that were the Jews to give up those rites, the observance of Jewish law, while living in a society that did not impose segregation and even granted them citizen rights, then political assimilation would lead to total assimilation, and Jewish identity would disappear. In the *Treatise*, he cites the case of the Babylonian exiles. "They turned their back on the entire Mosaic Law, consigned to oblivion the laws of their native land as being obviously pointless, and began to be assimilated to other nations."[66] In other words, the result of secularity and assimilation is not secular and assimilated Jews; it is secular and assimilated individuals who have left their Judaism behind. Spinoza also mentions in this context (perhaps a little too sanguinely) the case of the Jews of Spain, whose full political assimilation he sees as being conditional on their having given up their religion—understood as the observance of the Mosaic law—and the result of which was the disappearance of this group of Jews; "no trace of them was left," he says.[67] The fact that Spinoza here overlooks the laws of blood purity by which the Spanish themselves continued to distinguish true (Old) Christians from Jewish *conversos* (or New Christians) indicates that for him there is nothing to being a Jew other than the observance of the Mosaic law.

For Spinoza, then, the ceremonial laws are what is essential to Judaism. Judaism without a robust divine chosenness is relatively unproblematic. But there can be no Judaism unbounded by the observance of Jewish law. Take away the law of Moses and you take away the Jew. To put it another way, for Spinoza, to be a Jew is to be a ritually observant Jew. For what defines Jewish life for Spinoza just are the tenets of its religion and the set of ceremonial and other practices and laws that, with the destruction of the Temple, have lost their foundation. And what defines Jewish self-identity for him just is to belong to a Jewish community that is constituted by the self-conscious observance of those commandments.

Spinoza might seem uncharacteristically narrow-minded here. After all, Jewish identity in the absence of rigorous religious observance can be sustained—and, at least in the last two hundred years, has flourished—not only with selective observance of the *mitzvot* but, more important, by a sense of belonging to a shared genealogical and historical narrative and a common intellectual and cultural tradition. However, Spinoza's point—and it is, admittedly, a restrictive one—is that without the legalistic and liturgical context, without the objective framework and continuity provided by Torah, such a secular or cultural Judaism is an empty shell; it is not *Judaism*. Moreover, this is an opinion that would be shared by his contemporaries, for whom, in the absence of more and less observant denominations within Judaism (which arise only in the nineteenth century), the idea of a secular Jew was simply not on the horizon. Spinoza would not deny the obvious fact that any collection of people can find unity and group identity through historical and cultural circumstances. But if it should ever turn out that the *only* source of unity and identity for the Jewish people is a subjective feeling of belonging and nostalgic remembering, in addition to the hatred directed at them by others, then he would insist that, while individuals may assume or be given the label "Jewish," Judaism itself will have disappeared.[68]

Spinoza did not envision secular Judaism. To be a secular or assimilated Jew is, in his view, nonsense. It is to be a nonsectarian sectarian. For him, Judaism without an observance of its textually and historically defined tenets, laws, and ceremonies would be a masquerade. These laws and rituals—along with gentile anti-Semitism—are what have preserved Judaism since the destruction of the Temple, and what now constitute its essence. Of course, Spinoza had great contempt for traditional sectarian religions, and Judaism in particular. And he did argue that Jewish law is no longer binding on contemporary Jews. Perhaps in this sense he unwittingly opened the door for a secular or even Reform Judaism. But he also had a very strict understanding of what was to count as Judaism. Spinoza may have been a religious reformer, but what he envisioned was not reform *within* Judaism. Rather, what he had in mind was a universal rational religion that eschewed meaningless, superstitious rituals and focused instead on a few simple moral principles, above all, to love one's neighbor as oneself.

There is another persistent myth about Spinoza's religion, one based partly on the company he kept and partly on some remarks he makes in the *Treatise*. It has been claimed that after he was "expelled from the people of Israel," as the text of his *herem* puts it, Spinoza became a Christian, perhaps joining one of the dissident Reformed sects that flourished in the Netherlands and to which many of his friends and collaborators belonged.

Among Spinoza's closest companions from the mid-1650s on were the Mennonites Simon Joosten de Vries, Pieter Balling, and Jarig Jelles, all of whom were associated with the Collegiant groups that met in Amsterdam and Rijnsburg. There is also some reason to think that Spinoza had contacts with a number of English Quakers in Amsterdam at this time.[69] His relationships with these various *Chrétiens sans église*[70] has been taken to indicate that Spinoza either formally converted to Christianity in one of its radical Protestant forms or at least became a practicing Christian.[71]

There can be no doubt that his personal connections with Christian religious reformers—who rejected ecclesiastic hierarchy, eliminated ritual from their gatherings, and advocated the "inner light" as the true guide to God—were extremely influential in the development of Spinoza's own religious (and political) views. Many of Spinoza's comments in the *Treatise* on true religion and its distinction from traditional organized religion reflect the beliefs and practices of these pious dissenters. And any reader of the *Treatise* will be struck by Spinoza's respectful treatment of the Christian Gospels and the high praise that he reserves for Jesus as the prophet who excelled all others—including Moses—as well as his admiration for the Apostle Paul.

Spinoza never subjects the New Testament to the kind of rigorous and extended textual and historical critique that he gives to the Hebrew Bible. In contrast with his rather dismissive attitude toward much of Hebrew Scripture and his deflationary account of the Old Testament prophets, Spinoza has many positive things to say about the Christian Gospels and their authors. The apostles, he argues, expound their doctrines (or, rather, "Christ's doctrine") in a manner "entirely different" from the Hebrew prophets. In fact, they appear to have functioned more like teachers than prophets, operating through reason and persuasion (as if "conducting a discussion") rather than imagination and dogmatic assertion. Moreover, they worked from natural knowledge and often spoke only according to their own opinions, without the authoritative certainty found in a prophet's pronouncements. "The letters of the Apostles were composed only according to the natural light."[72]

Spinoza holds Paul especially in high esteem. While a prophet, he was also, it seems, close to being a philosopher, engaging others with wisdom. In this, he was unlike Moses, "the greatest of the prophets, who did not make any proper argument." Paul preached as one endowed with knowledge. With the other apostles, he worked in a rational manner to spread the message of Jesus and encourage and strengthen the religious faith of his audience.[73]

Why Spinoza should approach the Christian Gospels so differently from the way in which he deals with the books of Hebrew Scripture—and so respectfully—is something of a puzzle. He suggests at one point that he is not qualified to give these texts the kind of thorough critical examination to which he has subjected the Hebrew writings.

> Now it would be time to examine the books of the New Testament in the same way. But because I am told that this has been done by men who are most learned both in the sciences and especially in the languages, because I do not have so exact a knowledge of the Greek language that I might dare to undertake this task, and finally, because we are lacking copies of the books which were written in the Hebrew language I prefer to refrain from this difficult business.[74]

This is a bit disingenuous, however. Spinoza's lack of Greek does not stop him from having substantive things to say about the doctrines of the New Testament throughout the *Treatise*.[75] At the same time, he claims that "the native language of the Apostles is none other than Syriac," and even suggests that what we have in the Gospels is a Greek translation of a Syriac original.[76] Spinoza also insists, earlier in the *Treatise*, that the language that is essential for making sense of the Christian Gospels is Hebrew, not Greek.

> Because all the authors, both of the Old Testament and the New, were Hebrews, it is certain that the History of the Hebrew language is necessary above all others, not only for understanding the books of the Old Testament, which were written in this language, but also for understanding those of the New Testament. For although they have been made common to all in other languages, nevertheless they express themselves in a Hebrew manner.[77]

A more likely explanation for Spinoza's reluctance to deal at length with the Christian Gospels is also the most obvious one. Simply by virtue of his upbringing, Spinoza is much more versed in Hebrew Scripture and the Jewish commentary tradition than he is in the Christian literature. Moreover, as suggested above, it may also be that when Spinoza does address the Gospels he gives them a more respectful treatment so as not to turn an important part of his audience against him. He needed to tread carefully before those whom he hoped to persuade with the *Treatise* and co-opt into his project of religious and political reform. He could not risk alienating Amsterdam regents, liberal theologians, and members of dissident Reformed sects, none of whom would have been receptive to an appeal made by someone who denigrated Christ's apostles.[78] As Leo Strauss famously argues this point, "the *Treatise* is addressed to Christians," especially those Spinoza wanted to convert to philosophy, and it was "infinitely less dangerous to attack the Old Testament than the New."[79]

This does not imply that there is, as Strauss calls it, a "hidden teaching" in the *Treatise*; that Spinoza, out of fear of persecution and concern for the piety of the masses, is trying to hide the truth from many readers (while surreptitiously communicating it to the cognoscenti), and that the *Treatise* is therefore an "exoteric" work that demands "reading between the lines."[80] Rather, it suggests only that Spinoza, like so many authors, is working with a rhetorical strategy geared toward drawing in his audience, and thus does not always mean exactly what he says or say everything that he thinks.

So there may be good reasons, apart from his alleged ignorance of Greek, for Spinoza's relatively gentle treatment of the Christian Gospels and favorable view of the teachings of the apostles. But the notion that Spinoza himself converted to Christianity is not one of them.

There is, in fact, no evidence whatsoever for the idea that Spinoza became a Christian, not even as a fellow traveler. Given everything he says about the deleterious effects of organized religion on the freedom and happiness of individuals and on the well-being of society, it is a thoroughly implausible hypothesis. And a careful reader of the *Treatise* will see that Christianity, not as a collection of texts but as a sectarian religion, receives no kinder treatment from Spinoza than Judaism.

It is true that, in the *Treatise*, Spinoza does give Jesus pride of place among all the prophets. His revelations are qualitatively

different from, and superior to, those of Moses and the other Hebrew prophets. What distinguishes Jesus' prophesizing is the
immediacy of his grasp of God's word. According to Hebrew
Scripture, by which "we are required to make a distinction between the prophesying of Moses and that of other prophets," only
Moses had a direct revelation from God. He exceeded Jeremiah,
Ezekiel, Isaiah, and the others because, while they experienced
their revelations through the imagination, in dreams and illusory visions, Moses heard God's real voice, and even saw "his back
parts" (but not his face).[81]

Jesus, however, surpassed even Moses. He communed with
God not merely face-to-face (or, rather, face-to-backside) but
"mind to mind." Neither the imagination nor even the sensory
faculties were involved in Jesus' revelations. He perceived the
word of God immediately, through an intuitive mental grasp of
the divine message.

> We may quite clearly understand that God can communicate with
> man without mediation, for he communicates his essence to our
> minds without employing corporeal means. Nevertheless, a man
> who can perceive by pure intuition that which is not contained in
> the basic principles of our cognition and cannot be deduced there-
> from must needs possess a mind whose excellence far surpasses the
> human mind.

Spinoza is not allowing that human beings can have superhuman
(or supernatural) minds. Rather, there are some individuals whose
immediate grasp of certain truths is so unusual and so unique that
there is no obvious explanation for their talent (although we can
be sure that a natural explanation does exist).

> I do not believe that anyone has attained such a degree of perfection
> surpassing all others except Christ. To him, God's ordinances lead-
> ing men to salvation were revealed not by words or by visions, but
> directly, so that God manifested himself to the Apostles through the
> mind of Christ as he once did to Moses through an audible voice.
> The Voice of Christ can thus be called the Voice of God in the same

way as that which Moses heard. In that sense it can also be said that the Wisdom of God—that is, wisdom that is more than human—took on human nature in Christ, and that Christ was the way of salvation.[82]

Spinoza, of course, knows that Christianity proclaims (with what he regards as dubious scriptural authority) that there was something supernaturally divine about Jesus Christ, that he was "more than human" in a literal and metaphysical sense. But the naturalism of his philosophy will not allow for any such thing. As he says in a letter to Oldenburg, "as to the additional teaching of certain churches, that God took upon himself human nature, I have expressly indicated that I do not understand what they say. Indeed, to tell the truth, they seem to me to speak no less absurdly than one who might tell me that a circle has taken on the nature of a square." More generally, to the extent that Christians base their faith on the belief in miracles, he tells his English friend, "they rest their case . . . on ignorance, which is the source of all wickedness, and thus they turn their faith, true as it may be, into superstition."[83]

Christ's superiority as a prophet lies not in any supernatural gifts or miraculous powers, but only in the depth of his moral insight and his pedagogical skill. What makes him "the mouthpiece of God" is that he, more than anyone else, perceived God's word—religion's true ethical message, to love God and one's fellow human beings—truly and adequately. Instead of knowing this universal truth to be the supreme religious principle because he had visions from which he was able to derive that lesson or because he deduced it from some other principles, he understood it through an intuitive knowledge of God or Nature.

> This fact, that God revealed himself to Christ, or to Christ's mind, directly, and not through words and images as in the case of the prophets, can have only this meaning, that Christ perceived truly, or understood, what was revealed. For it is when a thing is perceived by pure thought, without words or images, that it is understood.[84]

What was exceptional about Christ, what Spinoza means when he says that Jesus communicated with God "mind to mind," is that he was endowed with a unique perspicuity of moral insight and that he was a gifted ethical teacher. It is in this perfectly naturalistic sense, and this sense only, that Spinoza accepts the idea that "Christ is the way of salvation." Therefore, anyone who, regardless of his ignorance of Scripture, nonetheless holds the proper beliefs about what is good and right and pursues a virtuous way of life, "is absolutely blessed and has within him the spirit of Christ."[85] Similarly, all talk of Jesus' resurrection must, when properly understood, have only a "spiritual" meaning. Jesus was a moral exemplar, and the doctrines of the incarnation and resurrection should be interpreted as saying that "in his life and death he provided an example of surpassing holiness, and that he raises his disciples from the dead in so far as they follow the example of his own life and death."[86] Anyone who, on the other hand, persecutes those who love justice and charity is "an enemy of Christ."[87]

Spinoza may have recommended christianity (or, better, Christism) as the path to blessedness, but he certainly did not become a Christian. The true faith has nothing to do with the superstitious dogmas or empty ceremonies of any sectarian worship.

Chapter 8

Faith, Reason, and the State

In popular accounts of the history of European philosophy, the seventeenth century is often referred to as the Age of Reason, presumably to distinguish it from the so-called Age of Faith, that is, the medieval period. But even a casual observer of the way in which ecclesiastic authority—both Catholic and Reformed—continued to police intellectual (and not just doctrinal) matters throughout the continent would be justified in having doubts about the appropriateness of the label.

Things did not start out auspiciously. In 1600, in Italy, Giordano Bruno was condemned by the Catholic Church for heresy and burned at the stake for daring to proclaim that the universe is infinite and that the earth is not the center of the cosmos. Sixteen years later, the same cleric who presided at Bruno's trial, Cardinal Roberto Bellarmine, warned Galileo to cease discussing Copernicanism. Despite having promised to obey, Galileo, a stubborn man, continued to argue publicly for the motion of the earth around a stationary sun. For his impudence he was hauled before the Holy Office in Rome in 1633, forced to confess the error of his ways, and sentenced to house arrest for the rest of his life. His *Dialogue Concerning Two Chief World Systems* was placed on the Index of Prohibited Books.

The Inquisition's treatment of Galileo was sufficiently troubling to Descartes, a thousand kilometers to the north, that, in the same year, he withheld his own cosmological work, *The World*, from publication.

I was beginning to revise [my treatise] and put it in the hands of a publisher, when I learned that some persons to whom I defer and who have hardly any less authority over my actions than my own reason has over my thoughts, had disapproved of a physical theory published a little before by someone else [i.e., Galileo]. I will not say that I accepted this theory, but only that before their condemnation I had noticed nothing in it that I could imagine to be prejudicial either to religion or to the state, and hence nothing that would have prevented me from publishing it myself, if reason had convinced me of it. This made me fear that there might be some mistake in one of my own theories. . . . That was enough to make me change my previous decision to publish my views.[1]

Many years later, when Descartes did offer a Copernican model of the universe in his *Principles of Philosophy*, he was very careful to present it as a mere "hypothesis or supposition" that, while it accounts for the astronomical appearances, "may be false and not the real truth."[2] Just to play it safe, he even proposed that the earth is stationary, but only because it maintains the same position relative to the matter that immediately surrounds it and that carries it around the sun.[3] The ruse only delayed the reckoning with the Church. In 1663, thirteen years after his death, Descartes's own writings were placed on the Index, where they were to remain "until corrected."[4]

Spinoza himself knew that, while the Calvinist Dutch Republic was generally more lenient with progressive, even "freethinking" intellectual trends than its Catholic neighbors, there were limits to the famed Dutch toleration. This was especially true in the first half of the century, before the period of the True Freedom inaugurated by De Witt's tenure as grand pensionary of the States of Holland. The University of Utrecht in the 1640s, to take just one example, was a major battleground in the debates over Copernicanism and Cartesianism. There was much resistance among the academic leadership (primarily conservative clergymen) to "dangerous innovations" in science and philosophy. Cartesian professors of medicine, physics, and other disciplines came in for rough treatment by the rector, Voetius, and his allies. Even in the 1660s, secular and generally liberal Dutch regents were susceptible to ecclesiastic-instigated acts of intellectual repression, as witnessed by the treatment of Koerbagh in Amsterdam. While Spinoza's friend was thrown into prison in 1669 by the municipal council, the case against him was pushed by the Reformed consistory.

It is not that the Catholic and Reformed churches were against science. Despite the textbook tale often told about the Galileo case, the notion that in this period religion was opposed to scientific progress in theory and practice has long been refuted as myth. A great deal of scientific activity in the Middle Ages and the early modern period—in physics, astronomy, mechanics, chemistry, and other areas—took place within the context of religious institutions, including Jesuit colleges and university faculties populated by perfectly orthodox ecclesiastics. These were generally, however, very conservative establishments, to say the least, and scientific and philosophical thinking had to respect certain boundaries set from outside their disciplines. The Catholic Church may have been a major supporter of scientific research, but the results of that science had to be consistent with its theological doctrines. Among Catholics, it was the pope and his appointed representatives—including local archbishops—who decided whether or not a theory about the cosmos or an account of terrestrial bodies was a danger to the faith; in the Protestant provinces of the Netherlands, it was up to the *predikanten* in the consistories and synods to guard against what the authorities at the University of Leiden called "the application of philosophy to the prejudice of theology."[5]

It is true that Bruno denied some central dogmas of Catholicism, including the Trinity; and Koerbagh seems to have made a concerted effort to mock sacred beliefs dear to both Catholic and Reformed faithful. But neither Galileo nor Descartes was interested in directly addressing religious themes. Descartes, in fact, went out of his way to avoid getting embroiled in theological disputes. He just wanted to be left alone to pursue his investigations into natural philosophy. How could a mere theory of matter or explanation of the laws of motion possibly be inconsistent with doctrines of theology or a threat to the faith?

Unfortunately, things were not so simple in the seventeenth century. Indeed, the question seems especially naive, and Descartes (despite his protests) could not have been very surprised at the reaction that his philosophical views elicited from theologians. To early modern churchmen, the problem with Cartesianism, or any "new" philosophical system, however mundane its pretensions, was not that its theories were empirically inadequate or suffered internal logical flaws. Rather, the attacks and proscriptions—such as the 1642 decree at Utrecht banning the teaching of any philosophy other than that of Aristotle—were motivated by what appeared, however obscurely to nonclerical eyes, to be a philosophy's religious implications.[6]

Some scientific theories, of course, were regarded by church authorities as directly inconsistent with truths about God and nature that they believed to be proclaimed, explicitly or implicitly, by Scripture. If the Bible asserts that on a day of battle the sun ceased its motion in the heavens, then obviously the Copernican model of a stationary sun must be rejected. But in other cases, the reason for ecclesiastic censorship of ostensibly secular ideas was more complex, particularly as the understanding of what properly belonged to church doctrine grew rather expansive. By this time, long-standing Aristotelian-Scholastic explanations of a number of Catholic and Reformed tenets had themselves practically achieved the status of religious dogma. Descartes thought he was merely doing metaphysics, but he learned very quickly what some Catholic clerics thought his new account of body meant for the real presence of Christ in the sacramental host.[7] The particular explanation of Eucharistic transubstantiation through neo-Aristotelian forms and qualities was so deeply entrenched in Catholic theology that it became an essential part of the mystery; to deny the Aristotelian account (as Descartes essentially did) was tantamount to denying the miracle itself.

Thus, the Catholic Church and the Reformed consistories, as guardians of the faith, monitored both religious affairs and philosophical and scientific ones. They presumed to have a say not only on what was a matter of piety but also on what was a matter of truth.

It is this notion that the limits to science and philosophy are to be determined by religious criteria, and especially by Scripture and its sectarian interpreters, that is a central object of Spinoza's attack in the *Treatise*. His point is that even to believe that there *can* be a conflict between knowledge-seeking disciplines, on the one hand, and the encouragement of piety, on the other hand, is to suffer a deep misunderstanding of the nature of faith and its relationship to truth and reason. The confusion and the intolerance this misunderstanding breeds infect not only the scientific academy and the philosopher's study but the political commonwealth at large. For Spinoza, the divide between faith and reason, between religion and philosophy, is as exclusive as that between the attributes of Thought and Extension in his metaphysics of nature.

In January 1665, Spinoza received his first letter from van Blijenburgh. The Dordrecht merchant, who knew Spinoza only from his work on Descartes's *Principles of Philosophy*, initiated the correspondence to learn more about Spinoza's views on evil; at this point, he obviously has no suspicion that the broader philosophy that Spinoza is harboring is one he would find truly disturbing. "I see that you will shortly publish the 'Metaphysical Thoughts' in an expanded form [i.e., the *Ethics*]. I very much look forward to both of these, for I have great expectations of them."[8] Five years later, van Blijenburgh will be shocked by what he reads in the *Treatise*, and he will go on to compose an extended refutation of that "blasphemous book."

In the January letter, which he wrote in Dutch, van Blijenburgh explains to Spinoza the "two general rules which always govern my endeavors to philosophize." One is "the clear and distinct conception of my intellect," something with which any good

Cartesian could agree. The second rule, though, concerns "the re-vealed Word, or will, of God," and it stipulates that "whenever it happens that after long consideration my natural knowledge seems either to be at variance with this Word or not very easily reconcilable with it, this Word has so much authority with me that I prefer to cast doubt on the conceptions I imagine to be clear rather than to set these above and in opposition to the truth which I find prescribed for me in that book."[9]

In the opening paragraph of his reply, Spinoza, writing back in Dutch (a language in which, he confesses, he has some trouble expressing himself), takes issue with just this rule. "I see that we disagree not only in the conclusions to be drawn by a chain of reasoning from first principles, but in those very same first prin-ciples, so that I hardly believe that our correspondence can be for our mutual instruction."[10] He goes on to explain that "since I am conscious that when an indisputable proof is presented to me, I find it impossible to entertain thoughts that cast doubt upon it, I entirely acquiesce in what my intellect shows me without any sus-picion that I am deceived therein, or that Holy Scripture, without my even examining it, can contradict it. For truth is not at odds with truth."

On the face of it, Spinoza seems in this letter to be offering what has been called a "dogmatic" approach to the relationship of faith and reason: that the principles of faith and the declarations of Scripture are to be understood in such a way that they are ac-commodated to the true pronouncements of science and philoso-phy. Much as Maimonides and Meijer argue that Scripture, as a revealed source of truth, should be interpreted figuratively when-ever a literal interpretation would be inconsistent with a ratio-nally demonstrated truth, so the dogmatist generally insists that truth is one, and that faith is to be adapted to reason. Van Blijen-burgh, by contrast, has adopted the so-called "skeptical" position, whereby reason—which skeptics traditionally argue is a weak and unreliable faculty, and particularly inadequate in such a transcen-dent and consequential domain as religion—must submit to faith when its discoveries do not mesh with truths revealed by God. If dogmatism gives priority to human reason, skepticism insists that reason must be subordinate to revelation.

Spinoza's letter to van Blijenburgh comes a few years before he would begin writing the *Treatise*. Either his remarks to van Blijenburgh do not reflect his considered view on the matter (and Spinoza may have had good reason to hide his real opinions from him), or his view developed after he put aside the *Ethics* to give his full attention to theological-political matters. Either way, it is clear that in the *Treatise* itself Spinoza rejects both dogmatism and skepticism.[11] He goes to great lengths to show that, in fact, philosophy and religion have absolutely nothing to do with one another. Philosophy is the pursuit of knowledge. Religious faith is about obedience and action. Philosophical propositions are assessed according to their truth-value; true theories expand our understanding of the world and of ourselves. The propositions of religion are assessed according to their piety and motivational value; they are supposed to inspire in us a love of God and ethical behavior toward others. This separation of the spheres of philosophy and faith is at the heart of Spinoza's argument for the theme of the *Treatise*: a defense of the "freedom of philosophizing."

As we have seen, the fundamental teaching of Scripture is a moral one: love your neighbor. This is also a principle discoverable by reason alone, for anyone sufficiently philosophical and capable of understanding what virtue truly is. But *that* Scripture teaches loving kindness as the word of God is not established by appealing to the book's conformity with any rational demonstration; rather, it is discovered by examining Scripture itself.

If this command is the supreme principle of true religion, as Spinoza insists, then the subordinate tenets of faith are limited only to those propositions that encourage obedience to it. "Faith requires not so much true dogmas as pious dogmas . . . it does not expressly demand true dogmatic belief, but only such beliefs as are necessary for obedience, that is, those that strengthen the will to love one's neighbor."[12] For those who will find their motivation for virtuous behavior in the Bible rather than in the demonstrations of the *Ethics*, they will learn from the prophetic writings just those things the belief in which are most useful, even necessary for encouraging the love of God and of one's fellow human beings.

In chapter fourteen of the *Treatise*, Spinoza enumerates what those basic beliefs are, as well as the reasons for thinking that these are necessary for obedience to God's law:

I. God, that is, a supreme being, exists, supremely just and merciful, the exemplar of true life; for whoever does not know or does not believe that he exists cannot obey him or know him as a Judge;

II. That God is one alone; for no one can doubt that this too is absolutely required for supreme devotion, admiration and love towards God; devotion, admiration and love arise only from the excellence of one by comparison with the others;

III. That God is omnipresent, and that all things are open to him; for if things were believed to be hidden from him, or people were not aware that he sees all, they would have doubts about the equity of his Justice, by which he directs all things, or at least they would not be aware of it;

IV. That God has supreme right and dominion over all things, and does nothing because he is compelled by a law, but acts only from his absolute good pleasure and special grace; for everyone is bound absolutely to obey him, but he is not bound to obey anyone;

V. That the worship of God and obedience to him consist only in justice and loving-kindness, or in the love of one's neighbor;

VI. That all and only those who obey God by living in this way are saved, the rest, who live under the control of the pleasures, being lost; if men did not firmly believe this, there would be no reason why they should prefer to obey God rather than their pleasures.

VII. Finally, that God pardons the sins of those who repent; for there is no one who does not sin; so if we did not maintain this, everyone would despair of his salvation, and there would be no reason why he would believe God to be merciful; moreover, whoever firmly believes that God, out of mercy and the grace by which he directs everything, pardons men's sins, and who for this reason is more inspired by the love of God, that person really knows Christ according to the Spirit, and Christ is in him.[13]

Spinoza's assumption is that only someone who believes that there is a free, just, and merciful God who knows all things and has power over all things, and especially who stands in judgment over his creatures, will willingly and consistently obey the divine command to love God and, imitating this representation of God in his own behavior, treat others with justice and charity. And the stature of these beliefs has nothing to do with their truth. In fact, they do not have to be true at all. Strictly speaking—that is, Spinozistically speaking—several of them are false (which is not surprising, given that Scripture's authors were not learned men). God (or Nature) is not just and merciful; it does not stand in judgment over us or issue pardon and punishment. And while the other beliefs may, when properly interpreted, be true (God or Nature is one, and is the all-powerful cause of everything), it is not their truth but their pragmatic efficacy that constitutes their value.

The articles of faith say nothing about incarnations, resurrections, virgin births, burning bushes, or the delights of paradise; nor do they touch on prayers, ceremonies, or rituals. They do not demand a belief in miracles, or even in a creationist account of the cosmos. Faith is silent when it comes to the physics of the heavens or the constitution of terrestrial bodies. It also leaves each individual free to conceive of God's nature as he wishes. "Whether [God] is fire, or spirit, or light, or thought, or something else, this is irrelevant to faith." On detailed questions of metaphysical theology, "it matters not what beliefs a man holds." One's views on such things can be true or they can be false, as long as they are sincerely believed. It all depends on what is most conducive to obedience, and this will be different for each person. "[E]very man is duty bound to adapt these religious dogmas to his own understanding and to interpret them for himself in whatever way makes him feel that he can the more readily accept them with full confidence and conviction."[14] What Spinoza calls his "universal" or "catholic" faith is a minimal one, geared expressly for maximizing ethical behavior and minimizing religious controversy.

Spinoza's insistence that these tenets are *necessary* for faith and true religion may seem odd, especially if some of them are false.[15]

One would expect him to say, rather, that the belief in God as powerful, just, and merciful is highly effective in encouraging obedience to God's word and the practice of justice and charity, and maybe even indispensable for the masses. But to claim that these propositions are necessary for faith might appear inconsistent with Spinoza's own view that some people can be led toward virtue and true religion through philosophical reflection rather than prophetic writings. How can these beliefs, amounting as they do to a very traditional, even anthropomorphic conception of a providential deity, be *essential* for obedience and salvation when the *Ethics* itself lays out a perfectly rational—and more secure— path to "blessedness" and the love of God?

However, the person who loves God and his neighbor out of an "intellectual or exact knowledge of God" is in a very different position from the person who does so without having achieved this supreme cognitive condition. The philosophically gifted person— and Spinoza does call such perfection a "gift"—does not really "obey" a command to love God and to act with justice and charity. He will enjoy the love of God and act constantly with virtue toward others as a natural, even necessary consequence of his true understanding of God or Nature. For him, salvation is not a matter of faith.

> Love of God is not obedience but a virtue necessarily present in a man who knows God aright, whereas obedience has regard to the will of him who commands, and not to necessity and truth. . . . We have shown that the divine commandments appear to us as commandments or ordinances only as long as we do not know their cause. Once this is known, they cease to be commandments, and we embrace them as eternal truths, not as commandments; that is, obedience forthwith passes into love, which arises from true knowledge by the same necessity as light arises from the sun. Therefore by the guidance of reason we can love God, but not obey Him; for by virtue of reason we can neither accept divine commandments as divine while not knowing their cause, nor can we conceive God as a ruler enacting laws.[16]

The person guided by reason knows that, in truth, God (or Nature) is not a lawgiver and does not issue commands; therefore, his just and charitable behavior is not, strictly speaking, a form of obedience (to laws) but an inevitable consequence of his intellectual virtue.[17]

Most people are not philosophers, however, and the point of Scripture is not to impart knowledge but to encourage obedience and strengthen the love of justice. As Scripture portrays God in anthropomorphic terms as a lawgiver, the nonphilosophical but pious person will, moved by faith, love God and his fellow human beings because he believes he is commanded to do so by God, and thus out of obedience and a sense of duty. Spinoza, while sometimes contemptuous of people who do their duty only out of fear of punishment or hope of reward, has made his peace with this. "God through his prophets asks no other knowledge of himself than the knowledge of his divine justice and charity, that is, such attributes of God as men find it possible to imitate by a definite rule of conduct."[18] Each person is free to read Scripture as he wishes and to believe of God (and of the natural world) what he wants, provided that his reading and beliefs are consistent with the prophets' primary moral message and effective in moving him to act with justice and charity—and (not incidentally) that he permit the same freedom to everyone else.

But just as philosophy (and what is true) does not determine what belongs to faith (and what best promotes obedience to God), so faith has no right to set limits to philosophizing. Religious authorities go well beyond their legitimate domain when they strive to control the pursuit of knowledge and determine what is to be accepted as true.

Faith allows to every man the utmost freedom to philosophize, and he may hold whatever opinions he pleases on any subjects whatsoever without imputation of evil. It condemns as heretics and schismatics only those who teach such beliefs as promote obstinacy, hatred, strife and anger, while it regards as the faithful only those who promote justice and charity to the best of their intellectual powers and capacity.[19]

The dogmatists are mistaken: faith is not the handmaiden of philosophy. But, despite what the skeptics say, neither is philosophy the handmaiden of faith. Religion has no right to demand anything more than the love of God and of one's fellow human beings or to insist on any beliefs other than those that are strictly necessary to foster such attitudes and behavior. The freedom of philosophizing extends even to philosophizing about God. To believe that the philosophical and scientific enterprises need to be policed by clerics and their boundaries set by religious dogma and the words of the prophets is to be guilty of a serious category mistake. "Between faith and theology on the one side and philosophy on the other there is no relation and no affinity."[20]

In his discussion of Scripture, Spinoza showed that Maimonides was wrong, and that the meanings of prophetic writings must not be forced to conform to reason and philosophy. Now he has shown that Cardinal Bellarmine was wrong, and that philosophy—whether it be natural philosophy or metaphysics—must not be forced to conform to faith. If, as Spinoza has argued, the Bible is not a source of philosophical or scientific truths but only of some very simple articles of religion, then it cannot be used to assess the claims of those secular disciplines and justify censorship of them. His position might be best summed up by Galileo's famous remark, over fifty years earlier, that the purpose of Scripture is "to teach us how one goes to heaven, not how heaven goes."[21]

Ecclesiastic meddling represents a threat not only to progress in philosophy and science but to the well-being of the state as well. In fact, the ability of clergy to exercise censorship over philosophical inquiry is directly proportional to their influence in domestic politics. Spinoza's argument in the *Treatise* for the freedom of philosophizing in the state is thus, at the same time, an argument for a state in which sectarian religious authorities have no influence over public affairs, including intellectual and cultural matters. In the end, Spinoza goes even further and argues that religion, to the extent that it is a matter of practice and public activity, is to be controlled by the secular leaders of society. He can make this case, however, only after an investigation into the nature of the state itself. Thus, in chapter sixteen, the *Treatise* takes a decidedly political direction.

Spinoza was a serious reader of ancient and modern political thought. His library included the complete works of Machiavelli, as well as writings by recent Dutch republican thinkers, such as Hugo Grotius and the brothers Pieter and Johan de la Court. By far the most important influence on Spinoza's political philosophy, however, were the works of Hobbes, both *De Cive*, which he owned, and *Leviathan*, which apparently he did not but which he read.

Hobbes, as we have seen, offers an account of the civil state that presents its theoretical (if not historical) origins in "the natural condition of mankind," or the state of nature.[22] This is a fictional condition that is assumed for the heuristic purpose of explaining the rationale of political obligation. The state of nature is a prepolitical environment, without any government or even social organization. It is characterized by the "war of every man against every man," where each individual follows the most basic law of nature and engages in the unbridled pursuit of self-interest. In these circumstances, everyone has the right to do whatever he can to protect and defend himself, and to obtain whatever he believes will aid his preservation and further his own good. In the state of nature, there is no right and no wrong, no justice or injustice. In the absence of any "common power to keep [men] in awe," violence and continual fear is the norm. It is a condition, Hobbes famously says in *Leviathan*, in which "the life of man [is] solitary, poor, nasty, brutish, and short."[23]

In such a state of affairs, "where every man is enemy to every man," reasonable people will eventually realize that self-preservation and the security of property are in fact best achieved not through perpetually defending themselves in conflict but through securing peace. The law of nature (or what Hobbes in *De Cive* calls the "dictate of reason"), then, also commands that one take positive steps to emerge from the state of nature. This is done by coming to an agreement of truce with others and voluntarily restraining the pursuit of self-interest. Rational individuals thereby choose to unite and give up the unlimited but uncertain rights they had in the state of nature. They commit to refraining from injuring each other and even to providing mutual assistance. Each is to behave in a manner conducive to the maintenance of their agreement, demonstrating self-control, utility, equity, courtesy, consideration, and other natural virtues—in short, they agree not to treat others in ways they would not want to be treated themselves.[24]

These proto-citizens, however, also realize that an agreement is only as good as the power behind it, and that there needs to be something in place besides conscience alone that keeps people from taking advantage of others when the desire and opportunity arise. "Consent or contracted society, without some common power whereby particular men may be ruled through fear of punishment, doth not suffice to make up that security, which is requisite to the exercise of natural justice."[25] Therefore, the parties to this truce go one step further and create by a kind of contract a formal commonwealth, with a designated sovereign power at its head. With this contract, they transfer all of their rights to the sovereign and confer upon it the authority to enforce the contract and punish transgressors. The sovereign has absolute power—and Hobbes does mean *absolute* power—in the now constituted polity; any other arrangement, with restrictions placed on the sovereign's power or the existence of alternative sources of authority in the state, would not allow the sovereign to effectively do what it has been established to do. The sovereign alone—whether it be one individual (monarchy), a council with restricted membership (aristocracy), or a representative body for the people at-large (democracy)—has the right to make laws and to provide all the sanctions necessary to ensure that the agreement that is the foundation of the state is observed and that peace and the common defense are maintained. The citizens, in turn, are henceforth bound to obey the sovereign and the laws it institutes.

In this way, the many wills that, in the state of nature, were opposed to each other are replaced by a single, all-governing will, that of the sovereign. In Hobbes's account, the citizens who enter into a political pact have given up much by submitting themselves to the absolute authority of the sovereign; but in doing so they have had returned to them, on more certain grounds, what they had been seeking in the first place. While fear is the primary motivation for entering into the political covenant, once that agreement is made, fear gives way to peace and security.

Spinoza's own considerations of the state also begin with the thought experiment of a state of nature, which he admits is "no more than theory," and the resulting social contract (*pactum*) among its members resembles that of Hobbes in many important respects.[26] Above all, what Hobbes and Spinoza, like other philosophers in the contractarian tradition, agree on is that the origin and legitimacy of government lie not in God's will—the core of the "divine right of kings" theory, proposed by the sixteenth-century French jurist Jean Bodin—but in a very human convention.

Like Hobbes, Spinoza sees all human beings as essentially motivated by self-interest. We are naturally, even necessarily, egoistic agents who will pursue anything and only that which we believe will contribute to our preservation and to an increase in our power. This is a fundamental principle of nature, one that in both the *Treatise* and the *Ethics* grounds the most basic right of every person to do what he can to survive and even to thrive. In the *Ethics* Spinoza writes that

> everyone exists by the highest right of nature, and consequently everyone, by the highest right of nature, does those things that follow from the necessity of his own nature. So everyone, by the highest right of nature, judges what is good and what is evil, considers his own advantage according to his own temperament, avenges himself, and strives to preserve what he loves and destroy what he hates.[27]

In the state of nature, where there is no government or even agreement among individuals, everyone is free to exercise this right and to pursue without restriction what one believes, rightly or wrongly, to be to one's advantage. The same idea introduces the political discussion in the *Treatise*.

Whatever every man, when he is considered as solely under the dominion of Nature, believes to be his advantage, whether under the
guidance of sound reason or under passion's sway, he may by sovereign natural right seek and get for himself by any means, by force,
deceit, entreaty or in any other way he best can, and he may consequently regard as his enemy anyone who tries to hinder him from
getting what he wants.[28]

If this striving for advantage were rationally directed, guided not
by passion and emotion but by true knowledge, then everyone
would pursue their natural right not only without injury or dis-
advantage to others but, on the contrary, by aiding others and
helping them live rightly. The rational person sees that coopera-
tion and generosity are in his own best interest. Sadly, as Spinoza
concedes in the *Ethics*, "it rarely happens that men live according
to the guidance of reason. Instead, their lives are so constituted
that they are usually envious and burdensome to one another."[29]
At the same time, human beings cannot but live among others.
Thus, unless the pursuit of self-interest among these unavoidably
coexisting individuals is somehow restrained, either by a person's
own reason or by some higher authority acting on reason's behalf,
aiming "only at the true good of men," daily existence will be an
insecure and risky enterprise, full of danger, anxiety, and constant
trouble. If everyone is free to do whatever he pleases, whether he
is motivated by justice and generosity or by anger and envy, then
life in the state of nature will be "wretched" and the original goal
of self-preservation difficulty to achieve for very long.

Individuals in such circumstances will eventually realize that
it is more advantageous for them to give up the unbridled pursuit
of self-interest and unite into "one body"—that is, a commonwealth—in which "the unrestricted right naturally possessed by
each individual should be put into common ownership, and that
this right should no longer be determined by the strength and
appetite of the individual, but by the power and will of all together."[30] Such a sacrifice of individual right and power is necessary to make possible the conditions for a "secure and good life."

Moreover, the members of this community will agree that the common will they have instituted must be directed by rational and universal principles, to better keep their various and often contrary irrational appetites in check.

This is the covenant that Spinoza in the *Treatise* sees as the justificatory origin of the state. Political obligation is, at least in principle if not in historical fact,[31] the result of a rational, voluntary agreement among individuals to hand over their right and power to pursue their own advantage to a common authority and to be governed by the will of all insofar as this will is guided by reason. What they receive in turn is peace, a more secure life, and the stable enjoyment of the goods they value.

If everyone behaved rationally all the time, then the observance of this agreement and respect for the common will would come naturally, since people would recognize that it is in their own interest to obey its commands, the laws. "If all men could be readily induced to be guided by reason alone and to recognize the supreme advantage and the necessity of the state's existence, everyone would entirely forswear deceit."[32] (In fact, at one point in the *Treatise* Spinoza says that perfectly rational individuals would not even need laws. "If men were so constituted by nature as to desire nothing but what is prescribed by true reason, society would stand in no need of any laws. Nothing would be required but to teach men true moral doctrine, and they would then act to their true advantage of their own accord, wholeheartedly and freely.")[33]

But in the absence of such universal rationality, the primary motivation among citizens for compliance with the agreement must be an affective one—that is, the fear that the evil consequences of disobeying the state are greater than whatever short-term advantage might thereby be gained. Thus, it is an essential part of the political contract that what is handed over to the community is the ability to enforce its will and punish transgressors. Political society can be maintained, Spinoza insists (in the political part of the *Ethics* that was probably composed *after* he had completed the *Treatise*), only when the state has "the power to prescribe a common rule of life, to make laws, and to maintain them—not by reason, which cannot restrain the affects, but by threats."[34]

In fact, like Hobbes, Spinoza believes that this social covenant will work only if the state has *absolute power* to pursue "the sovereign natural right over everything" that it has been granted. He says in the *Treatise* that "the sovereign power is bound by no law, and all must obey it in all matters; for this is what all must have covenanted tacitly or expressly when they transferred to it all their power of self-defense, that is, all their right." The individual citizens reserve no rights to themselves, since such a limitation on the sovereign's power would introduce a division of sovereignty in the state—there would be as many loci of authority as there are citizens—and thus bring about the state's eventual dissolution through civil discord. The parties to the contract have "submitted themselves absolutely to the will of the sovereign power . . . it is our duty to carry out all the orders of the sovereign power without exception, even if those orders are quite irrational. For reason bids us carry out even such orders, so as to choose the lesser of two evils."[35]

An all-powerful state with full authority to enforce its will. A sovereign who, through threats and fear, coerces obedience from its citizens. This hardly appears to be the vision of someone reputed to be a liberal and tolerant thinker. Has Spinoza taken the absolutist lessons of Hobbes too much to heart?[36]

There is, however, a crucial difference between the two political theorists. While Hobbes believes that sovereignty should be vested in a single individual and that monarchy is the most effective and stable form of polity, Spinoza believes that the purposes of the state are best served by democracy.[37] In Spinoza's ideal commonwealth, the right to determine what is in the common interest, issue laws, and enforce them is given to the people at-large. This is the message both of the *Treatise* and, more subtly, of the *Political Treatise*, composed several years later and left unfinished at the time of Spinoza's death.

Spinoza is sensitive to the charge that by giving absolute power to the state he has, in effect, enslaved its citizens. But he reassures us that "the danger involved in submitting oneself absolutely to the command and will of another [is] not such as to cause grave misgivings."[38] This is, in part, because the state's continued power to enforce its will is contingent on its issuing reasonable commands and aiming only at the public good with its laws. As soon as the sovereign becomes tyrannical and self-serving, its efficacy will inevitably diminish as citizens resist its authority and take back the power they originally gave to it; Spinoza believes that through the social contract citizens confer on the sovereign only their power, preserving their natural rights even in the state.[39] Thus, there is a natural check on tyrannical government, or so Spinoza (perhaps over-optimistically) believes.[40]

Moreover, the greater stability of democracy stems from the fact that it is, of all the forms of government, the least likely to behave unreasonably and alienate its citizens, "for it is practically impossible for the majority of a single assembly, if it is of some size, to agree on the same piece of folly."[41] Spinoza apparently assumes that the irrational and particularistic appetites of individuals will, in a democratic assembly, fall out of contention and the resulting "will" of the assembly will reflect a consensus that has as its object the rational well-being of the community. Because, as Spinoza shows in the *Ethics*, human beings "agree in nature" insofar as they "act according to the guidance of reason" and are at odds or "contrary to one another" only insofar as they are governed by passions,[42] it would be nearly impossible for a sufficiently large democratic assembly to agree on any proposed laws that express only the affect-guided, selfish desires of one or a few legislators; only rational laws will be likely to make it through the body's deliberative process. "It is the fundamental purpose of democracy to avoid the follies of appetite and to keep men within the bounds of reason, as far as possible, so that they may live in peace and harmony."[43] In a democracy, the sovereign consistently governs in the interest of the subjects, at least in theory. It enacts only laws that are commanded by reason and that are directed at "the welfare of the whole people."

Of equal importance is the fact that in a democracy, where "the entire community . . . [holds] the reins of government as a single body," the freedom of the citizens is maximized. This is because in obeying the sovereign they are obeying themselves. "Sovereignty is vested in all the citizens, and laws are sanctioned by common consent. In such a community the people would remain equally free whether laws were multiplied or diminished, since it would act not from another's bidding but from its own consent."[44] In a democracy, where the laws are made under the guidance of reason, not only is the will of the sovereign the will of the people, the will of the sovereign represents their *rational* will. In obeying the sovereign they are pursuing their own true self-interest (rather than being led by their irrational appetites) and living according to right reason. On the other hand, if sovereignty belongs to one man alone or to a small subset of citizens, conformity to the laws is more a matter of obedience in the strict sense, that is, submission to the authority of another or "action under orders." It is like what in the *Ethics* is called "bondage" to the passions, insofar as one is acting according the dictates of another.

Democracy, then, represents autonomy for its citizens, while monarchy and aristocracy are "an infringement of freedom" and risk degenerating into a kind of slavery, especially if the ruler does not act for the welfare of the people. Thus, Spinoza concludes, democracy is

> the most natural form of state, approaching most closely to that free-
> dom which nature grants to every man. For in a democratic state
> nobody transfers his natural right to another so completely that
> thereafter he is not to be consulted; he transfers it to the majority of
> the entire community of which he is a part.[45]

More than any other form of government, democracy preserves equality among citizens and the freedom of individuals.

In this important respect, the political philosophy of the *Treatise* was influenced less by Hobbes than by what Spinoza read in the treatises of the De la Court brothers that he so admired. Pieter and Johan were themselves conscientious students of *De Cive* and, later, *Leviathan*, and what Spinoza found in their Dutch writings—the *Political Discourses* and the *Observations on the State, or, The Political Balance*—was Hobbes filtered through Dutch republicanism. The

De la Courts agreed with the Englishman that the origins of the state lay in an agreement among individuals in a state of nature to confer authority on a central political power, and that its purpose is to restrain the passionate pursuit of self-interest and establish the conditions of peace and security. However, the De la Courts argued that this is best done by democracy, which is practically certain to issue rational laws in the interests of its citizens and where the "public will" is less likely to reflect only the private and self-interested will of the ruler alone.

Spinoza's discussion of democracy in the *Treatise* leaves much to be desired. He does not present in that work a model of how he envisions democracy working. There is no mention of the way in which his ideal democratic society is to be structured. Nor does Spinoza offer any detailed explanation of how the will of citizens is to get expressed in the will of the sovereign, whether by plebiscite in a direct democracy or through elected representatives, or who will be charged with executing that will. All of this was, presumably, to be covered in the chapters on democracy in the *Political Treatise*, a less theoretical and more "practical" and realist work, grounded in a conception of "men as they are [and not] as [one] would like them to be."[46] Unfortunately, Spinoza, having finished that book's chapters on monarchy and aristocracy, died after writing only a few paragraphs on democracy.

A political philosophy can be distinguished not only by where it places the locus of power or what it advocates as the best organization of society but also by what it regards as the purpose of the state. Classical liberals, such as John Locke, propose that government is there primarily to protect the life, liberty, and property of its citizens. The state's role, according to this variety of liberalism, is to provide for peace and security, the basic minimal conditions that will allow individuals freely to live the lives they choose and pursue what they deem to be of worth, but not to impose on them any substantive values or compel them to follow any particular conception of the good life.[47] For classical liberalism, the state is to remain neutral when it comes to competing views of how people should live, and must limit itself to making it possible for them to live how they want.

The republican tradition, by contrast, tends to emphasize the role of the state in modeling good citizens, and sometimes even in making them into good people. Plato's *Republic* offers only the most famous instance of this vision of the state. For Renaissance and early modern theorists of republicanism like Machiavelli and Montesquieu, government ought actively to be engaged in inculcating particular civic virtues among the people. More important than simply allowing citizens the liberty, and even providing them the means, to pursue their individual visions of the good life is the state's role in getting them to adopt for themselves, and act for the sake of, a common conception of the public good. Virtuous republican citizens identify their own personal well-being with the flourishing of their society.

Spinoza's political philosophy in the *Treatise* does not fit neatly into any category, liberal or otherwise (although this can be said for the political philosophy of practically every thinker in this period). But what is clear is that he envisions a substantive role for the sovereign, including a democratic one, in the moral lives of citizens. The purpose of the state is not merely to protect life and property or defend civil liberties, otherwise allowing people to do what they want and live according to whatever values they choose. The well-functioning commonwealth, for Spinoza, as it (theoretically) transitions individuals from the state of nature to an organized community, in fact does more than provide the basic peace and security that are the primary motivation for entering into the social contract in the first place. Under the auspices of the state, the people have the opportunity to increase their freedom and virtue, which for Spinoza is identical to living according to reason and acquiring greater control over the passions.

[The state's] ultimate purpose is not to exercise dominion nor to restrain men by fear and deprive them of independence, but on the contrary to free every man from fear so that he may live in security as far as is possible, that is, so that he may best preserve his own natural right to exist and to act, without harm to himself and to others. It is not, I repeat, the purpose of the state to transform men from rational beings into beasts or puppets, but rather to enable them to develop their mental and physical faculties in safety, to use their reason without restraint and to refrain from the strife and the vicious mutual abuse that are prompted by hatred, anger or deceit. Thus the purpose of the state is, in reality, freedom.[48]

By "freedom," Spinoza does not mean only what Isaiah Berlin called "negative freedom," or freedom from interference by others, but the positive autonomy that consists in acting from the guidance of reason rather than just responding affectively and heteronomously to external influences. A rational and free person does not simply pursue those things that make him feel momentary pleasure but chooses to do what he knows truly to be in his own best interest. Thus, while the state may be required to restrain the emotional appetites of citizens and thereby mitigate their differences and conflicts through threats implicit in the laws—especially when those citizens are newly liberated from the state of nature—its ultimate purpose is what Spinoza calls the "cultivation of reason."

The ideal state, democratically run and legislating under the guidance of reason, will help people develop into more rational individuals who exercise greater dominion over their own passions. It thereby makes up for natural human deficiencies and plays an educative and edifying role in their lives. As Spinoza says in the *Political Treatise*,

> If human nature were so constituted that men desired most of all what was most to their advantage, no special skill would be needed to secure harmony and trust. But since, admittedly, human nature is far otherwise constituted, the state must necessarily be so established that all men, both rulers and ruled, whether they will or no, will do what is in the interests of their common welfare; that is, either voluntarily or constrained by force or necessity, they will all live as reason prescribes.[49]

While citizens may start out as merely *obedient* to good laws (out of fear) and therefore acting only *in accordance with* what reason demands, they eventually, through good government, recognize the benevolent intentions behind the laws, internalize its normative content (the dictates of reason), and thus develop into rational citizens who are motivated by hope and dedicated and constant in their virtue. And it is the state's responsibility to make this happen. "Just as the vices of the subjects and their excessive license and willfulness are to be laid at the door of the commonwealth, so on the other hand their virtue and steadfast obedience to the laws must be attributed chiefly to the virtue and absolute right of the commonwealth."[50] Good behavior done out of fear of punishment is thereby replaced by justice and charity performed from a virtuous disposition, from right reason. The citizens are empowered by the state, literally, in the sense that so transformed they experience an increase in the power that for Spinoza constitutes the essence of any individual.[51] This, in turn, increases the power and stability of the state itself, as it is now composed of virtuous and rational citizens who identify their flourishing with that of their commonwealth.

Chapter 9

Libertas philosophandi

The First Amendment of the U.S. Constitution says that "Congress shall make no law respecting an establishment of religion, or prohibiting the free exercise thereof." This complex (and oft debated) proposition, comprised of both an "establishment" clause and a "free exercise" clause, is usually taken to be a clear and paradigmatic statement of the doctrine of separation of church and state. As Thomas Jefferson puts it, the First Amendment should be seen as "building a wall of separation between church and state."[1] The government may neither contribute to the promotion of any religious worship, but neither may it prevent people from observing any religious rites or ceremonies they wish.

Two hundred years earlier, freedom of religion was enshrined among the founding tenets of the United Provinces of the Netherlands. As we have seen, article thirteen of the Union of Utrecht states that "every individual should remain free in his religion, and no man should be molested or questioned on the subject of divine worship." The leaders of the Dutch Republic in the seventeenth century may not always have been faithful to this principle, and they certainly did not believe in the separation of church and state in the Netherlands, where the Reformed Church was, if not the *established* church, at least a formally privileged one. Still, there was for the period an unusually high freedom of religion in Holland and the other provinces (but not freedom *from* religion, since perceived atheists were, as Spinoza learned, sometimes persecuted with vehemence).

As the author of a "theological-political" work, and having prepared the ground in his discussions of prophecy, faith, Scripture, and political theory, Spinoza must finally address in the *Treatise* what he views as the proper relationship between the state and religion. It is often assumed that he was a strong early proponent of the separation of church and state, and that he, along with John Locke, laid the foundation for later programs of religious toleration. One commentator even writes that "the spirit of Spinoza lives on in the opening words of the First Amendment of the U.S. Constitution, the phrase referred to as the establishment clause."[2]

Nothing could be further from the truth.

The separation of church and state can mean a number of things. Spinoza did believe that when it comes to religious *belief*, people should be left alone to believe (or not believe) whatever they want. It is extraordinarily difficult to control people's beliefs anyway; there is no way to monitor, and very little one can do to manage, what goes on in their minds. True piety, "the inward worship of God," is an entirely personal matter. It should, as a matter not only of fact but of right, be left to the individual alone.

> Since [religion] consists in honesty and sincerity of heart rather than in outward actions, it does not pertain to the sphere of public law and authority. Honesty and sincerity of heart is not imposed on man by legal command or by the state's authority. It is an absolute fact that nobody can be constrained to a state of blessedness by force or law. . . . As the sovereign right to free opinion belongs to every man even in matters of religion, and it is inconceivable that any man can surrender this right, there also belongs to every man the sovereign right and supreme authority to judge freely with regard to religion, and consequently to explain it and interpret it for himself.[3]

As we shall see, Spinoza also argues that the free *expression* of one's religious beliefs, verbally or in writing, should be tolerated by the state. No one should be prosecuted for heresy or irreligion.

However, if the separation of church and state means what it is usually taken to mean in the free exercise and establishment clauses of the Constitution, that government may not regulate or

formally endorse any particular set of religious practices or outward forms of worship, then here Spinoza parts company with the
founders of the American republic.

In the properly ordered state, the sovereign power is charged
with all matters of public well-being. Any actions or practices
that enter into the public sphere and therefore may possibly affect
the welfare of the people and the commonwealth are the responsibility of the government. The state's laws and decrees must be
directed toward the peace, security, and stability of the polity, and
its legislators must take care to regulate institutions whose activities have some bearing on these. (By contrast, anything that is not
related to the public good, such as private belief, is not within the
sovereign's purview.)

It follows, then, that the sovereign's power extends not only to
the promulgation of civil laws but to laying down religious laws
as well, at least insofar as these are related to piety in the form of
public activities. The inner worship of God and the feelings of love
toward one's neighbors are to be left to the individual. But the
outer form in which this worship and love are to be practiced—
the rites and ceremonies observed and, especially, the expression
of the obedience of God and the love of one's neighbor through
justice and charity in action—falls within the public domain and,
thus, within the sovereign's sphere of authority.

> The welfare of the people is the highest law, to which all other laws,
> both human and divine, must be made to conform. But since it is the
> duty of the sovereign alone to decide what is necessary for the welfare
> of the people and the security of the state, and to command what it
> judges to be thus necessary, it follows that it is also the duty of the
> sovereign alone to decide what form piety towards ones' neighbor
> should take, that is, in what way every man is required to obey God.[4]

This means that the sovereign is responsible for what Spinoza calls
the "interpretation of religion." Individual citizens are free to read
and interpret the Bible for themselves and to take to heart, however they can (and with whatever metaphysical, theological, and
historical beliefs may help them), its exhortations to justice and

charity. But in a democracy, the governing assembly is to decide how God's law is to be translated into practice, since it has sole authority to decide what activities are consistent with the public welfare.

> No one can exercise piety toward his neighbor in accordance with God's command unless his piety and religion conform to the public good. But no private citizen can know what is good for the state except from the decrees of the sovereign, to whom alone it belongs to transact public business. Therefore, no one can practice piety aright nor obey God unless he obeys the decrees of the sovereign in all things.[5]

For the same reason, the sovereign is also the source of the authority of God's decrees in the state. Since God is, in truth, not a ruler or lawgiver, there are no laws, divine or otherwise, in a state of nature; before the formal institution of a polity, there is neither justice nor injustice, no piety and no sin. And there are no valid laws in the commonwealth that are not enacted by the sovereign, including all laws regarding the exercise of justice and charity—that is, the practice of true religion. Since, Spinoza says, "justice and charity can acquire the force of law and command only through the right of the state, I can readily draw the conclusion—since the state's right is vested in the sovereign alone—that religion can acquire the force of law only from the decree of those who have the right to command, and that God has no special kingdom over men save through the medium of those who hold sovereignty."[6]

Notice that Spinoza says that the organization and control of religion are the duty of the sovereign *alone*. Among those private citizens who are not qualified to make judgments about the public good and thus dictate outward forms of worship (including, presumably, ceremonial rites) are clergy. Spinoza has fully removed the supervision of religion from sectarian leaders and put it firmly in the hands of the civil authority. The sovereign is free to appoint ecclesiastics to act as its "ministers" in religious affairs, but these representatives serve at the pleasure of, and fully answer to, the secular authority.

Civil control of religious affairs, while no doubt offensive to early modern ecclesiastics, was in fact a prominent theme in seventeenth-century Dutch republican thought, and Spinoza was not alone in his views on this matter. Grotius, in his work *De imperio summarium potestatum circa sacra* (On the Command of the Highest Powers over Sacred Affairs), had proposed political regulation of preaching and worship,[7] while Pieter de la Court, foreshadowing Spinoza, insisted in his *Political Discourses* that the state, insofar as it is responsible for peace, security, and prosperity, should have power over all religious activities (while at the same time tolerating a diversity of religious *beliefs*). As we have seen, Hobbes, too, argued, not surprisingly, that the sovereign is to have absolute command over religion within its dominion: not just the organization and content of public preaching, but even in determining what is Scripture and what is the word of God. "There is . . . no other government in this life, neither of state nor religion, but temporal; nor teaching of any doctrine, lawful to any subject, which the governor, both of the state and of the religion, forbiddeth to be taught. And that governor must be one, or else there must needs follow faction and civil war in the commonwealth." There may be many pastors in a state, but they must all be subordinate to a single chief pastor. And "who that chief pastor is, according to the law of nature, hath been already shown, namely, that it is the civil sovereign."[8] The alternative to "this consolidation of the right politic and ecclesiastic" is, Hobbes believes, "civil troubles, divisions, and calamities of the nation."

For Spinoza, then, in the ideal state there is to be one and only one form of public devotion, and it is to be determined and supervised by the civil government.[9] His intention is most definitely *not* to institute a state religion with compulsory church attendance and religious observance. And he especially does not want the sovereign to dictate religious dogma (although it *is* the sovereign's responsibility to encourage among the masses an acceptance of those basic tenets of faith that are "necessary for obedience"). No one is to be forced to believe or to worship anything, to join any gathering or to engage in any ceremonial practices. Such enforced (and therefore false) piety and mandated conformity would not be consistent with the primary aim of the state (or of Spinoza's project): increasing the rationality and freedom of its citizens and insuring civic peace. Spinoza is not interested in seeing totalitarian control over people's lives. Rather, his position is based on the fear that, without such singular and secular control over religious matters, there is a real danger to the well-being of the commonwealth.

In Spinoza's view, the greatest threat to civil peace—both in theory and as ancient (biblical) and contemporary (Dutch) events have shown—is the divisions introduced into society by sectarian religion. The multiplication of large, unregulated religious bodies, even the existence of *one* sizable congregation independent of the official public one, poses a danger to even a powerful and prosperous society.[10] Organized religions set citizens against each other—Christians against Jews, Protestants against Catholics, Protestants against other Protestants—and, more important, against the state itself. As soon as there are alternative sources of authority besides the sovereign, the loyalty of citizens is divided. There are now states within the state. It becomes a legitimate question as to whether the citizens are devoted to the polity at large and the general welfare or to their more narrow sectarian causes. And a commonwealth within which there is such a schism of loyalties, with piety opposed to patriotism, is more likely to see civil discord. Its stability and ability to withstand internal and external enemies are seriously compromised. As Hobbes (quoting Matthew 6.24) succinctly puts it, "no man can serve two masters."[11]

The problem becomes particularly acute when the "religious functionaries" themselves seek influence over not just the hearts and minds of their congregants but the social and moral lives of citizens. It is inevitable that ecclesiastics, once allowed their independent sectarian domains, will encroach on the civil power and strive for supremacy over it. The result of such a usurpation of political authority is a division of sovereignty in the commonwealth and, in the end, its downfall.

This is precisely the lesson that Spinoza finds in ancient Israelite history. As long as political and religious authority were combined in one man (such as Moses) or one body acting on behalf of God (the true sovereign), the Hebrew commonwealth thrived as a theocracy. There was no confusion over to whom obedience was owed. A priestly caste existed, but its members were completely subordinate to the sovereign; they were consultants on religious matters, not leaders. After the monarchy was instituted under Saul, however, things deteriorated as power in the kingdom devolved into political and religious spheres. The kings were forced to recognize "a dominion within their dominion" as the priests exercised greater influence within and subsequently beyond the confines of the sanctuary. This was the beginning of the end.

> Anyone who seeks to deprive the sovereign of this authority [over religion] is attempting to divide the sovereignty; and as a result, as happened long ago in the case of the kings and priests of the Hebrews, there will inevitably arise strife and dissensions that can never be allayed.[12]

With the return from exile in Babylon and the restoration of independence in the Second Temple period, "the priests usurped the right of government, thereby holding absolute power." In a reading of biblical history that has clear resonance for the contemporary scene—where, in the late 1660s, the orthodox Calvinist elements in Dutch society exerted their considerable influence on behalf of the Orangist bloc and the return of the stadholder, and thus opposed the domestic and foreign policies of De Witt and the States party—Spinoza notes that "the priests became inflamed with the desire to combine secular and religious rule," with ruinous consequences for the Israelite commonwealth.[13] The Dutch Republic, heeding the lesson of the Kingdom of Judah, should not allow ecclesiastics to influence civic affairs.

> How disastrous it is for both religion and state to grant to religious functionaries any right to issue decrees or concern themselves with state business. Stability is far better assured if these officials are restricted to giving answers only when requested, and at other times

to teaching and practicing only what is acknowledged as customary and traditional.[14]

When priests and preachers acquire "the authority to issue decrees and to transact government business," their individual ambitions will know no bounds, and they will each seek "self-glorification both in religious and secular matters." They will fall out among themselves, increasing sectarian divisions in society. Corruption will necessarily follow, as the affairs of state will be run according to the self-interest of whichever sect happens to gain the reins of power. Meanwhile, the religion they enforce, now put to service for the perpetuation of their rule, will degenerate into "pernicious superstition."[15]

Is the political philosophy of the *Treatise* a liberalism? That is a difficult question to answer, in part because of the shifting and uncertain meaning of liberalism itself.[16] More to the point, it is not a helpful question when it comes to Spinoza. His account of the state and of religion is too multifaceted to be pigeonholed. Moreover, while the *Treatise* remains of great relevance today, it is also a response to very particular and very complex historical exigencies, and we do not do it justice by trying to make it fit some transhistorical category of theories.

What can be said is that Spinoza is, without question, one of history's most eloquent proponents of a secular, democratic society and the strongest advocate for freedom and toleration in the early modern period. And this brings us, at last, to the ultimate goal of the *Treatise*, enshrined in both the book's subtitle and in the argument of its final chapter: to show that "freedom to philosophize may not only be allowed without danger to piety and the stability of the republic, but that it cannot be refused without destroying the peace of the republic and piety itself."[17]

To begin with, there is the question of the toleration of *beliefs*. And what Spinoza has said already about the freedom of religious belief holds for all opinions whatsoever: they are to be absolutely free and unimpeded, both by necessity and by right. "It is impossible for the mind to be completely under another's control; for no one is able to transfer to another his natural right or faculty to reason freely and to form his own judgment on any matters whatsoever, nor can he be compelled to do so."[18] Indeed, any effort on the sovereign's part to rule over the beliefs and opinions of citizens can only backfire, as it will ultimately serve to undermine the sovereign's own authority. In a passage that strikes the reader as both obviously right and extraordinarily bold for its time, Spinoza writes that

> a government that attempts to control men's minds is regarded as tyrannical, and a sovereign is thought to wrong his subjects and infringe their right when he seeks to prescribe for every man what he should accept as true and reject as false, and what are the beliefs that will inspire him with devotion to God. All these are matters belonging to individual right, which no man can surrender even if he should so wish.

A sovereign is certainly free to try and limit what people think, but the result of such a foolhardy policy would be only to create resentment and opposition to its rule. "It is true that sovereigns can by their right treat as enemies all who do not absolutely agree with them on all matters, but the point at issue is not what is their right, but what is to their interest."[19] The freedom of opinion is, for Spinoza, an "inalienable right."

Still, the toleration of belief is easy, because it is necessary. Even Hobbes saw that citizens cannot be forced to believe anything. The more difficult case, the true test of a political philosopher's commitment to toleration, concerns the liberty of citizens to *express* those beliefs, either in speech or in writing. And here Spinoza goes further than anyone else in the seventeenth century.[20]

> Utter failure will attend any attempt in a commonwealth to force men to speak only as prescribed by the sovereign despite their different and opposing opinions. . . . The most tyrannical government

will be one where the individual is denied the freedom to express and
to communicate to others what he thinks, and a moderate government is one where this freedom is granted to every man.[21]

Spinoza's argument for freedom of expression is based both on the
right (or power) of citizens to speak as they desire and on the fact
that (as in the case of belief) it would be counterproductive for a
sovereign to try to restrain that freedom. No matter what laws are
enacted against speech and other means of expression, citizens will
continue to say what they believe (because they can), only now
they will do so in secret. "It is far beyond the bounds of possibility
that all men can be made to speak to order. On the contrary, the
greater the effort to deprive them of freedom of speech, the more
obstinately do they resist."[22] The result of the suppression of freedom is, once again, resentment and a weakening of the bonds that
unite subjects to sovereign. In Spinoza's view, intolerant laws lead
ultimately to anger, revenge, and sedition. The attempt to enforce
them is a "great danger to the state."

Spinoza also argues for freedom of expression on utilitarian
grounds. It is necessary for progress in the discovery of truth and
the growth of creativity. Without an open marketplace of ideas,
science, philosophy, and other disciplines are stifled in their development, to the technological, economic, and even aesthetic
detriment of society. In this respect, Spinoza's defense of liberty
foreshadows the one that John Stuart Mill would offer two centuries later in his essay *On Liberty*. As Spinoza puts it, "this freedom
[of expressing one's ideas] is of the first importance in fostering
the sciences and the arts, for it is only those whose judgment is
free and unbiased who can attain success in these fields."[23]

For Spinoza, then, there is to be no criminalization of ideas in
the well-ordered state. *Libertas philosophandi*, the freedom of philosophizing, must be upheld for the sake of a healthy, secure, and peaceful commonwealth and material and intellectual progress. "What
greater misfortune can be imagined for a state than that honorable
men should be exiled as miscreants because their opinions are at

variance with authority and they cannot disguise the fact? What can be more calamitous than that men should be regarded as enemies and put to death, not for any crime or misdeed, but for being of independent mind?"[24] One cannot but think that Spinoza had his friend Koerbagh in mind when he wrote these words.

Spinoza's views on liberty go beyond what was envisioned by another philosopher renowned for his defense of toleration: John Locke. Locke was primarily interested in the toleration within a society of a variety of religious ideas, so that individuals may enjoy the uninhibited personal communion with God in which religion consists. In "A Letter on Toleration," written in 1685, Locke argues that no religious group has the right to persecute those who belong to other sects. Membership in a community of believers is voluntary, and thus no church may use force (or engage the power of the state) to further its narrow sectarian aims. Theological dissent and different forms of worship are to be allowed, even encouraged, in the commonwealth.

Like Spinoza, Locke also makes his case for toleration through utilitarian considerations. Such freedom, insofar as it fosters the search after truth, brings great benefits for society, and not just intellectual ones. Locke was clearly impressed by the economic fruits of toleration that he saw in the Dutch Republic, where he was residing when he wrote the "Letter." However, Locke makes one significant exception to the general policy of openness for religious and secular ideas: there is to be no toleration of atheism and other forms of irreligion. Since atheists do not believe in God, they have no foundation for morality, and thus they cannot be trusted not to act in ways that are harmful to their fellow citizens. "Those are not at all to be tolerated who deny the being of God . . . promises, covenants, and oaths, which are bonds of human society, can have no hold upon an atheist."[25] While Locke's refusal to grant the same freedom to atheists that he provides for believers is therefore made on political and ethical rather than religious grounds—and apparently it is not only freedom of expression that is being denied to them but also freedom of belief, since their mere presence in the state is supposed to be a threat to its welfare—it nonetheless represents an inconsistency in his thought and a striking failure of toleration, one that is absent from Spinoza's account.

And yet Spinoza himself does not support *absolute* freedom of speech. He explicitly states that the expression of "seditious" ideas is *not* to be tolerated by the sovereign. There is to be no protection for speech that advocates the overthrow of the government, disobedience to its laws, or harm to fellow citizens. The people are free to argue for the repeal of laws they find unreasonable and oppressive, but they must do so peacefully and through rational argument. If their argument fails to persuade the sovereign to change the law, then that must be the end of the matter. What they may not do is "stir up popular hatred against [the sovereign or his representatives]."[26]

Absolutists about the freedom of speech will be troubled by these caveats on Spinoza's part, and rightly so. After all, who is to decide what kind of speech counts as seditious? May not the sovereign declare to be seditious simply those views with which it disagrees or that it finds contrary to its policies? Spinoza, presumably to allay such concerns, does offer a definition of "seditious political beliefs" as those that "*immediately* have the effect of annulling the covenant whereby everyone has surrendered his right to act just as he thinks fit."[27] The salient feature of such opinions is "the action that is implicit therein"—that is, they are more or less verbal incitements to act against the sovereign and thus they are directly contrary to the tacit social contract of citizenship. ("Other beliefs," he says, "in which there is no implication of actions such as the breaking of the covenant, the exaction of revenge, the indulgence of anger and so forth, are not seditious.")

But this still leaves a considerable gap for unreasonable censorship. Engaging in speech that is supposed to "immediately" contribute toward weakening the political compact could be done directly, by incendiary words intended to stir up civil disobedience. Or it could be done in a more subtle and indirect way, by spreading subversive beliefs about the sovereign (such as a rumor that its policies are treasonous, or even that its rule is illegitimate). Among the things that Spinoza says are not to be allowed is accusing a magistrate of injustice. If there is an "implication of action" or an "immediate" effect of "annulling the covenant" in this case, it is at best obscure.[28]

It thus seems a rather hazy boundary here between legitimate dissent and protest (which, for Spinoza, is protected) and being "an agitator and a rebel" (which is not). While Spinoza may feel that he has provided an unambiguous criterion and identified a small and well-circumscribed domain for what is to count as seditious speech, and thereby set a firewall against the arbitrary abuse of state power over expression, there appears to remain a loophole for a wily sovereign to engage in a potentially extensive suppression of ideas, including prior restraint of the press, the censorship of books, and even the prohibition of meetings.[29] Perhaps Spinoza should have more consistently followed the logic of his own reasoning by drawing the line not within the realm of belief (including its expression) but at the border of belief and true action, as he sometimes seems to do.

> It was only the right to act as he thought fit that each man surrendered, and not his right to reason and judge. So while to act against the sovereign's decree is definitely an infringement of his [the sovereign's] right, this is not the case with thinking, judging, and consequently with speaking, too.[30]

Although, again, Spinoza adds the warning: "provided one does no more than express or communicate one's opinion, defending it through rational conviction alone, not through deceit, anger, hatred, or the will to effect such changes in the state as he himself decides."[31]

Spinoza is certainly conscious of, and willing to allow for, some potentially unpleasant consequences entailed by the broad respect for civil liberties. There will be public disputes, even factionalism, as citizens express their opposing views on political, social, moral, and religious questions. This is, however, what comes with a healthy democratic and tolerant society. As he concedes, "what cannot be prohibited must necessarily be allowed, even if harm often ensues."[32] The proper state will be very much like Amsterdam itself, which, while not truly democratic, Spinoza greatly admires for the freedom it allows its denizens and the flourishing such toleration has brought the city.

> Take the city of Amsterdam, which enjoys the fruits of this freedom, to its own considerable prosperity and the admiration of the world. In this flourishing state, a city of the highest renown, men of every race and sect live in complete harmony; and before entrusting their property to some person they will want to know no more than this, whether he is rich or poor and whether he has been honest or dishonest in his dealings. As for religion or sect, that is of no account, because such considerations are regarded as irrelevant in a court of law; and no sect whatsoever is so hated that its adherents—provided that they injure no one, render to each what is his own, and live upright lives—are denied the protection of the civil authorities.[33]

It is surprising to see Spinoza writing this. One of his close friends has just died in prison, condemned by the city of Amsterdam— in a brutal act of intolerance at the instigation of the Calvinist consistory—for philosophical and religious ideas. So maybe there is a good deal of bitter irony in Spinoza's words here. On the other hand, Amsterdam was the most liberal and tolerant city in a republic renowned in its own time for religious and political toleration, and Spinoza, while aware of the city's shortcomings, also knew well and appreciated its virtues.

One can hope that perhaps Spinoza himself was uncomfortable with the restriction he had placed on freedom of speech, and that deep down he really was an absolutist on this matter. In the penultimate paragraph of the *Treatise*, he does draw a clear line between ideas and their expression, on the one hand, and actions, on the other hand, and insists—this time without any qualification— that the sovereign's authority should (if only out of prudence) be restricted to the latter: "The state can pursue no safer course than to regard piety and religion as consisting solely in the exercise of charity and just dealing, and that the right of the sovereign, both in religious and secular spheres, should be restricted to men's actions, with everyone being allowed to think what he will and to say what he thinks."[34] This sentence, a wonderful statement of the principle of toleration, is perhaps the real lesson of the *Treatise*, and should be that for which Spinoza is remembered.

Chapter 10

The Onslaught

When Spinoza's first publication, his exposition of Descartes's philosophy, appeared in 1663, the title-page indicated that the book was published in Amsterdam, "in the quarter commonly called the Dirk van Assensteeg." Later called the Dirk van Hasseltsteeg, the "quarter" is in fact a short and narrow, winding street in the center of the city that runs off the Nieuwezijds Voorburgwal and beside a cul-de-sac once known for its pastry shops (appropriately named the Suiker Bakkerssteeg, or Sugar Bakers' Street).

It was out of his home on this street that Jan Rieuwertsz[1] ran a well-known bookstore and publishing business. Born in 1616 to a merchant family, Rieuwertsz originally opened the shop called Book of Martyrs in 1640 in another part of town. He moved it to the Van Assensteeg and took up publishing as well nine years later, soon after losing his first wife.[2] Within a short period of time, Rieuwertsz had gained a reputation as an *uitdrukker* of liberal, even radical books, including writings by progressive philosophers and dissenting Reformed theologians. He was the publisher of a Dutch translation of Descartes's oeuvres (whose philosophy, he predicted in his preface, would be "to some readers like sand in the eyes"[3]), as well as works by the Mennonite pastor and Collegiant leader Galenus Abrahamsz, and by Dirck Camphuysen, a well-known Remonstrant and poet in the first half of the century who was a hero to Collegiants for his reformist views. (Rieuwertsz, closely allied with the Amsterdam Collegiant circle, was also believed to harbor Socinian—that is, antitrinitarian—tendencies, and even of holding meetings of this heretical sect in his home.) The owner of the Book of Martyrs was willing to publish political and religious material that no other publisher would touch. As one nineteenth-century scholar puts it, "anyone experiencing the need to publish ideas that were opposed to received opinion found refuge *chez* Jan Rieuwertsz."[4]

This was the Amsterdam publisher, already suspect in the eyes of the authorities, to whom Spinoza, now living in Voorburg, personally brought the manuscript of his just completed *Tractatus Theologico-Politicus* in early 1669. By this time, the two men had probably known each other for more than fifteen years, since Spinoza first began associating with members of the city's Mennonite community, such as the mercantile agent Pieter Balling and the grocer Jarig Jelles (whose *Confession of Universal Faith* Rieuwertsz published). In the mid-1660s, Rieuwertsz was among the participants in the Amsterdam group (led by Lodewijk Meijer and Adriaan Koerbagh) that was devoted to studying the manuscript of Spinoza's *Ethics*—a regular gathering that most likely met in his shop, which functioned as a kind of salon for left-wing ideas—and was clearly a great admirer of the philosopher. Spinoza, in turn, placed a good deal of trust in the publisher. Rieuwertsz served as an intermediary for Spinoza's correspondence; once Spinoza had permanently left Amsterdam, he occasionally used Rieuwertsz's address as a postal box, particularly for letters from abroad. And when the philosopher visited Amsterdam, he appears to have lodged in Rieuwertsz's house.[5]

Rieuwertsz was one of over a hundred publishers or printers in Amsterdam, a city infamous for flooding Europe with subversive literature—political, religious, even erotic tracts—in many languages.[6] This was a source of dismay to Dutch authorities, particularly when these clandestine writings, often critical of monarchical regimes or ecclesiastic power, caused trouble for foreign powers (especially England and France) by stirring up democratic sentiments or spreading freethinking ideas. Over the course of the seventeenth century, they therefore made various, but not always successful, efforts to control what came off the Dutch Republic's many presses.

In the late sixteenth century, no book or pamphlet could be published in the province of Holland without permission of the States of Holland; this "privilege," granted after the contents of the work had been examined and approved, had to be printed in the book itself.[7] In the first decades of the seventeenth century, the States General became increasingly interested in books that were likely to cause problems "in both ecclesiastical and political affairs," culminating in a 1615 edict intended to encourage provincial and municipal bodies to engage in the preventive censorship of offensive works.

By 1650, however, with a marked increase in the number of books and pamphlets being prepared for publication—and, in many cases, simply being published without being submitted for official approval—neither the province of Holland nor the States General was able to keep up, and so they no longer required publishers to submit manuscripts for approval prior to publication. Printers henceforth had only to register their businesses with the local magistrates, as well as swear an oath that they would hand over any suspicious writings that had been submitted to them and that in their opinion might be a danger to the state or to piety. The control of the presses in the Dutch Republic in the second half of the century was a generally decentralized affair, with the States General ceding authority to the individual provinces to manage things, and the provincial States in turn leaving it up to the cities and towns to keep an eye on their local publishers. Consequently, there was a great deal of inconsistency throughout the Republic in the enforcement of censorship, whether before or after publication. What might be severely repressed in Groningen could well find easy distribution in Amsterdam or Leiden.

When Spinoza was handing his manuscript over to Rieuwertsz in 1669, the Dutch Republic, and especially Holland, was enjoying a period of general freedom of the press, but it was certainly not an absolute liberty to publish anything. In the preceding ten years, over thirty books or pamphlets had been proscribed by the secular authorities, the second-highest number for a decade since the revolt of the Netherlands in 1580.[8] Even the Amsterdam regents had their limits, bowing sometimes to political pressure from above, sometimes to local ecclesiastic influence.

A canny businessman, Rieuwertsz had learned over the years that he needed to be cautious, especially given the kinds of things he put out. At one point, he was forced to deny any connection with a certain book, despite the fact that it bore his name as publisher on the title-page. Religious authorities, in particular, were always on the lookout for writings that would threaten the spiritual well-being of their flocks. They kept a particularly close eye on Rieuwertsz. In March 1669, the Amsterdam consistory notes that

> it has been reported that the writings of various Socinians have been printed together in-folio, altogether in six or seven volumes, and have also been available for purchase in this city. The assembly, with deep sorrow, learns about this blasphemous heresy boldly rearing its head and judges it of the highest importance to remain as vigilant as it possibly can. It should undertake very precise inquiries as to the identity of the authors, the means by which such works have been sold and printed, and any information that might prove useful for deciding what must be done to gain an exact report. We note, in particular, that particular attention should be paid to the shop of Jan Rieuwertsz on the Dirk van Assensteeg.[9]

Such surveillance was evidently undertaken. Several weeks later, the consistory received a report that "diverse persons, of all sorts, have been seen coming out of the shop of Jan Rieuwertsz engaged in singular conversations."[10]

But there were ways around the Calvinist watchdogs in Amsterdam. The more liberal regents, particularly in this period of the True Freedom, were often able to resist the pressure exerted by clerics who wanted to see a work banned or an author punished. They could simply turn a blind eye to books or pamphlets that the more orthodox elements of society deemed religiously or morally subversive, or, in the case of anonymous publications, at least stall any action by claiming that they did not know who had written it—even when where there really was no question about the author's identity. (Part of the problem for Koerbagh was that

he *did* put his name on the cover of his book.) Still, given the frequent changes in Dutch foreign alliances and domestic politics, as
well as the waxing and waning influence of the *predikanten*, there
was no telling what kind of response a book might receive in a
particular year.

In this political environment, as shifting and unpredictable
as the Dutch weather, the author and publisher of the *Tractatus
Theologico-Politicus* were not going to take any chances. Fortunately, Rieuwertsz knew exactly how to play it safe—not so much
in what he published, but in how he published it.

The first copies of the *Treatise*, in-quarto, appeared in early January 1670, perhaps from the press belonging to the printer Pieter
Arentsz, with whom Rieuwertzs had begun collaborating in
1669.[11] To avoid a fine, or worse, and to give the municipal authorities a ready excuse, when harangued by the Reformed leadership, that they would prosecute the responsible parties *if only they
knew who they were*, the cover page of the *Treatise* bore the name of
no author. Moreover, the place of publication was falsely listed as
Hamburg, not Amsterdam, and the name of the publisher given
was "Henricus Künraht." (The title page also contained a quotation from the First Letter of John: "Through this we might know
that we dwell in God and that God dwells in us: he has imparted
his Spirit to us" [4.13].)

"Künraht," or Heinrich Künrath, was a German alchemist and
a member of the Rosicrucians in the second half of the sixteenth
century. While a minor figure in history, his works were not entirely unknown in the seventeenth century, and even enjoyed some
popularity with the renewed interest in alchemy.[12] In later editions of the *Treatise*, especially those in which it was bound with
other works (including Meijer's *Philosophy, Interpreter of Holy Scripture*), Rieuwertsz would replace the Künraht name with different
pseudonyms, including "Jacobus Paulli," "Isaacus Herculis," and
"Carolus Gratiani."

All of this was, of course, an attempt to throw off the authorities. When Meijer's book was published in 1666—probably by Rieuwertsz—the listed city of publication was "Eleutheropolis," which everyone knew to be Amsterdam. By placing the origin of Spinoza's *Treatise* in Hamburg, Rieuwertsz was taking even greater precautions than usual. He obviously knew that he had an incendiary work on his hands.

The ruse worked for a while, although if it was employed only to provide plausible deniability for publisher, author, and sympathetic regents it may not have been intended really to fool anyone for very long.

It is not exactly clear when Spinoza was first unmasked as the author of the book. An early published identification occurred in the spring of 1673 with the appearance of *La Religion des Hollandois*, by Jean-Baptiste Stouppe. Stouppe had been a French Reformed minister in London, but later entered military service under the Prince of Condé during the French occupation of the Netherlands. He was shocked by what he saw and read during his time in the Republic, and his book is an indictment of the Dutch for their lax piety and unreasonable toleration of religious differences. He is especially troubled by the absence of any efforts by Dutch theologians to counter Spinoza, "a man who was born Jewish . . . who has neither renounced the Jewish religion nor embraced the Christian religion: he is thus a very bad Jew, and a no better Christian." This Spinoza, Stouppe continues, "has some years ago produced a book in Latin, whose title is *Tractatus Theologico Politicus*, in which he seems to have the principal goal of destroying all religions and particularly the Jewish and Christian ones, and of introducing atheism, libertinage and the freedom of all religions."[13]

Word that Spinoza was the author of the *Treatise*, however, was circulating well before Stouppe's treatise. In what is perhaps the earliest known identification, in June 1670, Friedrich Ludwig Mieg, a professor at the University of Heidelberg, alerted an academic colleague to the fact that the book was the work of "Spinoza, a former Jew," the same man "whose exposition in the geometric method of Cartesian philosophy I possess."[14] Later that summer, in

August, Johan Melchior, a pastor in a small village near Bonn and later a professor of theology at Duisberg, wrote a "refutation" of the *Treatise* in Latin (it was not published until 1671, in Utrecht). In a letter to a friend, "containing a censure of a book titled *Tractatus Theologico-Politicus*," Melchior says that the *irreligiosus* author of this book is one "Zinospa" or "Xinospa," adding (like Mieg) that this is the same man who some years before wrote a work on the philosophy of Descartes.[15] We do not know how Mieg or Melchior, in his German backwater, came by this information.

It was not only abroad that Spinoza's name, among others (including Meijer's), was early on connected to the *Treatise*. Also in the summer of 1670, Samuel Desmarets, who was a professor in Groningen, was figuring out that the author of the "atrocious" book was "Spinoza, ex-Jew, blasphemer and formal atheist."[16] At around the same time, Johann Ludwig Fabricius, a German traveler in the Netherlands, wrote to Baron Johann Christian von Boineburg (the philosopher Leibniz's employer and patron) in Mainz about the *Treatise*. In his letter, Fabricius—who, acting on behalf of the elector of Palatine, would later invite Spinoza to move to Heidelberg to take up a professorship there, an invitation that the philosopher declined—speculated about the origin of the work. Among the candidates he was considering as its likely author—and this must have been something Fabricius heard from locals during his sojourn in the Republic—was Spinoza.[17] In April 1671, a more certain Johann Georg Graevius, professor of rhetoric at the University of Utrecht and a sympathizer to Cartesian philosophy, also wrote to Leibniz about "this pestilential book whose title is *Tractatus Theologico-Politicus*." Its author, "having followed the footsteps of Hobbes," was "a Jew named Spinoza who was recently excommunicated because of his monstrous opinions."[18] (This indicates, as well, that Leibniz, who had acquired a copy of what he called the "intolerably licentious" *Treatise* several months after its publication, knew by the spring of 1671 at the latest that Spinoza was its author.)[19]

Regardless of how Graevius and others ended up associating Spinoza with the anonymous treatise, it must have been common enough knowledge by November 1671. That is when Spinoza identifies himself as the work's author in correspondence with Leibniz, to whose introductory letter he was responding. Usually a very cautious man—his signet ring read *Caute*—he revealed this fact to a person he did not know at all, with no hesitation or even a warning that Leibniz should keep the information to himself.[20]

In the first few months of 1670, however, nobody (aside from Spinoza's tight circle of friends) seemed to know who had written this scandalous work—a book that denied the divinity of the Bible, ruled out the possibility of miracles, identified God's providence with the laws of nature, deflated the revelations of the prophets, and reduced religion to a simple moral code. Certainly the authorities had no idea who its impudent author was. None of the many ecclesiastic or civil resolutions about the *Treatise* that were promulgated in the months following publication makes any mention of Spinoza's name.

The church consistory of Utrecht was only the first in a long line of Reformed bodies to express alarm about "a profane, blasphemous book [that] has appeared, titled *Theological-political treatise concerning the freedom of philosophizing in the state*." Its members resolved, on April 8, 1670, that the city's burgemeesters—who, a few years earlier, had acted against the books by Meijer and Koerbagh—be requested to take "appropriate preventive measures" against this new work. Three days later, the consistory seemed satisfied with at least the preliminary results: "The burgemeesters have been spoken to about the book . . . and their Honors have agreed that the book should be delivered to the honorable town council."[21] The Utrecht town council was, at the time, controlled by a more liberal, States party faction, and while they appear eventually to have complied with the consistory's request, it would take them more than a year to do so.

One month after the Utrecht consistory's resolution, the Reformed consistory of Leiden followed suit.

> Be it resolved that, since a well-known book has come to light, with the name *Theological-political treatise*, its content and the

monstrosities or obscenities [therein] should be demonstrated to the burgemeesters. Earnestly seeking that the book be seized and suppressed, the directors and the two presiding *predikanten* are delegated to do this.

Again, the consistory got its way. The three-man delegation to the town council was successful in raising the alarm. One week later, the burgemeesters ordered that the town's sheriff raid the bookshops and seize all copies of the *Treatise*.[22]

The resolutions of the consistories of Utrecht and Leiden were soon followed by similar motions by the local church bodies of Haarlem, in May, and Amsterdam, in June. The Amsterdam consistory, as we have seen, wanted the *Treatise* subsumed under earlier legislation in which the States of Holland (along with those of Zeeland and Utrecht, as well as the States General) banned "Socinian" books, or those believed to further the general program of the sect that flourished under the Polish theologian Faustus Socinus (1539–1604). By the mid-seventeenth century, the term "Socinian" came to refer not only to antitrinitarianism but to any doctrine that appeared to recommend a skeptical attitude toward Jesus' divinity and the denial of a robust divine providence. The 1653 edict by the secular authorities provided strong and effective measures, still in force in the late 1660s, when various *Sociniaensche Boecken* (including those of Meijer and Koerbagh) were seized from bookstores. The Amsterdam clerics considered Spinoza's *Treatise* properly to belong to this category, and through their delegation of Brothers Philips Huijbertsz and Lucas van der Heiden to the district synod were appealing to the older States' legislation in the hope of spurring the civic leaders to do something about it.

By the summer, things had progressed from the municipal to the district and then to the provincial ecclesiastic levels, as the Reformed synods, in response to complaints from the consistories, debated what to do. In July, the district synod for The Hague asked the provincial Synod of South Holland for a way to deal with the *Treatise*, as well as with "any other treatise of idolatry and superstition."[23] The provincial synod found the *Treatise* to be "as obscene and blasphemous a book as, to our knowledge, the world has ever seen, and over which the Synod should be greatly distressed," and resolved "immediately to take the most vigilant measures against it." At the same time, they alerted local magistrates and urged them to "suppress and forbid" the printing and distribution of the *Treatise* and "all such books."

Similarly, that same month, the synod for the Amsterdam district, proclaiming the *Treatise*—with its "monstrous and abominable" content—to be "blasphemous and dangerous," approved of the city consistory's request that the book be banned under the rubric of the earlier anti-Socinian legislation against "licentious book publishing," and forwarded this idea to the Synod of North Holland. There the representatives from Amsterdam read out excerpts from Spinoza's book (presumably in Dutch translation), no doubt to the horror of the assembled brothers.[24]

In August, the North and South Holland Synods, "heartily abominating that obscene book," took their case to the States of Holland in The Hague. For all their bluster, the ecclesiastic bodies had no power to take any action on their own in civic affairs. The *predikanten* themselves could neither halt printings nor order sheriffs to raid bookstores. All they could do was recommend—or, rather, demand—action by the secular authorities.

On March 24, 1670, the States of Holland referred the matter to the Hof van Holland, the province's highest judicial court. It was quite some time before the tribunal, also in The Hague, rendered its verdict, but the result was, at least at this intermediate stage, what the synods were hoping for. One year later, on April 16, 1671, the high court confirmed the Reformed ministers' collective view that the *Treatise*, along with some other infamous books (including an anthology of true Socinian writings), were illegal, according to the States' earlier edicts.

> We have, pursuant to Your Noble Great Mightinesses' [the delegates to the States of Holland] directive, examined the content of the request that has been transmitted by the deputies of the North and South Holland Synods. In that request they complain very much against the

printing and dissemination of various blasphemous books, and especially the books titled *Bibiotheca Fr. Polon*, who are called unitarians,
the famous book of Hobbes, titled *Leviathan*, and further the book
titled *Philosophy Interpreter of Holy Scripture*, and also the book titled
Theological-Political Treatise, and they ask with the greatest respect and
great desire that Your Noble Great Mightinesses agree to commit
not only to a prompt and effective remedy, according to the highest
wisdom, for the confiscation of the aforementioned slanderous books,
and in particular the slanderous book titled *Theological-Political Treatise*, but also that an official edict be issued, whereby the door for the
importing of such soul-corrupting books be closed once and for all.
Afterwards we then forwarded to Your Noble Great Mightinesses on
the 15th of this month our advice from 12 December of 1670, regarding the book titled *Bibl. Fratr. polon.* [the Socinian anthology] and the
book titled *Leviathan*, so we desired to refer to it in this matter. As for
the two other books, and especially the *Theological-Political Treatise*,
which contains many blasphemous thoughts, as Your Noble Great
Mightinesses can see from the enclosed excerpts, we are of the opinion that . . . the printing, importing, and dissemination of such blasphemous books directly contradicts Your Noble Great Mightinesses'
edict of 19 September 1653.

The court therefore directed the States of Holland to formally ban
these troubling works through an act of law.

[I]n order to avoid the reproach that such books are printed, dis-
seminated, and sold here, Your Noble Great Mightinesses should
through a particular edict forbid the printing, importing, disseminating, and selling the above-named soul-corrupting books, attach-
ing a strong punishment thereto, and order the officials of each city
to find out the authors, printers, importers, and distributors, and,
having discovered them, take measures against them without any
leniency, as the content of the aforementioned edict allows and as is
found appropriate.[25]

The court is, in effect, telling the States of Holland to create new
proscriptive legislation aimed directly at these recently published

books. (The objects of their ire, in the case of *Leviathan*, were the Latin and Dutch translations.) The justices apparently believed that this would be a more effective approach than simply relying on an eighteen-year-old law that, one might object, only tenuously covered the new cases.

The States of Holland (and Westfriesland), for its part, seems not to have been particularly eager to take action. On April 24, its delegates concluded that the "memo" (*missive*) from the Hof "be further examined and considered" by an appointed committee, which (in addition to some members of the Hof) would include "the gentlemen from Leiden, Amsterdam, Gouda, Rotterdam, Alkmaar, and Hoorn," among whom was Johan de Witt himself.[26]

It was a classic delaying tactic. Rather than issue a new law—as the synods, seconded by the high court of justice, requested—simply refer the question to another committee. The States of Holland was dragging its feet. Perhaps its regent members, seeing repressive legislation as a greater threat to the peace of the Republic than licentious books, were reluctant to engage in the censorship of publications. Or maybe, while sympathetic to the concerns of the religious alarmists, they did not want to call even more attention to these works through public decrees.[27] It is uncertain to what extent De Witt, still grand pensionary of the province of Holland and thus holder of what was, de facto, the most powerful office in the Republic, was personally responsible for protecting the *Treatise* from legal condemnation. It is unlikely that, given his own deteriorating political situation—he was regarded by his Orangist opponents as an incompetent leader, and even as a traitor to his country—he would have stuck his neck out very far to protect a work that was the object of such unanimous ecclesiastic vilification.[28]

By the end of the summer of 1672, after the French invasion of the Netherlands, De Witt would be dead, viciously murdered by an angry mob. Meanwhile, with the States-appointed committee still deliberating—or procrastinating—over what to do about the *Treatise*, and almost two years since the ecclesiastic bodies had submitted their resolutions, the clerics were growing impatient. The deputies from the North and South Holland Synods had earlier written directly to De Witt and asked him point-blank, with "an urgent petition"—submitted with excerpts from the *Treatise*—to get the slow-moving States to act. Now, they are ready to bypass the legislative route altogether and see things handled by the judiciary and local magistrates. In July, the South Holland Synod, disappointed that "no decree has come down" from The Hague, "concludes that at this time the matter should no longer be brought to the state, but that redress should be sought from the Hof or the respective magistrates."[29]

If the provincial synods were frustrated, the local consistories and district synods were at their wits' end. The *classis* of Amsterdam, ever more concerned about what it saw as the pernicious influence of the *Treatise* on public spirituality and morality, complained in July 1672 that it has "strived now for so many years in all ways, as is suitable, and did what it could to arouse fear in men" regarding the "insolences" and "abominable teachings" of books that "destroy the soul," especially "the most godless book *Theological-Political Treatise*." This work, along with writings of Hobbes and Meijer, are responsible for "the increase of cry-aloud-to-heaven transgressions, slanders of God's name, blasphemies, curses, Sabbath shaming, desecrations, contempt of religion, dishonor, and such." These troubles "are so far from being eliminated that rather they are daily being increased, against which the almighty God will issue his anger from heaven; and already the appearance of his anger pours upon our dear fatherland." The district synod's members are desperate for some remedy for these pestilential writings—their impatience is palpable in the extant reports—but no one seems to be doing anything about them.[30]

The efforts by municipal and provincial church leaders, tired of waiting for action from the States, to seek more immediate redress through local civil authorities met with some success. In September 1671, the Utrecht district synod reports that the town council has finally complied with its demand. "The *Theological-Political Treatise* has been confiscated."[31] One year later, in August 1672, the deputies of the Synod of North Holland approached the pensionary of Leiden, a man named Burgersdijck, hoping to persuade him to do something in his town. They presented him with excerpts from the *Treatise*, and "he promised to do his duty in regard to this matter, so that a good conclusion should be achieved."[32] One year later, Burgersdijck reported back to the synod that (as the synod representatives tell their colleagues) "already much has been done with respect to" the *Theological-Political Treatise*. He also explained that he and other officials "are constantly taken up in demand of other commissions, so that until now they could not have executed their charge on this matter. However," the representatives' report concludes, "he now undertakes to do his duty."[33] In other words, chasing after a book was not the pensionary's top priority, but he will see what he can do about it.

What all of this shows, as Jonathan Israel has argued, is that, while efforts to enact province- or Republic-wide bans of the *Treatise* only very slowly bore fruit, the suppression of the *Treatise* was nonetheless able to proceed "on a piecemeal, local basis from the very outset."[34] In those Dutch cities where the judiciary and law enforcement were willing to cooperate with the Reformed authorities, it may have been very difficult to find a copy of the *Treatise*, at least on the shelves of local booksellers.[35]

The efficacy of censorship at the municipal level is shown by the fact that Rieuwertsz, after publishing two Latin editions (in 1670 and 1672) with anonymous but straightforward titles, began trying even more devious routes. In 1673 he bound together Spinoza's *Treatise* and Meijer's *Philosophy, Interpreter of Holy Scripture* in a single octavo volume. This time, in addition to a false publisher, the title pages contained false titles and authors. One such joint edition appeared as the *Opera Chirurgica Omnia* (Complete Chemical Writings) of Francisco Henriquez de Villacorta, Medical Doctor, printed with permission of the Spanish King Charles II and published in Amsterdam by "J. Paulli." This was probably destined for readers in the Spanish Netherlands. Another edition carried the title *Danielis Heinsii P. P. Operum Historicum Collectio*, or Collection of the Historical Works of Daniel Heinsius (Heinsius was a well-known Dutch classical scholar in the first half of the

seventeenth century). The title page of a third version was billed
as the complete medical writings of Francisco dele Boe Sylvius, "A
Most Famous Doctor among the Dutch."

With these new evasive moves by Spinoza and Rieuwertsz, the
Treatise had truly entered the realm of clandestine literature.[36]

At long last, in December 1673, the States of Holland, responding to the high court's recommendation, gave the *predikanten* what
they had been looking for. The catalyst seems to have been these
deceptively packaged volumes, which alarmed the secular authorities even more than the anonymous editions.

> The deputies [to the States of Holland] from the city of Leiden, in
> the name of and on behalf of their colleagues, have made known to
> this gathering that those colleagues have come to learn that recently
> the *Theological-Political Treatise* and the *Philosophy Interpreter of Holy
> Scripture* have both been published in an octavo edition somewhere
> in these lands, and disseminated in a single volume under false
> titles; one volume carries the title: *Francisco de le Boe Sylvii Opera
> Medica omnia* . . . and another the title *Danielis Heynsii P. P. Operum
> Historicorum Collectio.* . . . They request that immediate measures be
> considered by Your Noble Mightinesses and put into effect, through
> which such kinds of deceit might be countered. Accordingly, after
> deliberations, it is agreed and concluded that . . . a decree be estab-
> lished on how and in what way the aforementioned and other such
> deceits with respect to the publication of forbidden and irreligious
> books, which tend to be undertaken with false titles, could and
> should best be defended against. At the same time the President
> and counselors of the Hof should be informed so that they might
> issue such a command and take care that the above-named writings
> be immediately seized and suppressed everywhere in this province
> that they are available.[37]

Six months later, in July 1674, the counselors of the Hof followed
through on the States' directive.

> Having examined their contents, we find that not only do these books
> undermine the teachings of the true Christian Reformed religion,

but they also overflow with blasphemies against God and his attributes, and his worshipful trinity, against the divinity of Jesus Christ and his true mission, along with the fundamental dogmas of the true Christian religion, and in effect the authority of Holy Scripture, so seeking to bring all this into contempt and to introduce doubt into weak, unstable minds, all of which goes directly against resolutions and edicts repeatedly issued against them by these lands. Thus, in order to prevent this harmful poison and to hinder as much as possible anyone from being misled by it, we have judged it to be our duty to condemn and proclaim the aforementioned books as blasphemous and soul-harming books, full of groundless and dangerous opinions and abominations that injure true religion and true worship. Accordingly, we hereby forbid everyone and anyone from printing, disseminating or selling, by auction or otherwise, such or similar books, under the punishment that has been established by the edict of the lands, and especially through the edict of 19 September 1653. We further enjoin that everyone whom this concerns should abide by it, and that this be known and posted everywhere it is heard and in the same language.

Spinoza's *Theological-Political Treatise* was now officially banned in the Dutch Republic.

The edict of the Hof appears under the name of Willem Hendrik, who ("by the grace of God") has been Prince of Orange and Nassau and is now, as Willem III, occupant of the newly reinstated office of stadholder in Holland and other provinces (and later to be king of England). The period of the True Freedom was over. With De Witt gone and his States party allies in a weakened position, there were fewer obstacles in the way of the hard-core Reformed ministers seeking to exercise oversight of the Republic's political and intellectual life. It was exactly the eventuality Spinoza so feared and against which he warned in the *Treatise*.

For some time, the liberal De Witt had in fact been regarded as Spinoza's protector. A few of his critics went so far as to see him as Spinoza's co-conspirator, even co-author. A telling remark appears in a catalogue of the books reportedly found in De Witt's library.

Published as an anonymous pamphlet by one of De Witt's enemies, the list of books was intended to demonstrate the criminal character of the late grand pensionary. Beside item no. 33, *Tractatus Theologico-Politicus*, is the following note: "Forged in hell by the apostate Jew working together with the devil, and published with the knowledge and complicity of M. Jan."[38]

Perhaps more disturbing to Spinoza than the response by Dutch ecclesiastic bodies, which he probably anticipated, were the attacks by intellectuals, both domestic and foreign. In correspondence to each other and in published works, university theologians and philosophers offered unremittingly negative reactions to the *Treatise*. These came even from quarters where Spinoza might reasonably have expected a sympathetic hearing.

The first reviews appeared abroad, and very soon after the publication of the *Treatise*.[38] In May 1670, the German theologian Jakob Thomasius fulminated against a recent, anonymously published book. Its author, he claimed in his *Adversus anonymum de libertate philosophandi* (Against the Anonymous [Treatise] on the Freedom of Philosophizing), the first published "refutation" of the *Treatise*, is an atheist and his work "a godless document" that should be immediately banned in all countries. Thomasius's former student, Leibniz, writing to his erstwhile professor in Leipzig, congratulated him for the way in which

> you have dealt with the intolerably licentious book on the liberty to philosophize in the way it deserved. It seems that the author follows closely not only the politics, but also the religion of Hobbes. . . . For there is nothing in the astounding critique of Sacred Scripture put into effect by this audacious man, the seeds of which have not been sowed by Hobbes in an entire chapter of *Leviathan*.[40]

Leibniz composed this in October 1670, one year before he wrote to Spinoza directly, seeking to ingratiate himself with his Dutch philosophical colleague and (despite—or perhaps because of—having learned from Graevius that it was Spinoza who was the author of the *Treatise*) expressing admiration for his "achievements."[41]

Closer to home, there was van Blijenburgh, the philosophically inclined merchant and regent who, in 1665, had so earnestly entreated Spinoza to explain the principles of his philosophy. Nine years after their exchange of letters (and a brief meeting), van Blijenburgh wrote his own commentary on the *Treatise*. "This atheistic book," he complained in *The Truth of the Christian Religion and the Authority of Holy Scripture Affirmed Against the Arguments of the Impious, or A Refutation of the Blasphemous Book Titled Theological-Political Treatise*, "is full of studious abominations and an accumulation of opinions which have been forged in hell, which every reasonable person, indeed every Christian should find abhorrent."[42]

The attacks did not come only from the more conservative side of the political and religious spectrum. Remonstrants, and even Collegiants—who had a clear stake in the campaign for religious toleration in the Republic—joined the battle. Jacob Batelier, a Remonstrant minister in The Hague, composed his attack on the *Treatise*, the *Vindiciae Miraculorum* (In Defense of Miracles), just before he died in 1672 (it was published the following year), while Johannes Bredenburg, a Collegiant businessman from Rotterdam with Cartesian sympathies, wrote his *Enervatio Tractatus Theologico-Politici* (Refutation of the Theological-Political Treatise) in 1675. What bothered Batelier, for whom Spinoza was an atheist bent on corrupting others, was the way in which the causal determinism of the *Treatise* undermined divine and human freedom and eliminated the manifestation of God's providence through real miraculous events. Bredenburg objected vehemently to Spinoza's conception of God (at least as far as he could decipher this from the *Treatise* alone), his method of scriptural interpretation and, like Batelier (and many others), the determinism or "fatalism" at the heart of the account of miracles. He argued, moreover, that Spinoza's reduction of religion to moral maxims and his denial that the divine commandments have authentic truth value were all harmful to true religion and the worship of God.[43]

Ironically, also among these early opponents of the *Treatise* was Frans Kuyper, the Socinian compiler of the *Bibliotheca Fratrum Polonorum* (Library of Polish Brothers), which was so often condemned in tandem with the *Treatise*. This former Remonstrant minister, now a Collegiant and radical book publisher in Amsterdam and Rotterdam, viciously attacked the work as "atheistic." If this was a desperate act of self-preservation intended to distance his own publications from that of Spinoza, it was unlikely to succeed.[44] Kuyper had published an explicitly Socinian anthology, one directly counter to the 1653 legislation. Thus, the problem was not a matter of his book being too close to Spinoza's but of Spinoza's book being too close to his!

Even individuals whom Spinoza could rightly regard as long-standing friends apparently turned on him after they had read the *Treatise*. Oldenburg obtained a copy of "the treatise on Scripture" soon after its publication. While no doubt excited finally to see the book that, some years earlier, Spinoza told him he was starting on "my views regarding Scripture,"[45] its contents clearly alarmed him. Although the letter in which he expresses to Spinoza his initial reaction is no longer extant, it must have been extremely harsh, for it would be five years before he wrote again, with a letter in which he practically apologizes for what he calls his "premature" judgment of the work. Still, it is clear that Oldenburg, without question a man of science and devoted to the new philosophy of nature, remains concerned that the *Treatise* "tends to the endangerment of religion," particularly "those [passages] which appear to treat in an ambiguous way of God and Nature, which many people consider you have confused with each other." Moreover, Oldenburg warns Spinoza,

> many are of the opinion that you take away the authority and validity of miracles, which almost all Christians are convinced form the sole basis on which the certainty of Divine Revelation can rest. Furthermore, they say that you are concealing your opinion with regard to Jesus Christ, Redeemer of the World, sole Mediator for mankind, and of his Incarnation and Atonement.[46]

Oldenburg is under the impression that Spinoza intends to "moderate those passages in the *Theological-Political Treatise* which have proved a stumbling-block to readers." In particular, he expects him to disavow what appears to be "a fatalistic necessity in all things and actions," a view that would "do away with the practice of religious virtue . . . and sever the sinews of all law, all virtue and religion."[47] He was greatly distressed, then, to find out that, in the end, all Spinoza had to offer was a clarification explaining why in the *Treatise* he did indeed embrace such a determinism in nature and denial of miracles.[48]

Spinoza probably did not expect too much understanding from Oldenburg, whom he knew to be an Englishman of conventional faith. But he certainly did hope for better things from more progressive Dutch colleagues. Thus, he was particularly disappointed by the way in which Cartesians—generally, a politically liberal and intellectually tolerant group who had themselves suffered censorship at the universities—attacked the *Treatise*.

Regnier van Mansvelt, a professor at the University of Utrecht widely known for his own exposition of Descartes's philosophy, insisted in his *Adversus Anonymum Theologico-politicum* of 1674 that the work was harmful to all religions and "ought to be buried forever in an eternal oblivion."[49] He was particularly bothered by the idea that Scripture is not a source of truths. "There can be no [need for] accommodation between two truths that are true per se. For each comes from God. The true always corresponds with the true without any accommodation."[50] Similarly, as we have seen, Lambert van Velthuysen, in his correspondence with Spinoza mediated by Jacob Ostens, came down hard on the *Treatise*. This liberal physician and amateur Cartesian philosopher simply could not tolerate the denial of miracles, the demotion of the prophets, or the way in which Scripture was robbed of its divinity and authority. In his harsh remarks to Ostens (presumably intended for Spinoza) in 1671, Van Velthuysen insists that "the doctrine of the political-theologian . . . banishes and thoroughly subverts all worship and religion, prompts atheism by stealth, or envisages such a God as cannot move men to reverence for his divinity, since he himself is subject to fate; no room is left for divine governance and providence, and the assignment of punishment and reward is entirely abolished."[51]

To be sure, there was a political dimension to the Cartesian assault on the *Treatise*, as Spinoza himself knew. Their attacks were a tactical maneuver intended to distinguish themselves from this dangerous atheist in the minds of their own powerful ecclesiastic and academic opponents. "The stupid Cartesians," Spinoza wrote to Oldenburg in 1675, "in order to remove suspicion from themselves because they are thought to be on my side, ceased not to denounce everywhere my opinions and my writings, and still continue to do so."[52] The Cartesians had to show that there was in fact no connection between Descartes's philosophy (of which Spinoza was, much to their dismay, the decade's most famous expositor) and the doctrines of the *Treatise*, that Spinoza's ideas were not the ultimate logical conclusion of Cartesian principles. Van Velthuysen in particular was concerned that Spinoza's Bible hermeneutic—with its emphasis on the rational examination of the text and the inquiry into the historical context of its composition—would seem rather similar to his own, and that Spinoza would thereby drag him down with him.[53]

Whether they were bothered by the *Treatise*'s treatment of prophecy, miracles, the Bible, or God himself, all of Spinoza's critics—conservative and liberal—believed him to be an atheist and a freethinker, and the book to be a fount of irreligion and immorality. Even De Witt, the only person demonized by the Calvinist/Orangist camp more than Spinoza was, had nothing good to say about the *Treatise*. He was reportedly worried especially about its effect on the morality of common people, who would no longer believe in "reward and punishment after this life" and thus presumably feel free to behave in licentious ways.[54] Although Spinoza was a natural political ally for De Witt and the States party, the *Treatise* was much too radical for this liberal politician's taste.

It is no mystery why the *Treatise* occasioned such a vitriolic backlash from so many corners of the philosophical, political, religious, and intellectual world in the seventeenth century. Sectarian theologians were clearly taken aback by the boldness of Spinoza's attack on the basic doctrinal foundations of their religions. After all, where would Christianity (and Judaism and Islam) be without the belief in miracles, divine prophecy, and the truth of Scripture? Reformed and Catholic ecclesiastics in Europe (and especially the Netherlands) were also threatened by Spinoza's attempt to undermine their growing influence in political and civic affairs. At the same time, secular leaders would have seen Spinoza's ideas as an assault on their authority—since the notion of a broadly tolerant, thoroughly secular, liberal democracy was not yet on the political horizon—and even on public order and morality (since without the belief in a providential God, why would anyone behave morally?). Meanwhile, philosophical moderates and those on the left saw in the *Treatise* their worst nightmare: a truly radical work that, because it would be perceived as the natural extension of their own ideas, would bring down upon them the full power of church and state.

Despite his annoyance with the Cartesians, Spinoza seems to have been able to deal with the attacks against the *Treatise* with his usual stoic equanimity. He complained about being misunderstood, of course; and he resented the unfair and highly personal way in which he was treated by his many critics. There is even a flash of anger in his first response to Van Velthuysen's critique: "I can hardly bring myself to answer that man's letter."[55] But he did not waste much time composing replies. He was generally dismissive toward the numerous books and pamphlets written against him, and he regarded their authors as uninformed and motivated by malice.[56] His reaction to Van Mansvelt's book, expressed in a letter to Jelles in 1674, is characteristic.

The book which the Utrecht professor wrote against mine and has been published after his death, I have seen in a bookseller's window. From the little that I then read of it, I judged it not worth reading through, and far less answering. So I left the book lying there, and its author to remain such as he was. I smiled as I reflected that the ignorant are usually the most venturesome and most ready to write. It seemed to me that the [gap in text] set out their wares for sale in the same way as do shopkeepers, who always display the worse first. They say the devil is a crafty fellow, but in my opinion these people's resourcefulness far surpasses him in cunning.[57]

Spinoza initially had hopes that the *Treatise*, with its defense of the freedom of philosophizing, would pave the way for publication (and a welcome reception) of the *Ethics*. It was a serious miscalculation. The critical onslaught directed at the *Treatise* was so great that he realized that the *Ethics* now could not possibly get a fair hearing. He tells Oldenburg in September 1675 that "I was setting out for Amsterdam, intending to put into print the book of which I had written to you [the *Ethics*]. While I was engaged in this business, a rumor became widespread that a certain book of mine about God was in the press, and that in it I endeavor to show that there is no God. This rumor found credence with so many. So certain theologians, who may have started this rumor, seized the opportunity to complain of me before the Prince and the magistrates." Concerned about the alarm generated by these reports that the author of the *Treatise* was about to publish a book about God, "I decided to postpone the publication I had in hand until I should see how matters turn out."[58]

A few years earlier, in 1671, before the Hof van Holland had formally condemned the *Treatise*, Spinoza also put a halt to plans to bring out a Dutch translation of the work. A vernacular edition, capable of spreading his subversive and impious ideas to the masses, would surely inflame the authorities beyond even their current fever pitch. When he heard that some people,[59] without having consulted him, were in the process of preparing a Dutch version, Spinoza was afraid it would hasten a ban. He immediately wrote to Jelles to get him to intervene. "I beg you most earnestly please to look into this and, if possible, to stop the printing. This is not only my request, but that of many of my good friends who would not wish to see the book banned, as will undoubtedly happen if it is published in Dutch."[60] A Dutch translation of the *Treatise* would not appear in print until 1693; its publisher was Jan Rieuwertsz, the Younger.

Meanwhile, a French translation of the *Treatise* was published—again, in clandestine editions—in 1678. Among the false titles given the volume were *The Key to the Sanctuary, by a learned man of our century* and *Curious Reflections, by a disinterested soul on the matters of the highest importance for public and private salvation.* An English translation of the *Treatise* was not produced until 1689, and there was no German edition until 1806.

The irrepressible Rieuwertsz continued his radical publishing activities throughout the ecclesiastic and secular trials of the *Treatise*. As far as we know, his business did not suffer. Although the authorities remained suspicious and continued to keep a close watch on him, he appears not to have been seriously harassed or suffered any legal troubles. This was probably because, despite the fact that the political winds had shifted in the Republic and the conservative Orangists were now, with the installation of Willem III, in power at the provincial and national levels, Amsterdam remained in the hands of more liberal regents. Still, no one could have been more surprised than Rieuwertsz himself when he was appointed the official municipal printer of Amsterdam in 1675. The post was given to him by the city treasurer, Johannes Hudde, a devoted Cartesian.

In February 1677, Spinoza died, at the age of forty-four. The philosopher's friends gave Rieuwertsz the unpublished writings and letters they found among his possessions. Rieuwertsz published these in two editions: the Latin *Opera Posthuma* and, once they were translated, the Dutch *Nagelate Schriften*. This brought renewed attention to his shop, including an investigation by the apostolic vicar and chief of Catholic clergy in the Netherlands, Jan van Neercassel. Writing to his superiors in Rome, van Neercassel notes that the publisher of Spinoza's works "is accustomed to bringing out, through his press, every imaginable bizarre and impious thing composed by exotic and impious minds." When confronted by van Neercassel, Rieuwertsz denied having published Spinoza's late writings. "The publisher is a boldfaced liar," van Neercassel notes. "When interrogated by me about his [Spinoza's] unpublished works, he responded that no manuscript had been found besides some annotations on Descartes."[61]

As for the *Treatise* itself, it enjoyed great fame and tremendous infamy throughout Europe in the decades after its publication. A few hailed it as the harbinger of enlightenment; many more continued the campaign of vilification, regarding it as the most dangerous book ever published. In 1679, it was placed on the Catholic Church's Index of Prohibited Books, along with the *Ethics*, the *Political Treatise*, and Spinoza's correspondence. By contrast, there was in the seventeenth century almost no response to the *Treatise* from Jewish quarters; not even the Spanish and Portuguese Jews of Amsterdam bothered to compose a response to it, if only to distance themselves from their most problematic son.[62] The *Treatise* did, however, have a considerable role in the rise of the *Haskalah*, or Jewish Enlightenment, in the eighteenth century.[63]

It is tempting to think that Spinoza failed in his aim in composing the *Treatise*. If, as he said to Oldenburg in the autumn of 1665 when beginning the book, he was writing in order to counter "the prejudices of theologians," respond to "the opinion of me held by common people, who constantly accuse me of atheism," and "vindicate completely . . . the freedom to philosophize and to say what we think" and undermine the way in which this freedom "is suppressed by the excessive authority and egotism of preachers,"[64] then it would have to be said that Spinoza achieved only one of his initial goals, the construction of a strong and eloquent defense of the freedom of thought and expression. He certainly reached his intended audience with the *Treatise*, but it did not have the consequences he wanted. Rather than opening up the door to greater liberty to philosophize—including the possibility of publishing his own philosophy!—Spinoza seems mainly to have succeeded in mobilizing the entire world, including Dutch liberals, against himself.

This would, of course, be an unfair judgment based on a short-sighted perspective. Without a doubt, the *Theological-Political Treatise* is one of the most important and influential books in the history of philosophy, in religious and political thought, and even in Bible studies. More than any other work, it laid the foundation for modern critical and historical approaches to the Bible. And while often overlooked in books on the history of political thought, the *Treatise* also has a proud and well-deserved place in the rise of democratic theory, civil liberties, and political liberalism. The ideas of the *Treatise* inspired republican revolutionaries in England, America, and France, and it encouraged early modern anticlerical and antisectarian movements.

To the extent that we are committed to the ideal of a secular society free of ecclesiastic influence and governed by toleration, liberty, and a conception of civic virtue; and insofar as we think of true religious piety as consisting in treating other human beings with dignity and respect, and regard the Bible simply as a profound work of human literature with a universal moral message, we are the heirs of Spinoza's scandalous treatise.

A Note on Texts and Translations

The original Latin text of the *Tractatus Theologico-Politicus* was published in 1670 by Jan Rieuwertsz in Amsterdam. The standard edition has for some time been the one prepared by Carl Gebhardt in *Spinoza Opera* (originally published in 1925). This edition of Spinoza's works is now in the process of being superseded by the *Oeuvres complètes*, a more thorough critical edition being prepared under the auspices of the Association des Amis de Spinoza. Volume three, dedicated to the *Tractatus*, has already appeared (1999), with the text established by Fokke Akkerman and a French translation and critical apparatus by Jacqueline Lagrée and Pierre-François Moreau (published by the Presses Universitaires de France). However, because the Gebhardt edition is so widely accessible and used, especially among Anglo-American readers; and since the Akkerman volume includes the pagination from both the original edition and Gebhardt, I have in the notes provided primary citations to the Gebhardt Latin edition.

Edwin Curley is currently in the process of completing volume two of his English translation of Spinoza's writings, *The Collected Works of Spinoza* (Princeton University Press), which will include the *Treatise* and the correspondence after 1665. When the volume appears, this will be the standard translation. Professor Curley has kindly shared his manuscript with me. Meanwhile, the second (and corrected) edition of the translation by Samuel Shirley (Hackett Publishing) is widely available. Because Curley's translation has not yet appeared, I am not able to provide page citations from it. Most of the translations of passages from the *Treatise* in this book come from the Shirley translation; some come from the Curley translation. The passages from Curley's translation, including those that correspond to my use of Shirley's translation,

will be easily locatable because Curley is including the pagination from the Gebhardt edition. The translations from the *Ethics*
and other works (including the correspondence through 1665) are
from Curley, volume one (Spinoza 1985); the translations from the
correspondence after 1665 are from Samuel Shirley, *Spinoza: The
Letters* (Hackett).

The translations of all other Latin, French, and Dutch texts are
my own, unless indicated otherwise.

Abbreviations

The following abbreviations are used in the notes to refer to works by Spinoza and others:

1. Works by or on Spinoza

C   *The Collected Works of Spinoza.* Vol. 1. Trans. Edwin Curley. Princeton, NJ:
        Princeton University Press, 1985.
Ep.   "Epistle," from Spinoza's correspondence.
FW   *Die Lebensgeschichte Spinozas. Zweite, stark erweiterte und vollständig neu
        kommentierte Auflage der Ausgabe von Jakob Freudenthal.* 2 vols. Ed. Jakob
        Freudenthal and Manfred Walther. Stuttgart: Frommann-Holzboog,
        2006.
G   *Spinoza Opera.* 4 vols. Ed. Carl Gebhardt. Heidelberg: Carl Winters
        Universitätsverlag, 1925; reprinted 1972.
S   *Theological-Political Treatise.* 2nd ed. Trans. Samuel Shirley. Indianapolis:
        Hackett, 2001.
SL   *Spinoza: The Letters.* Trans. Samuel Shirley. Indianapolis: Hackett, 1995.
SM   *Complete Works.* Trans. Samuel Shirley; ed. Michael Morgan. Indianapolis:
        Hackett, 2002.
TTP   *Tractatus Theologico-Politicus*

2. Works by Others

A. LEIBNIZ
GP   *Philosophische Schriften.* 7 vols. Ed. C. I. Gerhardt. Berlin: Weidmann,
        1875–90; reprinted Hildesheim: Georg Olms, 1978.
H   *Theodicy: Essays on the Goodness of God, the Freedom of Man, and the Origin of
        Evil.* Trans. E. M. Huggard. La Salle, IL: Open Court, 1985.
L   *Philosophical Papers and Letters.* 2nd ed. Ed.-trans. Leroy Loemker.
        Dordrecht: D. Reidel, 1969.

B. DESCARTES
AT   *Oeuvres de Descartes.* 12 vols. Ed. Charles Adam and Paul Tannery. Paris:
        J. Vrin, 1974–83.
CSM   *The Philosophical Writings of Descartes.* 2 vols. Ed.-trans. John Cottingham,
        Robert Stoothoff, and Dugald Murdoch. Cambridge: Cambridge
        University Press, 1985.

Notes

Preface

1. See Israel 2001a.

2. There are some very notable exceptions to this; in particular, see Strauss 1997 (originally published in Germany in 1930). More recently, see Curley 1990a, Curley 1994, and Verbeek 2003.

3. Fields other than philosophy (e.g., Jewish studies, political science, history, literary studies) have been much kinder to the *Treatise*, particularly in the past twenty-five years; see, for example, Smith 1997 and Levene 2004.

4. Such a study has been undertaken at great length by the historian Jonathan Israel in a series of monumental volumes—see Israel 2001a and Israel 2006.

Chapter 1: Prologue

1. Huijbertsz is, in Dutch patronymic usage, short for "Huijbertszoon," or "Huijbert's son."

2. Amsterdam Municipal Archives, Archive 376, inv. no. 12, p.116. My thanks to Odette Vlessing for bringing this archival material to my attention.

3. Amsterdam Municipal Archives, Nieuwe Kerk Archives, no. 376/12, p. 110; FW, doc. 93, I.289.

4. Amsterdam Municipal Archives, Notary deed 1557A, fol. 91, notary Jan Volkaertsz. Oli, 18 March 1649.

5. Amsterdam Municipal Archives, Nieuwe Kerk Archives, no. 379/101; FW, doc. 96, I.291.

6. Amsterdam Municipal Archives, Nieuwe Kerk Archives, no. 379/101; FW, doc. 97, I.292.

7. This biographical sketch is drawn from Nadler 1999.

8. By the late 1630s there was also a sizable population of Central and Eastern European (or Ashkenazic) Jews in Amsterdam.

9. *Treatise on the Emendation of the Intellect*, G II.5; C I.7.

10. The Hebrew text is no longer extant, but the Portuguese version is found in the Book of Ordinances (*Livro dos Acordos de Naçao e Ascamot*), Municipal Archives of the City of Amsterdam, Archives for the Portuguese Jewish Community in Amsterdam, Archive 334, no. 19, fol. 408.

11. The text used for the *herem* had been brought back to Amsterdam from Venice by Rabbi Saul Levi Mortera almost forty years earlier, ostensibly to be used in case an intramural congregational dispute in 1619 could not be resolved amicably.

12. Spinoza's friends, who edited his works and letters for publication immediately after his death, seem to have destroyed all letters that were not of mainly philosophical (as opposed to biographical and personal) interest.

13. Freudenthal 1899, 5.

14. Freudenthal 1899, 7.

15. Revah 1959, 32–33.

16. The text of Brother Tomas's deposition (in Revah 1959, 32) reads as follows:

He knew both Dr. Prado, a physician, whose first name was Juan but whose Jewish name he did not know, who had studied at Alcala, and a certain de Espinosa, who he thinks was a native of one of the villages of Holland, for he had studied at Leiden and was a good philosopher. These two persons had professed the Law of Moses, and the synagogue had expelled and isolated them because they had reached the point of atheism. And they themselves told the witness that they had been circumcised and that they had observed the law of the Jews, and that they had changed their mind because it seemed to them that the said law was not true and that souls died with their bodies and that there is no God except philosophically. And that is why they were expelled from the synagogue; and, while they regretted the absence of the charity that they used to receive from the synagogue and the communication with other Jews, they were happy to be atheists, since they thought that God exists only philosophically . . . and that souls died with their bodies and that thus they had no need for faith.

17. The original text of Maltranilla's testimony is in Revah 1959, 67.

18. Mendes 1975, 60–61.

19. Freudenthal 1899, 8.

20. This treatise was not included in the Latin or Dutch collections of Spinoza's writings published by his friends after his death, and was only rediscovered in Dutch manuscripts in the nineteenth century.

21. Throughout this book, 'Nature' (with a uppercase N) is used to refer to the metaphysical substance of Spinoza's universe, which is identical with God; 'nature' (lowercase n) is used to refer to what we ordinarily think of as "nature": the empirical world, with all its familiar items, events, and laws, all of which is caused by and belongs to Nature.

22. *Ethics* III, Preface, G II.138; C I.492.

23. *Ethics* IV, Appendix, G II.276; C I.593–94.

Chapter 2: The Theological-Political Problem

1. Ep. 1, G IV.5; C I.163.

2. Oldenburg's letter is a reply to a previous but nonextant letter by Spinoza, from September 4. In that letter Spinoza presumably outlined his ideas for his new treatise.

3. Ep. 29, G IV.165; SL 183.

4. Ep. 30.

5. This philosophical background was necessary, but certainly not sufficient, for understanding the theses and arguments of the *Ethics*; many well-schooled contemporaries, including Leibniz, did not fully understand Spinoza.

6. For a good discussion of Spinoza's audience with the *Treatise*, see Frankel 1999 and Smith 1997, chap. 2. Smith agrees with Strauss about the esoteric features of the *Treatise*, but I believe that Lagrée (2004), who insists that we should read Spinoza *à la lettre*, is closer to the truth: "Spinoza écrit ce qu'il pense et pense ce qu'il écrit" (10). It is true that Spinoza does not say *everything* that he thinks, particularly about Christianity; he certainly pulls his punches in his discussion of Christian Scripture, as Ed Curley has reminded me. But this does not, in my estimation, amount to an esoteric message.

7. TTP, Preface, G III.12; S 7.

8. Frankel (1999), in fact, argues that the intended audience of the *Treatise* was indeed the theologians, at least those who were not corrupt and prejudiced ("learned ecclesiastics") and who thus might have read it with at least a partly open mind. "Spinoza addresses himself primarily to clergy and theologians who can influence the multitude and discourage their perverse interpretations of Scripture" (902).

9. TTP, Preface, G III.12; S 7.

10. TTP, Preface, G III.12; S 8.

11. The phrase is from Kolakowski 1969.

12. TTP, Preface, G III.12; S 8.

13. Hsia and Van Nierop 2002, 75.

14. See Israel 1995, chap. 27. See also Hsia and Van Nierop 2002.

15. Israel 1995, 639, 759–60. See also Blom 1981.

16. See chapter 8.

17. *Leviathan*, III.39, Hobbes 1994, 316.

18. There has been much debate over whether Hobbes is in fact an atheist. See Martinich 1992 and Curley 1996a and 1996b.

19. *Leviathan*, IV.44, Hobbes 1994, 411.

20. Aubrey 1898, I.357, modified according to the emendation suggested by V. de S. Pinto and accepted by Curley (Hobbes 1994, lxviii).

21. Verbeek (2003, 9–10) suggests that the *Treatise* might in fact be seen as a commentary on *Leviathan*.

22. TTP, G III.89; S 78.

23. See Bayle in FW, I.62; Colerus's early biography of Spinoza, FW, I.132; and the report by Solomon van Til, FW, I.399.

Chapter 3: Rasphuis

1. Sellin 1944, 27.

2. Sellin 1944, 41. On the Rasphuis, see also Weissman 1908.

3. For Koerbagh's biography and an account of his ordeal, see Meinsma 1983, 240–77, and Vandenbossche 1978.

4. Jongeneelen 1987, 248.

5. Jongeneelen 1987, 249–50.

6. Vandenbossche 1978, 9–10.

7. Jongeneelen 1987.

8. Meinsma 1983, 269.

9. Meinsma 1983, 252–53.

10. Meinsma 1983, 266.

11. For the text of this judgment, see FW I.286.

12. Sellin 1944, chap. 9.

13. On Spinoza's relationship with Koerbagh, see Vandenbossche 1978.

14. FW I.285–86.

15. Israel 1995, 663.

16. FW I.280.

17. Ep. 43, G IV.220; SL 238.

18. Ep. 30.

19. TTP, Preface, G III.7; S 3.

Chapter 4: Gods and Prophets

1. Thus, in a letter to Albert Burgh, Spinoza calls Judaism, Catholicism, and Islam "superstition" (Ep. 76). See also Epistle 73, a letter to Oldenburg, where Spinoza says that "the chief distinction I make between religion and superstition is that the latter is founded on ignorance, the former on wisdom" (G IV.307–8; SL 333).

2. See Nussbaum 1986.

3. TTP, Preface, G III.5–6; S 1–2.

4. TTP, Preface, G III.6–7; S 2–3.

5. TTP, Preface, G III.8–9; S 4.

6. *Leviathan* I.12, Hobbes 1994, 70.

7. The relationship between Hobbes and Spinoza (especially *Leviathan* and the *Theological-Political Treatise*) on this and other matters has been studied by Curley (1992), Malcolm (2002), and Verbeek (2003), among others.

8. *Ethics* IP15S[I], G II.57; C 421.

9. *Ethics* I, Appendix, G II.78; C I.439–40.

10. *Ethics* I, Appendix, G II.78–79; C I.440–41.

11. Ep. 23, G IV.148; SL 166.

12. Ep. 56, G IV.260; SL 277.

13. *Ethics* I, Appendix, G II.80; C I.442.

14. The only exceptions are Spinoza's friends, who since the mid-1660s had been reading the *Ethics* in a manuscript version that circulated among them.

15. As Altmann (1978, 1) says, "the question whether prophecy is a natural phenomenon or a divine gift goes back to classical antiquity."

16. On Spinoza and Maimonides, see Wolfson 1934, Harvey 1981, Levy 1989, Ravven 2001, Nadler 2002, and Fraenkel 2006.

17. *Guide* II.36, Maimonides 1963, 369.

18. *Guide* II.36, Maimonides 1963, 372.

19. *Guide* II.37, Maimonides 1963, 374.

20. *Guide* II.38, Maimonides 1963, 377.

21. *Guide* II.32, Maimonides 1963, 361.

22. Aside from being the source of the overflow, God's role in prophecy seems to be limited only to *preventing*, by a special act, someone from becoming a prophet who was otherwise on his way naturally to reaching the condition of prophecy; see *Guide* II.32, Maimonides 1963, 361. This preventative divine intervention can, however, be seen as Maimonides' way of introducing some element of divine choice into the phenomenon of prophecy. For discussions of Maimonides on prophecy, see Reines 1969, Kellner 1977, Altmann 1978, and Kreisel 2001, chap. 3, among many others.

23. See Kreisel 2001 for a survey of medieval Jewish and Arabic philosophical views on prophecy.

24. TTP I, G III.15; S 9. The word Spinoza uses here for "knowledge" is *cognitio*.

25. TTP I, G III.15; S 9.

26. *Ethics* IIP40s2.

27. TTP I, G III.15; S 9.

28. TTP I, G III.16; S 10.

29. TTP I, G III.21; S 14.

30. TTP I, G III.28; S 20.

31. TTP II, G III.35; S 26.

32. TTP II, G III.35; S 26

33. TTP II, G III.32; S 23.

34. TTP I, G III.28; S 20.

35. For studies of the role of the imagination in Spinoza's epistemology, see Moreau 1994 and Malinowski-Charles 2004.

36. TTP II, G III.31, 37; S 23, 28.

37. TTP I, G III.23; S 16.

38. TTP I, G III.27; S 19. "Exceeding the normal" is Shirley's translation of *supra communem*.

39. TTP II, G III.29; S 21.

40. TTP II, G III.42; S 32–33.

Chapter 5: Miracles

1. Müller 1714, 3. I first learned of Müller's role here from Israel 2001a, 218.

2. Müller 1714, 8.

3. Müller 1714, 13.

4. Israel 2001a, 218.

5. Aubrey 1898, I.357.

6. The doctrine of occasionalism, according to which God is the only causal agent in the universe and all natural phenomena have God's will as their efficacious cause, might be thought to be an exception to this. But even that doctrine's most prominent partisan, Nicolas Malebranche, insisted that the goal of science is to discover the

correlations within nature between events (as they are moved by God) in the physical world, and that appeals to God's will have no place within physics proper.

7. Descartes goes so far as to say that "everything is guided by divine providence, whose eternal decree is infallible and immutable to such an extent that, except for matters it has determined to be dependent on our free will, we must consider everything that affects us to occur of necessity and as it were by fate, so that it would be wrong for us to desire things to happen in any other way" (*Passions of the Soul* II.146, AT XI.439; CSM I.380). It is a further question as to whether this is an example of Descartes paying mere lip service to piety or something he seriously believes.

8. Such considerations were capable of making a programmatic difference for science. Malebranche, for example, just because of his occasionalism, believed that the role of the scientist is not to look for causal powers (all of which lie in God alone) but to investigate nature's regularities (i.e., the effects of divine activity) and formulate the laws that describe them. Metaphysical insights might also make a difference in the conclusions reached by science. Thus, Leibniz insisted that, because Descartes and Malebranche misunderstood the difference in nature of God's activity with respect to motion and rest, they were led to a false account of some of the basic laws of motion and impact. For a discussion of these issues, see Nadler 1998.

9. See, for example, Thomas Aquinas, *Summa Contra Gentiles*, chap. 101, where he distinguishes among three degrees of miracles, according to whether the event is or is not, in principle, within nature's power.

10. Maimonides, *Commentary on the Mishnah*, "Eight Chapters" (Introduction to Pirke Avot), chap. 8; translation from Maimonides 1972, 383.

11. See his *Diverse Thoughts on the Occasion of the Comet*, §§ 65–67.

12. See his reply to Bayle of 1698 (GP IV.520), and *Theodicy*, § 207 (GP VI.240–41). For a discussion of this, see Rutherford 1993.

13. See items 6 and 7 of the summary of the propositions of the *Discourse on Metaphysics* that Leibniz sent to Arnauld (GP II.12).

14. *Metaphysics*, XII.6–7.

15. Ackerman 2009.

16. G I.267; C I.333.

17. TTP VI, G III.81–2; S 71–72.

18. TTP VI, G III.82–3; S 72–73.

19. TTP VI, G III.83; S 73.

20. This is, of course, an unhelpfully brief sketch of the structure of Spinoza's metaphysics. For a more extensive analysis, see Nadler 2006. For alternative accounts, see Curley 1969 and Bennett 1984.

21. *Ethics* IP29.

22. Some scholars are unhappy with reading Spinoza in this way, and they hope to rescue him from necessitarianism. See Curley and Walski 1999. They are responding to Garrett 1991, who argues for a necessitarian reading. The fear is that with necessitarianism comes the loss of a number of crucial distinctions—between necessary and contingent truths, between essential and accidental properties of things—and an inability to account for such important conceptual tools as

counterfactuals; see Bennett 1984, 111–24. Bennett grants, though, that it is hard to avoid the conclusion that Spinoza's considered position ("what Spinoza consciously, explicitly held") was the necessitarian one (123).

23. *Ethics* IP33.

24. G I.266; C I.332.

25. *Ethics* I, Appendix, G II.81; C I.443–44.

26. Spinoza's recognition of this, confirmed for him by the outrage generated by the *Treatise*, certainly contributed to his decision not to publish the *Ethics* in his lifetime.

27. Again, while I reject the Straussian reading of the *Treatise* and the idea that one has to "read between the lines," I do believe that Spinoza does not say in the work everything that he thinks; the view of God and Nature in the *Ethics* is one of the things that Spinoza holds back—not completely, but to a large degree. One difference between my reading and a Straussian reading is that I do not believe that the deeper metaphysical theology is part of some esoteric message of the *Treatise*.

28. TTP VI, G III.83; S 73.

29. Ep. 75, G IV.313; SL 338. Spinoza says *miracula & ignorantiam pro aequipollentibus sumpsi*.

30. TTP VI, G III.83–84; S 73.

31. TTP VI, G III.90; S 79.

32. Most current scholarship on Spinoza on miracles takes this same line, although with subtle differences. See Curley 1985, Walther 1994, Israel 2001a, 218, and Batnitzky 2003–4. For a contrary position, see Hunter 2004, in which it is argued that Spinoza did believe that true miracles are possible.

33. *Enquiry Concerning Human Understanding* X.1, Hume 1975, 114. In a footnote to this page, he provides a more restrictive definition: "a transgression of a law of nature by a particular volition of the Deity, or by the interposition of some invisible agent."

34. I am grateful to Ed Curley for helping me make this point more clear.

35. TTP VI, G III.82–83; S 72–73.

36. TTP VI, G III.87; S 76.

37. Koerbagh 1668, 447: "Mirakel: wonderwerk, wonderdaad. De Godsgeleerden willen dat een wonderwerk zal zijn iets 't geen tegen of boven de natuur geschied 't welk valsch is want daar en kan niet tegen of boven de natuur geschieden."

38. See Vandenbossche 1978, 12.

39. Compare, for example, Reines 1974, where it is argued that Maimonides' true view is that miracles are not possible, with Langermann 2004, in which it is argued that Maimonides' view developed over time, and that in *Guide of the Perplexed* Maimonides does believe that miracles are possible.

40. *Guide* II.29, Maimonides 1963, 345.

41. This is the reading offered by Reines (1974), and I find it a convincing one.

42. *Mishneh Torah*, Hilhot Yesodei ha-Torah, II.2.

43. *Guide* II.28, Maimonides 1963, 335. Ackerman suggests that for Maimonides miracles represent only a temporary change in nature, and that he is still concerned to maintain their possibility, if not their actual occurrence (2009, 377).

A fuller examination of Maimonides on miracles would have to take into account his highly defensive discussion of the miracle of resurrection, particularly in his "Treatise on Resurrection."

44. *Leviathan* III.32, Hobbes 1994, 247–49.

45. *Leviathan* III.37, Hobbes 1994, 293–94.

46. *Leviathan* III.37, Hobbes 1994, 294.

47. See *Leviathan* III.9. Ed Curley has suggested to me that Hobbes' concession that there was a period in the past when miracles did in fact occur should not be taken seriously—since it would mean that it is reasonable to believe in miracles in cases where the evidence is very weak and dependent on very old testimony but not in cases where the evidence is relatively strong (because more recent)—but rather is an accommodation to his more orthodox readers.

48. *Leviathan* III.37, Hobbes 1994, 294.

49. There is great debate among Hobbes scholars on how to read his view on miracles. See Curley 1992, Martinich 1992, and Whipple 2008.

50. *Leviathan* III.37, Hobbes 1994, 296–97.

51. *Leviathan* XXXVII.12, Hobbes, 1994, 299.

52. *Leviathan* III.37, Hobbes 1994, 299.

53. Martinich (1992, 239–41) argues that Hobbes has two conflicting views on miracles, one of which is designed "to reconcile religion with science without compromising science."

54. Maimonides, in fact, downplays the central providential role of miracles and their religious value; see, for example, the passage quoted above from *Mishneh Torah*, Hilhot Yesodei ha-Torah, II.2, as well as VII.7–VIII.3.

55. TTP VI, G III.81; S 71.

56. TTP VI, G III.89; S 78.

57. TTP VI, G III.85–86; S 75.

58. See, for example, Maimonides, *Guide of the Perplexed* III.17–18. For a general study of medieval Jewish rationalist views of providence, see Nadler 2009b.

59. *Ethics* VP6s.

60. *Ethics* IVP67.

61. At one point, Spinoza says that human virtue just *is* happiness: "Blessedness is not the reward of virtue, but virtue itself" (*Ethics* VP42).

62. TTP III, G III.46; S 36.

Chapter 6: Scripture

1. For an extensive survey of this tradition, see Saebø 2000 and 2008.

2. See especially Friedman 1987.

3. *Leviathan* III.xxxiii.21, Hobbes 1994, 259.

4. Babylonian Talmud, Bava Batra 14b.

5. Ibn Ezra 1976, 2:213–15; 2001, 5:3.

6. TTP VIII, G III.118; S 106. For an assessment of Spinoza's reading of Ibn Ezra on the question of Mosaic authorship, see Harvey 2010.

7. See Malcolm 2002, 402–10.

8. Malcolm 2002, 408.

9. Spinoza uses the term 'Pharisees' to refer even to latter-day Jews.

10. TTP VIII, G III.118; S 105.

11. See Zac 1965, 8–9.

12. TTP VII, G III.97; S 86.

13. TTP VII, G III.98; S 87.

14. TTP VIII, G III.122; S 109.

15. TTP VIII, G III.123; S 110.

16. TTP VIII, G III.125; S 112.

17. TTP VIII, G III.125–26; S 112–13.

18. TTP VIII, G III.127; S 113.

19. TTP IX, G III.131; S 118.

20. TTP X, G III.150; S 136.

21. TTP IX, G III.132; S 118.

22. TTP IX, G III.134; S 120–21.

23. TTP IX, G III.133; S 120; the lacuna on the years of Saul's reign is in Spinoza's text.

24. Hobbes, unlike Spinoza, could not have known Ibn Ezra's "arguments" firsthand, since he did not know Hebrew; but it is possible he could have heard about them from others.

25. *Leviathan* III.33, Hobbes 1994, 252–56.

26. Spinoza, of course, rejects the idea that this document has as its original foundation a supernatural act of revelation; most likely, so does Hobbes.

27. *Leviathan* III.33, Hobbes 1994, 259.

28. La Peyrère could have met Hobbes in Paris, as both were members of the intellectual circle of Marin Mersenne, and, as Popkin (1987, 84–6) has speculated, he could have met Spinoza in Amsterdam, through Rabbi Menasseh ben Israel.

29. La Peyrère 1656, 208.

30. La Peyrère 1656, 210.

31. La Peyrère 1656, 208.

32. Popkin 1996, 391.

33. *De Cive* XVII.16.

34. Malcolm (2002, 392, 397) says that "the conclusions to be drawn [about] the relationship between the arguments of Hobbes, La Peyrère, and Spinoza are, at first sight, frustratingly inconclusive," but leans toward the conclusion that Spinoza arrived at his views independently of the others. Smith (1997, 57) says that "the extent of La Peyrère's influence on Spinoza is largely a matter for conjecture." While Popkin (1987) argues for La Peyrère's influence on Spinoza, Curley (1994) rejects the idea.

35. The seventeenth-century exegete Richard Simon says of La Peyrère, "il ne savoit ni Grec ni Hebreu" (Simon 1730, II.30).

36. Popkin (1985, 1996) suggests that the Quaker Samuel Fisher, who was in Amsterdam in the 1650s, should be included among important antecedents and possible influences on Spinoza.

37. TTP IX, G III.133; S 120. Spinoza is here referring to 1 Samuel 13.1, but I believe his point is meant to be generalized to Hebrew Scripture as a whole.

Spinoza's critical attention in the central chapters of the *Treatise* is primarily focused on the books of the Hebrew Bible. He does not subject the Christian gospels to as rigorous or extended a historical examination. Indeed, in contrast to his rather dismissive attitude toward much of Hebrew Scripture and the Old Testament prophets, Spinoza has many positive things to say about the New Testament and its authors. I return to this issue in chapter 7.

38. TTP IX, G III.135; S 122.

39. G I.131; C I.229.

40. *Philosophia S. Scripturis Interpres* (henceforth PSSI), chap. III, sec. 6, Meyer 2005, 44–45.

41. PSSI IV.5, Meyer 2005, 93.

42. PSSI IV.7, Meyer 2005, 97.

43. PSSI V.1, Meyer 2005, 105.

44. PSSI VI.1, Meyer 2005, 113.

45. PSSI, Epilogue, Meyer 2005, 238–39.

46. Meyer 2005, 262. For a discussion of the controversies around the PSSI, see Israel 2001a, 200–217.

47. Luther 1989, 78–79.

48. See his letter to the Grand Duchess Christina, in Galileo 1989, 89–93.

49. G I.265; C I.331.

50. *Guide* I.35, Maimonides 1963, I.81.

51. *Guide* II.25, Maimonides 1963, II.328.

52. For a discussion of Jewish rationalism in the interpretation of Hebrew Scripture, see Nadler 2005a.

53. TTP VII, G III.116; S 102.

54. TTP VII, G III.115; S 102.

55. TTP VII, G III.114; S 101.

56. Spinoza explicitly criticizes this approach for its obscurity in TTP VII, G III.112; S 99.

57. TTP VII, G III.97–98; S 86–87.

58. TTP Preface, G III.9; S 5.

59. TTP VII, G III.100; S 88.

60. TTP VII, G III.111; S 97.

61. TTP VII, G III.98; S 87.

62. TTP VII, G III.99; S 87.

63. There is no copy of this work in Spinoza's library, but we know that he was familiar with it; see Ep. 2, where he is quite critical of Bacon.

64. See Ep. 11 and 13.

65. TTP VII, G III.102; S 90.

66. It is another question whether the scientific method for discovering "definitions" described in the *Treatise* really is consistent both with Spinoza's discussion of scientific method elsewhere and with his account of the knowledge of essences in the *Ethics*. For a discussion of Spinoza on scientific method, see Savan 1986 and Gabbey 1996.

67. See *Principles of Philosophy* II.36–40.

68. TTP VII, G III.98; S 87.
69. TTP VII, G III.99; S 87.
70. TTP VII, G III.112; S 99.
71. PSSI V.1–2, Meyer 2005, 105.
72. PSSI XVI.6, Meyer 2005, 217.
73. TTP VII, G III.117; S 103–4.
74. TTP VII, G III.100; S 88.
75. TTP VII, G III.101–2; S 90.
76. TTP VII, G III.110; S 97.
77. TTP VII, G III.102; S 90.
78. TTP VII, G III.102; S 90–91.
79. TTP VII, G III.102; S 91.

80. *Disputationes Theologiae prior refutatoria libelli de philosophia Interprete Scripturae* (1667), III.11; Maresius was writing, of course, against Meijer's views. For a discussion of Maresius, see Preus 2001, 94–98.

81. TTP VII, G III.100–1; S 89.
82. Ep. 19, G IV.92; SL 135.
83. TTP VII, G III.100–1; S 88–89.
84. TTP VII, G III.103; S 91–92.
85. TTP VII, G III.106; S 94.
86. TTP VII, G III.111; S 98.
87. TTP XII, G III.159; S 146.
88. TTP VII, G III.99; S 88.
89. TTP XII, G III.160; S 146.
90. TTP XII, G III.160; S 147.
91. TTP XII, G III.161; S 147. See also TTP V, G III.79; S 68:

The only value [of historical narratives] lies in the lesson conveyed, in which respect alone some narratives can be superior to others. So the narratives of the Old and New Testament differ in excellence from non-sacred writings and from one another to the extent that they inspire salutary beliefs. Therefore if a man reads the narratives of Holy Scripture and has complete faith in them, and yet pays no heed to the lesson that Scripture thereby aims to convey, and leads no better life, he might just as well have read the Koran or a poetic drama or at any rate ordinary history, giving the same attention as common people do to such writings.

92. TTP V, G III.79; S 68.
93. TTP X, G III.145; S 131.
94. TTP XII, G III.163; S 149.

Chapter 7: Judaism, Christianity, and True Religion

1. Ep. 42, G IV.218; SL 236.
2. Ep. 43, G IV.219; SL 237.
3. Ep. 43, G IV.220; SL 238.

4. TTP V, G III.75; S 64.

5. TTP V, G III.73–74; S 63.

6. TTP V, G III.70; S 60.

7. TTP V, G III.76; S 65.

8. In his correspondence, Spinoza has even harsher things to say about the Eucharist. In a letter to Albert Burgh, a one-time friend and now a devout Catholic convert fervently trying to get Spinoza to give up his evil ways, Spinoza writes, "O young man bereft of understanding, who has bewitched you, so that you believe you are eating that highest and eternal being, and have him in your intestines?" He refers to this sacrament and other Catholic rites as "absurd errors" (Ep. 76, G IV.323). For a study of this letter and what it says about Spinoza's attitude toward Christianity, see Curley 2010.

9. TTP V, G III.78; S 67.

10. TTP IV, G III.60; S 50.

11. For Spinoza's demonstation of this, see *Ethics* IVP31–37. For a discussion of the way in which the pursuit of one's own perfection is supposed to lead to virtuous behavior toward others, see Della Rocca 2004.

12. TTP IV, G III.60–61; S 50–51.

13. TTP IV, G III.68; S 57.

14. TTP IV, G III.61; S 51.

15. *Ethics* IIIP13s. Hate, similarly, is sadness accompanied by a conception of the object that is the cause of sadness. One hates the object that brings about a deterioration in one's condition or the person who causes one harm.

16. *Ethics* VP30.

17. *Ethics* VP27d.

18. *Ethics* VP32s.

19. *Mishneh Torah*, Hilchot Teshuvah, X.1–3.

20. *Mishneh Torah*, Hilchot Teshuvah, X.6.

21. *Guide* III.51, Maimonides 1963, 620.

22. *Guide* III.51, Maimonides 1963, 620.

23. *Guide* III.52, Maimonides 1963, 629.

24. *Guide* III.52, Maimonides 1963, 630.

25. It may be that Maimonides' conception of the fear and awe experienced by the sage is not indicative of a more traditionally religious attitude on Maimonides' part but rather is something for which he can provide a reductive, intellectualist explanation in keeping with his general rationalism; see, for example, *Mishneh Torah*, Hilchot Yesodai ha-Torah, II.1–2. Be that as it may, there is no counterpart—not even a nominal one—in Spinoza to Maimonides' account of the fear and awe experienced by the philosopher and prophet before God.

26. TTP XII, G III.158; S 145.

27. TTP XIII, G III.167; S 153.

28. TTP IV, G III.64; S 53.

29. TTP XIII, G III.171; S 156.

30. TTP XII, G III.165; S 151.

31. TTP XIII, G III.170; S 156.

32. TTP XIII, G III.171; S 156.

33. TTP XIII, G III.171; S 156–57.

34. In supplementary note 34 to the *Treatise*, Spinoza distinguishes obedience proper, which "has regard to the will of him who commands," from the love of God that follows intellectual virtue "in a man who knows God aright" (G III.264; S 238). Thus, strictly speaking, the philosophically virtuous man who acts with true religion and behaves with justice and charity is not doing so out of obedience.

35. TTP XV, G III.188; S 172.

36. TTP XIII, G III.172; S 157.

37. TTP V, G III.79; S 68.

38. TTP V, G III.80; S 70.

39. TTP V, G III.79; S 68.

40. TTP XII, G III.165; S 151.

41. Ep. 73, G IV.307–8; SL 333.

42. TTP XII, G III.159; S 145.

43. For a critical overview of some assessments of Spinoza's relationship to Judaism, see Nadler 2009a.

44. See the letter to Burgh, where he characterizes Roman Catholicism as "pernicious superstition" (Ep. 76, G IV.323).

45. I do not believe, however, that Spinoza's harsh treatment of Judaism in the *Treatise* is to be seen as a strategy of ingratiating himself with Christians by adopting an anti-Semitic attitude.

46. Revah 1959, 67.

47. This raises the question of whether, with the re-establishment of a Jewish state in Israel, Jewish law has regained the political foundation that it lost with the end of the ancient kingdom. I suspect that Spinoza's answer to this is "no." First, without a rebuilding of the Temple and the reinstatement of Temple worship and a priestly caste, all of the commandments related to such matters remain obsolete. Second, the laws instituted by Moses and executed by later Israelite sovereigns were not just laws for *a* Jewish state but for the stability and prosperity of a particular Jewish state under specific historic and geopolitical conditions; these conditions no longer obtain, and so Mosaic law is no longer necessary to provide for the well-being of a Jewish state.

48. TTP V, G III.72; S 62–63.

49. Maimonides, for example, says that election is not instituted by the covenant, but is a reward for observing it. For a discussion of the election of Israel, see Novak 1995.

50. There is a rabbinic tradition according to which God did not choose Israel but Israel chose God; see Babylonian Talmud, Avodah Zerah 2b–3a.

51. *The Kuzari* I.27.

52. TTP III, G III.45; S 36.

53. TTP III, G III.45–46; S 36.

54. TTP III, G III.47; S 37. 'Wise' here is how Curley and Shirley translate *prudens*.

55. This distinction between God's "external" and "internal" help is, I believe, Spinoza's adaptation of what medieval Jewish philosophers called "general providence" and "special providence"; see Nadler 2005b.

56. TTP III, G III.47–48; S 38.

57. TTP III, G III.47–48; S 39.

58. TTP III, G III.50; S 42.

59. TTP III, G III.56; S 45.

60. For a discussion of Spinoza on the election of Israel, see Novak 1995, chap. 1.

61. Bodian 2009.

62. Huygens 1893, VI.81.

63. *Treatise* III, G III.56; S 45.

64. TTP III, G III.57; S 45.

65. TTP III, G III.57; S 45. Spinoza in this passage adds hatred of the Jews (and circumcision) as contributing factors, but it is obvious that hatred of the Jews can exist only once the Jews have constituted themselves as a separate people through their ceremonial laws.

66. TTP V, G III.72; S 62.

67. TTP III, G III.56–57; S 46.

68. For an interesting discussion on these questions of Jewish identity, see Judt 2010. Judt suggests that Judaism (especially in the United States) is, in many respects, no longer a "lived condition" but has been reduced to remembering the Holocaust and "Israelophilia." "Modern-day Jews," he claims, "live in preserved memory. Being Jewish largely consists of remembering what it meant to be Jewish."

69. See Popkin 1984 and 1985.

70. The phrase is from Kolakowski 1969.

71. See, for example, Hunter 2005. For a critical review of Hunter, see Melamed 2007. No one has suggested that Spinoza had anything to do with Catholic Christianity, and for good reason (as he explicitly calls Catholicism a "pernicious superstition" [Ep. 67, G IV.323]). But as Curley (2010) argues, Spinoza not only rejects the Catholic Church, "but does so in terms which imply a rejection of all forms of organized Christianity" (13).

72. TTP XI, G III.155; S 142.

73. TTP XI, G III.155; S 141–42.

74. TTP X, G III.151; S 137.

75. A point nicely made by Frankel (2001).

76. TTP, Supplementary Note 26.

77. TTP VII, G III.100; S 88.

78. See, for example, Pollock 1880, 336–38; Strauss 1997, 21; and Smith 1997, 105. See also Frankel 2001, which addresses this question from a different perspective.

79. Strauss 1947–48, 119–20.

80. I strongly disagree with Strauss (and sympathetic scholars) on this point (see, for example, Smith 1997). Emphasizing one thing rather than another and being reticent on some topics for the sake of reaching your audience is one thing; implanting a secret message behind a more accessible but false cover story out of fear of persecution is another. Nor do I believe that insisting on the exoteric/esoteric distinction in the *Treatise* is necessary for Strauss to make what is admittedly the valuable point that Spinoza's respectful treatment of the Christian

Gospels is a function of his trying not to alienate a potentially sympathetic Christian audience. For an effective critique of Strauss, see Harris 1978.

81. TTP I, G III.19; S 12. It is not clear how this is consistent with Spinoza's assumption that Moses believed God to have no resemblance to visible things.

82. TTP I, G III.20–1; S 13–14.

83. Ep. 73, G IV.309; SL 333.

84. TTP IV, G III.64–65; S 54.

85. TTP V, G III.79; S 68. I thus disagree with the suggestion often made by scholars that Spinoza is not sincere in his praise of Jesus because the things he says about Jesus are inconsistent with his own philosophical tenets. I believe that the things Spinoza says about Jesus, when properly understood, are perfectly consistent with his metaphysical and epistemological views.

86. Ep. 75, G IV.315; SL 338–39.

87. TTP XIV, G III.176; S 161. "Enemy of Christ" is Shirley's translation of *Antichristus*; Curley opts for the more literal "Antichrist."

Chapter 8: Faith, Reason, and the State

1. *Discourse on Method* VI, AT VI.60; CSM I.141–42.

2. *Principles of Philosophy* III.19, AT VIII-1.86; CSM I.251.

3. *Principles of Philosophy* III.26: "The earth is at rest in its own heaven, but nonetheless it is carried along by it."

4. The problem in Descartes's case seems not to have been Copernicanism but the perceived incompatibility of his metaphysics of matter with the Catholic understanding of Eucharistic transubstantiation. For a discussion of this, see Armogathe 1977. For an argument that this same issue was behind the condemnation of Galileo, see Redondi 1989.

5. Malcolm 2002, 45.

6. For an examination of the controversies at Utrecht, see Verbeek 1992.

7. Some of these theologians were even generally sympathetic readers who would become Cartesians themselves, such as the French Jansenist Antoine Arnauld; see his Fourth Objections to Descartes's *Meditations*, AT VII.196–218; CSM II.138–53.

8. Ep. 20, G IV.124–25; SL 150.

9. Ep. 20, G IV.97; SL 137.

10. Ep. 21, G IV.126; SL 151.

11. This point is well put by Strauss (1965).

12. TTP XIV, G III.176; S 161.

13. TTP XIV, G III.177–78; S 162 (translation modified).

14. TTP XIV, G III.178–79; S 162–63.

15. That Spinoza considers these tenets to be strictly necessary conditions for faith is clear from his statement that "faith must be defined as the holding of certain beliefs about God such that, without these beliefs, there cannot be obedience to God, and if this obedience is posited, these beliefs are necessarily posited" (TTP XIV, G III.175; S 160).

16. TTP, Supplementary Note 34, G III.264; S 238–39. This is among the *adnotationes* that Spinoza composed after the publication of the *Treatise* and which he intended to be incorporated into a subsequent edition. For a discussion of their composition and status, see Akkerman 2005.

17. For a good discussion of this point, see Garber 2008, 175–76.

18. TTP XIII, G III.170; S 156.

19. TTP XIV, G III.179–80; S 164.

20. TTP XIV, G III.179; S 164. The Latin says that *inter fidem sive Theologiam & Philosophiam nullum esse commercium nullamve affinitatem.*

21. Letter to the Grand Duchess Christina (Galileo 1989, 96).

22. At one point in *Leviathan*, Hobbes suggests that a state of nature not only has existed in the past, but currently exists in the present, among "the savage people in many places in America" (I.13, Hobbes 1994, 77).

23. *Leviathan* I.13, Hobbes 1994, 76. There are some differences between Hobbes' account of the state in *De Cive* and his account in *Leviathan*, in some cases for historical reasons; see Sommerville 1992. For my purposes here, these differences are trivial.

24. See *De Cive* III.

25. *De Cive* V.5, Hobbes 1991, 169.

26. For comparative discussions of Spinoza and Hobbes, see Matheron 1969, 151–79; Machery 1992; Curley 1992, 1996a, and 1996c; Malcolm 2002, chap. 2; and Verbeek 2003. Verbeek suggests that the *Treatise* is, among other things, a commentary on *Leviathan* (8–10). There is an entire issue of *Studia Spinozana* (1987) devoted to Spinoza and Hobbes.

27. *Ethics* IVP37s2.

28. TTP XVI, G III.190; S 174,

29. *Ethics* IVP35s.

30. TTP XVI, G III.191; S 175.

31. Actually, Spinoza does believe that there was a historical moment that very closely approximated the theoretical state of nature. When Moses led the Israelites out of Egypt, their condition was tantamount to a state of nature, since they were citizens of no commonwealth and thus were without any government or sovereign.

32. TTP XVI, G III.192; S 176. See also *Ethics* IVP72, where he says that a person guided by reason will never lie.

33. TTP V, G III.73; S 63.

34. *Ethics* IVP37s2.

35. TTP XVI, G III.193–94; S 177.

36. For an argument that Hobbes was not, in fact, a totalitarian, but rather allows for a significant degree of toleration in the state, see Ryan 1988 and Curley 2007.

37. This is not, of course, the only difference between Spinoza and Hobbes in political theory. For example, as both Curley (1996c) and Malcolm (2002) point out, for Hobbes one transfers to the state one's rights, whereas for Spinoza what is conveyed is power; Spinoza himself remarks on this as "the difference between Hobbes and myself" (Ep. 50). And Spinoza certainly allows for more freedoms among citizens—including, most importantly, freedom of expression—than Hobbes.

38. TTP XVI, G III.194; S 177.

39. I must confess I am not sure how to reconcile this with Spinoza's claim, noted earlier, that in the state the citizens have transferred "all their right" to the sovereign. Presumably there is a distinction between the *power* conferred on the sovereign and *right* reserved to the citizen. But Spinoza's frequent conflation of power and right only confuses the issue.

40. Hobbes, in fact, would agree with this. The more a sovereign exercises arbitrary power or issues commands that are contrary to the interests of the people, the more difficult it will be to sustain its authority; see Hobbes 1990, 62.

41. TTP XVI, G III.194; S 178.

42. *Ethics* IVP34, 35.

43. TTP XVI, G III.194; S 178. Curley (1996c, 317–18) suggests that Spinoza's confidence in democracy is incongruent with his low opinion of the multitude.

44. TTP V, G III.74; S 63–64.

45. TTP XVI, G III.195; S 179.

46. TP I.1, G III.273; SM 680.

47. See, for example, Locke's *Two Treatises of Government*. However, there is a great deal of debate among Locke scholars as to whether Locke, when he says that government has "no other end but preservation," means that the state's only role is to protect the rights of individuals from infringement by others (what Isaiah Berlin calls "negative liberty") or that the state is to provide positive conditions for the public good; see, for example, Nozick 1974 and Tuckness 2002.

48. TTP XX, G III.240–41; S 223.

49. TP VI.3, G III.297–98; SM 701.

50. TP V.3, G III.295; SM 699. For an excellent study of this aspect of Spinoza's political thought, see Steinberg 2009. That Spinoza, on the other hand, more properly fits in the classical liberal tradition is argued by Den Uyl (1983) and Smith (1997).

51. It is commonly assumed that this represents another important difference between Spinoza and Hobbes, for whom (it is claimed) the state's role is simply to provide safety and security and to protect the lives and possessions of citizens from the predation of others. To the extent that this is true, Spinoza's view again is closer to that of the De la Court brothers, for whom a good state makes its citizens more rational and virtuous and thereby increases their freedom; see Nyden-Bullock 1999. I am not convinced, however, that this is an accurate reading of Hobbes. In *De Cive*, he insists that by the "safety" provided by the state what is meant is "not the sole preservation of life in what condition soever, but in order to its happiness. For to this end did men freely assemble themselves and institute a government, that they might, as much as their human condition would afford, live delightfully." The sovereign, in other words, is to act so that its subjects "may be strong in body and mind" (XIII.4, Hobbes 1991, 259). In fact, for Hobbes the sovereign is to exercise control over the teaching of religious and moral doctrines, insofar as it sees itself as responsible not only for the temporal happiness and well-being of its citizens but for their eternal salvation as well (XIII.5; XV.16–18).

Chapter 9: *Libertas philosophandi*

1. Letter to Danbury Baptist Association, 1802.

2. Goldstein 2006, 11.

3. TTP VII, G III.117; S 103.

4. TTP XIX, G III.232; S 215–16.

5. TTP XIX, G III.232–33; S 216.

6. TTP XIX, G III.229; S 213.

7. See Malcolm 2002, 41.

8. *Leviathan* III.29.v, Hobbes 1994, 316.

9. It might be argued that what Spinoza is insisting upon is something weaker than this: not a single form of public worship but only the idea that all forms of public worship—and there may be many—must nonetheless be consistent with the civil laws and public welfare, as these are determined by the sovereign. Thus, he says that "no one can obey God unless his practice of piety . . . conforms with the public good" (TTP XIX, G III.232; S 216). Rather than being the establisher of religion, government would thereby be only its watchdog. But it seems to me that Spinoza does intend the stronger claim, that there is to be only one form of public worship, when he says, just before that passage, that "it is the duty of the sovereign alone to decide what form piety towards one's neighbor should take." On the other hand, as Michael Della Rocca has pointed out to me, the form of public worship dictated by the state may be so generic that it is compatible with a plurality of religions (though not with all religions), with the result that Spinoza's ideal state may, in the end, be tolerant of a wide variety of illegitimate religious devotions as long as those are consistent with the general form of worship that the state requires.

10. In the *Political Treatise*, Spinoza does allow that there can be independent religious sects in the state. However, there will be restrictions: "Large congregations should be forbidden, and so, while those who are attached to another religion [besides the state religion] are to be allowed to build as many churches as they wish, they are to be small, of some fixed dimensions, and some distance apart." The houses of worship of the "national religion," by contrast, "should be large and costly" (VIII.46, G III.345; SM 740).

11. *De Cive* VI.11, Hobbes 1991, 179–80: "For no man can serve two masters; nor is he less, but rather more a master, whom we believe we are to obey for fear of damnation, than he whom we obey for fear of temporal death."

12. TTP XIX, G III.235; S 218.

13. TTP XVII, G III.221; S 203–4.

14. TTP XVIII, G III.225; S 208.

15. TTP XVIII, G III.222; S 205–6.

16. Among those who argue for Spinoza's political thought as a liberalism are Feuer (1958), Den Uyl and Warner (1987), and Smith (1997).

17. See also TTP XX, G III.247; S 229. Some good recent discussions of Spinoza and toleration are Rosenthal 2000, 2001, and 2003 and Steinberg 2010.

18. TTP XX, G III.239; S 222.

19. TTP XX, G III.240; S 223.

20. Hobbes explicitly denies freedom of speech, and insists that the sovereign should exercise careful control over what ideas are expressed in the commonwealth. "It is annexed to the sovereignty to be judge of what opinions and doctrines are averse, and what conducing, to peace; and consequently, on what occasions, how far, and what men are to be trusted withal, in speaking to multitudes of people, and who shall examine the doctrines of all books before they be published" (*Leviathan* II.xvii.9; Hobbes 1994, 113).

21. TTP XX, G III.240; S 223.

22. TTP XX, G III.243; S 226.

23. TTP XX, G III.243; S 226.

24. TTP XX, G III.245; S 227.

25. From Locke's "A Third Letter for Toleration," quoted in Israel 2001a, 266. For a comparative discussion of Locke and Spinoza on toleration, see Israel 2001a, 265–70.

26. TTP XX, G III.241; S 224.

27. TTP XX, G III.242; S 225 (my emphasis).

28. It is not clear, then, that Spinoza's position really amounts to the view, as Israel (for example) reads it, that the expression of opinions "only becomes subversive and hence liable for punishment . . . if it directly obstructs implementation of laws and decrees" (2006, 158; see also Balibar 1998, 27).

29. In this respect, it may be that while Spinoza's views on toleration seem much more liberal than those of Hobbes, when the sovereign's ability to censor ideas in the name of public peace and political stability are taken into account, the two thinkers in fact are not that far apart; see note 20 above.

30. TTP XX, G III.241; S 224.

31. It might be argued that Spinoza does, in fact, draw the line between what the sovereign can and cannot legitimately monitor between ideas and action because the *expression* of ideas falls under the latter (since such expression, whether in speech or in a publication, is a public act). It would then be perfectly consistent with his principles of toleration for Spinoza to allow the sovereign to censor speech; this is how Garber (2008, 170), at least, sees it. However, Spinoza does not actually argue in this way. He does not say that the expression of ideas is an action, and therefore is in the domain of the sovereign's control. Rather, he argues that those expressions that have an "action that is implicit therein"—that is, speech that is a call or incitement to action—are subject to government control, and thus he maintains the distinction between ideas (and their expression) and action.

32. TTP XX, G III.243; S 225.

33. TTP XX, G III.245–46; S 228.

34. TTP XX, G III.247; S 229.

Chapter 10: The Onslaught

1. His full name was Jan Rieuwertszoon, or "Rieuwert's son."

2. For Rieuwertsz's biography, see Meinsma 1983, 118–20, and Manusov-Verhage 2005.

3. See Manusov-Verhage 2005, 245–46.

4. Meinsma 1983, 118.

5. Meinsma 1983, 276.

6. See Israel 2001b.

7. For a study of book censorship in the seventeenth-century Dutch Republic, see Groenveld 1987.

8. See the chart in Groenveld 1987, 74.

9. Meinsma 1983, 275–76.

10. Meinsma 1983, 276.

11. This, at least, is the suggestion by Manusov-Verhage 2005, 238. For questions about the printing of the *Treatise*, see Gerritsen 2005. Gerritsen suggests that the printer was Johannes van Sommeren, while Meinsma (1983, 276) and Bamberger (2003), following Colerus's early account, claim that it was Christoffel Koenraad, on the Egelentiersgracht.

12. See Manusov-Verhage 2005, 244–45, and Singer 1937–38.

13. Stouppe 1673, 66. On Stouppe and his reaction to the *Treatise*, see Popkin 1995. Popkin is wrong, however, to call Stouppe's 1673 treatise "the first published reaction" to the *Treatise*, since Melchior's "refutation" was published in 1671.

14. Freudenthal 1899, doc. III.6, 193.

15. Meinsma 1983, 279–80.

16. Israel 2001a, 210.

17. See Otto 1994, 18–20.

18. Leibniz 1923–, I.1.142.

19. See Leibniz's letter to Thomasius of September 1670 in Leibniz 1993, 261. Laerke (2008, 96), however, suggests that Leibniz was at this time not entirely confident in Graevius's identification of Spinoza as the author. Goldenbaum (1999) believes that Leibniz knew Spinoza's identity even earlier, soon after acquiring the book.

20. Ep. 46.

21. FW, docs. 88 and 89, I.287–88.

22. FW, docs. 90–92, I.288–89.

23. FW, doc. 94, I.290.

24. FW, doc. 96, I.291–92.

25. FW, doc. 98, I.293–94.

26. FW, doc. 99, I.295.

27. This is the suggestion by Israel 2001a, 277.

28. Israel (1996) suggests that "the reluctance of the States of Holland to issue a new edict . . . presumably was due, at least in some measure, to a lack of enthusiasm on De Witt's part" (10).

29. FW, doc. 103, I.299.

30. FW, doc. 104, I.300.

31. FW, doc. 101, I.298.

32. FW, doc. 105, I.301.

33. FW, doc. 113, I.311.

34. Israel 1996, 10.

35. Israel (1996) insists that "Spinoza's *Tractatus Theologico-Politicus* was never freely in circulation, or on sale, in the United Provinces, not even in the first few months after its publication, even though there was no formal ban against the work by the States of Holland until July 1674" (10–11).

36. For a study of editions of the *Treatise*, see Kingma and Offenberg 1977 and Israel 2001a, 279–83.

37. FW, doc. 115, I.313.

38. FW, doc. 106, I.302.

39. Meinsma (1983) suggests this was because Rieuwertsz sent most of his early stock abroad, so as to have few enough on hand to make it plausible when he told the authorities that it was published not in his shop but in Hamburg (279). For a study of early reactions to the TTP by Dutch intellectuals, see Israel 2010.

40. Leibniz 1923–, II.1(2).106.

41. Ep. 45.

42. FW, I.138.

43. On Bredenburg's critique of Spinoza, see Van Bunge 1989, Van Bunge 1995, and Scribano 1995.

44. Israel 2001a, 348–49.

45. Ep. 30.

46. Ep. 71.

47. Ep. 74.

48. Ep. 75.

49. FW, I.138.

50. Van Mansvelt 1674, 259.

51. G IV.218; SL 236.

52. Ep. 68.

53. Van Velthuysen wrote his *Dissertatio de usu rationis in rebus theologicis* in 1668. For a discussion of this aspect of Van Velthuysen's critique of Spinoza, see Van Bunge 1995, 57. See also Blom 1991.

54. Israel 2001a, 278.

55. Ep. 43, G IV.219; SL 237.

56. See, for example, his response (in the first paragraph of a letter to Ostens) to Velthuysen's critique: "I shall . . . show how perversely he has misinterpreted by meaning—whether from malice or ignorance, I cannot say" (Ep. 43).

57. Ep. 50.

58. Ep. 68.

59. These were certainly acquaintances of Spinoza, either Johannes Bouw-meester or (more likely) Jan Hendriksz Glazenmaker, commissioned by Rieuwertsz.

60. Ep. 44.

61. For the text of van Neercassel's report, see Manusov-Verhage 2005, 238.

62. Isaac Orobio de Castro, a member of the Amsterdam Portuguese congrega-tion, did compose a work in which he offers a critique of the *Ethics*—the *Certamen*

Philosophicum Propugnatae Veritatis Divinae ac Naturalis Adversus J. Bredenburgi Principia, published in 1684—but Orobio's case is an exception, and his concern was not with the *Treatise*.

63. The most thorough and important examination of the legacy of the *Treatise* is Israel 2001a and 2006. See also Smith 1997, chap. 7, and Sorkin 2010.

64. Ep. 30.

Bibliography

Ackerman, Ari. 2009. "Miracles." In *The Cambridge History of Jewish Philosophy: From Antiquity Through the Seventeenth Century*, ed. Steven Nadler and Tamar Rudavsky, 362–87. Cambridge: Cambridge University Press.

Akkerman, Fokke. 2005. "*Tractatus theologico-politicus*: Texte latin, traductions néerlandaises et *Adnotationes*." In *Spinoza to the Letter: Studies in Words, Texts and Books*, ed. Fokke Akkerman and Piet Steenbakkers, 209–36. Leiden: Brill.

Altmann, Alexander. 1978. "Maimonides and Thomas Aquinas: Natural or Divine Prophecy?" *Association for Jewish Studies Review* 3:1–19.

Armogathe, Jean-Robert. 1977. *Theologia Cartesiana: L'Explication physique de l'Eucharistie chez Descartes et Dom Desgabets*. The Hague: Martinus Nijhoff.

Aubrey, John. 1898. *Brief Lives*. Ed. Andrew Clark. Oxford: Clarendon Press.

Balibar, Etienne. 1998. *Spinoza and Politics*. London: Verso.

Bamberger, Fritz. 2003. *Spinoza and Anti-Spinoza Literature: The Printed Literature of Spinozism, 1665–1832*. Cincinnati: Hebrew Union College Press.

Batnitzky, Leora. 2003–4. "Spinoza's Critique of Miracles." *Cardozo Law Review* 25:507–18.

Bennett, Jonathan. 1984. *A Study of Spinoza's Ethics*. Indianapolis: Hackett.

Blom, Hans. 1981. "Spinoza en De La Court." *Mededelingen vanwege het Spinozahuis* 42.

———. 1991. "Lambert van Velthuysen et le naturalisme." *Cahiers Spinoza* 6:203–12.

Bodian, Miriam. 2009. "Crypto-Jewish Criticism of Tradition and Its Echoes in Jewish Communities." In *Religion or Ethnicity? Jewish Identities in Evolution*, ed. Zvi Gitelman, 35–58. New Brunswick, NJ: Rutgers University Press.

Chalier, Catherine. 2006. *Spinoza, Lecteur de Maïmonide*. Paris: Cerf.

Curley, Edwin. 1969. *Spinoza's Metaphysics: An Essay in Interpretation*. Cambridge, MA: Harvard University Press.

———. 1985. "Spinoza on Miracles." In *Proceedings of the First Italian International Congress on Spinoza*, ed. E. Giancotti, 421–38. Naples: Bibliopolis.

———. 1990a. "Notes on a Neglected Masterpiece II: The *Theological-Political Treatise* as a Prolegomenon to the *Ethics*." In *Central Themes in Early Modern Philosophy*, ed. J. A. Cover and M. Kulstad, 109–60. Indianapolis: Hackett.

———. 1990b. "*Homo Audax*: Leibniz, Oldenburg, and the TTP." *Studia Leibnitiana Supplementa: Leibniz' Auseinandersetzung mit Vorgängern und Zeitgenossen*, ed. Ingrid Marchewitz and Albert Heinekamp, 277–312. Stuttgart: Franz Steiner Verlag.

———. 1992. "'I Durst Not Write So Boldly,' or, How to Read Hobbes' Theological-Political Treatise." In *Hobbes e Spinoza*, ed. E. Giancotti. Naples: Bibliopolis.

————. 1994. "Notes on a Neglected Masterpiece: Spinoza and the Science of Hermeneutics." In *Spinoza: The Enduring Questions*, ed. Graeme Hunter, 64–99. Toronto: University of Toronto Press.

————. 1996a. "Calvin and Hobbes, or, Hobbes as an Orthodox Christian." *Journal of the History of Philosophy* 34:257–71.

————. 1996b. "Reply to Professor Martinich." *Journal of the History of Philosophy* 34:285–87.

————. 1996c. "Kissinger, Spinoza and Genghis Khan." In *The Cambridge Companion to Spinoza*, ed. Don Garrett 1996, 315–42. Cambridge: Cambridge University Press.

————. 2007. "Hobbes and the Cause of Religious Toleration." In *The Cambridge Companion to Hobbes' Leviathan*, ed. Patricia Springborg, 309–36. Cambridge: Cambridge University Press.

————. 2010. "Spinoza's Exchange with Albert Burgh." In *Spinoza's Theological-Political Treatise: A Critical Guide*, ed. Yitzhak Melamed and Michael Rosenthal, 11–28. Cambridge: Cambridge University Press.

Curley, Edwin, and Gregory Walski. 1999. "Spinoza's Necessitarianism Reconsidered." In *New Essays on the Rationalists*, ed. Rocco J. Gennaro and Charles Huenemann, 241–62. Oxford: Oxford University Press.

Della Rocca, Michael. 2004. "Egoism and the Imitation of Affects in Spinoza." In *Spinoza on Reason and the "Free Man,"* ed. Yirmiyahu Yovel and Gideon Segal, 123–48. New York: Little Room Press.

Den Uyl, Douglas. 1983. *Power, State and Freedom: An Interpretation of Spinoza's Political Philosophy*. Assen: Van Gorcum.

Den Uyl, Douglas, and Stuart D. Warner. 1987. "Liberalism and Hobbes and Spinoza." *Studia Spinozana* 3:261–317.

Descartes, René. 1974–83. *Oeuvres de Descartes*. 12 vols. Ed. Charles Adam and Paul Tannery. Paris: J. Vrin.

————. 1985. *The Philosophical Writings of Descartes*. 2 vols. Trans. John Cottingham, Robert Stoothoff, and Dugald Murdoch. Cambridge: Cambridge University Press.

Feuer, Lewis Samuel. 1958. *Spinoza and the Rise of Liberalism*. Boston: Beacon Press.

Fraenkel, Carlos. 2006. "Maimonides' God and Spinoza's *Deus sive Natura*." *Journal of the History of Philosophy* 44:169–215.

Frankel, Steven. 1999. "Politics and Rhetoric: The Intended Audience of Spinoza's *Tractatus Theologico-Politicus*." *Review of Metaphysics* 52:897–924.

————. 2001. "The Invention of Liberal Theology: Spinoza's Theological-Political Analysis of Moses and Jesus." *Review of Politics* 63:287–315.

Freudenthal, Jakob. 1899. *Die Lebensgeschichte Spinoza's in Quellenschriften, Urkunden und Nichtamtlichen Nachrichten*. Leipzig: Verlag Von Veit.

Freudenthal, Jakob (and Manfred Walther). 2006. *Die Lebensgeschichte Spinozas. Zweite, stark erweiterte und vollständig neu kommentierte Auflage der Ausgabe von Jakob Freudenthal*, 2 vols. Stuttgart: Frommann-Holzboog.

Friedman, Richard Elliott. 1987. *Who Wrote the Bible?* New York: Simon and Schuster.

Gabbey, Alan. 1996. "Spinoza Natural Science and Methodology." In *The Cambridge Companion to Spinoza*, ed. Don Garrett, 142–91. Cambridge: Cambridge University Press.

Galileo Galilei. 1989. *The Galileo Affair: A Documentary History*, ed. Maurice A. Finocchiaro. Berkeley and Los Angeles: University of California Press.

Garber, Daniel. 2008. "Should Spinoza Have Published His Philosophy?" In *Interpreting Spinoza: Critical Essays*, ed. Charlie Huenemann. New York: Cambridge University Press.

Garrett, Don. 1991. "Spinoza's Necessitarianism." In *God and Nature in Spinoza's Metaphysics*, ed. Yirmiyahu Yovel. Leiden: Brill.

Gerritsen, Johan. 2005. "Printing Spinoza: Some Questions." In *Spinoza to the Letter: Studies in Words, Texts and Books*, ed. Fokke Akkerman and Piet Steenbakkers, 251–62. Leiden: Brill.

Goldenbaum, Ursula. 1999. "Die *Commentatiuncula de judice* als Leibnizens erste philosophische Auseinandersetzung mit Spinoza nebst der Mitteilung über ein neuaufgefundenes Leibnizstück." In *Labora Diligenter: Potsdamer Arbeitstagung zur Leibnizforschung*, ed. Martin Fontius, Hartmut Rudolph, and Gary Smits. *Studia Leibnitiana Sonderheft* 29:61–107. Stuttgart: Franz Steiner.

Goldstein, Rebecca Newberger. 2006. *Betraying Spinoza: The Renegade Jew Who Gave Us Modernity*. New York: Shocken Books.

Groenveld, S. 1987. "The Mecca of Authors? States Assemblies and Censorship in the Seventeenth-Century Dutch Republic." In *Too Mighty to Be Free: Censorship and the Press in Britain and the Netherlands*, ed. A. C. Duke and C. A. Tamse. Zutphen: De Walburg.

Harris, Errol. 1978. "Is There an Esoteric Doctrine in the *Tractatus Theologico-Politicus?*" *Mededelingen vanwege het Spinozahuis* 38. Leiden: Brill.

Harvey, Warren Zev. 1981. "A Portrait of Spinoza as a Maimonidean." *Journal of the History of Philosophy* 19:151–72.

———. 2010. "Spinoza on Ibn Ezra's "Secret of the Twelve." In *Spinoza's Theological-Political Treatise: A Critical Guide*, ed. Yitzhak Melamed and Michael Rosenthal, 41–55. Cambridge: Cambridge University Press.

Hobbes, Thomas. 1990. *Behemoth*. Ed. Stephen Holmes. Chicago: University of Chicago Press.

———. 1991. *Man and Citizen*. Ed. Bernard Gert. Indianapolis: Hackett.

———. 1994. *Leviathan*. Ed. Edwin Curley. Indianapolis: Hackett.

Hsia, R. Po-Chia, and H.F.K. Van Nierop. 2002. *Calvinism and Religious Toleration in the Dutch Golden Age*. Cambridge: Cambridge University Press.

Hume, David. 1975. *Enquiries Concerning Human Understanding and Concerning the Principles of Morals*. Ed. L. A. Selby-Bigge. Oxford: Oxford University Press.

Hunter, Graeme. 2004. "Spinoza on Miracles." *International Journal for Philosophy of Religion* 56:41–51.

———. 2005. *Radical Protestantism in Spinoza's Thought*. Hampshire, UK: Ashgate.

Huygens, Christiaan. 1893. *Oeuvres completes*. 22 vols. The Hague: Martinus Nijhoff.

Ibn Ezra, Abraham. 1976. *Perushei ha-Torah*. 2 vols. Jerusalem: Mossad Harav Kook.

————. 2001. *Commentary on the Pentateuch.* 5 vols. Ed. H. Norman Strickman and Arthur M. Silver. New York: Menorah.

Israel, Jonathan. 1995. *The Dutch Republic: Its Rise, Greatness, and Fall, 1477–1806.* Oxford: Oxford University Press.

————. 1996. "The Banning of Spinoza's Works in the Dutch Republic (1670–1678). In *Disguised and Overt Spinozism Around 1700,* ed. Wiep van Bunge and Wim Klever, 3–14. Leiden: Brill.

————. 2001a. *Radical Enlightenment: Philosophy and the Making of Modernity 1650–1750.* Oxford: Oxford University Press.

————. 2001b. "The Publishing of Forbidden Philosophical Works in the Dutch Republic (1666–1710) and their European Distribution." In *The Bookshop of the World: The Role of the Low Countries in the Book Trade 1473–1941,* ed. Lotte Hellinga, Alastair Duke, Jacob Harskamp, and Theo Hermans, 233–43. Houten: Hes & De Graaf.

————. 2006. *Enlightenment Contested: Philosophy, Modernity and the Emancipation of Man 1670–1752.* Oxford: Oxford University Press.

————. 2010. "The Early Dutch and German Reaction to the *Tractatus Theologico-Politicus*: Foreshadowing the Enlightenment's More General Spinoza Reception." In *Spinoza's* Theological-Political Treatise: *A Critical Guide,* ed. Yitzhak Melamed and Michael Rosenthal, 72–100. Cambridge: Cambridge University Press.

Jongeneelen, Gerrit H. 1987. "An Unknown Pamphlet of Adriaan Koerbagh." *Studia Spinozana* 78:405–15.

Judt, Tony. 2010. "On Being Austere and Being Jewish." *New York Review of Books,* May 13, 20–22.

Kellner, Menachem. 1977. "Maimonides and Gersonides on Mosaic Prophecy." *Speculum* 52:62–79.

Kingma, J., and A. Offenberg. 1977. "Bibliography of Spinoza's Works Up to 1800." *Studia Rosenthaliana* 11:1–32.

Koerbagh, Adriaen. 1668. *Een Bloemhof van allerley lieflijkheyd sonder verdriet.* Amsterdam.

————. 1974. *Een Ligt schijnende in duystere plaatsen.* Ed. H. Vandenbosche. Brussels.

Kogan, Barry. 2009. "Understanding Prophecy: Four Traditions." In *The Cambridge History of Jewish Philosophy: From Antiquity through the Seventeenth Century,* ed. Steven Nadler and Tamar Rudavsky, 481–523. Cambridge: Cambridge University Press.

Kolakowski, Leszek 1969. *Chrétiens sans Eglise.* Paris: Gallimard.

Kreisel, Howard. 1984. "Miracles in Medieval Jewish Philosophy." *The Jewish Quarterly Review* 75:99–133.

————. 2001. *Prophecy: The History of an Idea in Medieval Jewish Philosophy.* Dordrecht: Kluwer.

Laerke, Møgens. 2008. *Leibniz Lecteur de Spinoza: La genèse d'une opposition complexe.* Paris: Honoré Champion.

Lagrée, Jacqueline. 1988. "Sens et verité: Philosophie et théologie chez L. Meyer et Spinoza." *Studia Spinozana* 4:75–89.

————. 2004. *Spinoza et le débat religieux.* Rennes: Presses Universitaires de Rennes.

Langermann, Y. Tzvi. 2004. "Maimonides and Miracles: The Growth of a (Dis)
Belief." *Jewish History* 18:147–72.

La Peyrère, Isaac. 1656. *Men before Adam*. London.

Leibniz, Gottfried Wilhelm. 1875–90. *Philosophische Schriften*. 7 vols. Ed. C. I.
Gerhardt. Berlin: Weidman.

———. 1923–. *Samtliche Schriften und Briefe*. Berlin: Akademie-Verlag.

———. 1993. *Leibniz-Thomasius. Correspondance 1663–1672*. Ed. R. Bodéus. Paris:
J. Vrin.

Levene, Nancy. 2004. *Spinoza's Revelation: Religion, Democracy, and Reason*. Cambridge: Cambridge University Press.

Levy, Ze'ev. 1989. *Baruch or Benedict: On Some Jewish Aspects of Spinoza's Philosophy*.
Frankfurt: Peter Lang.

Luther, Martin. 1989. *Basic Theological Writings*. Ed. Timothy F. Will. Minneapolis:
Fortress.

Machery, Pierre. 1992. "A Propos de la différence entre Hobbes et Spinoza." In
Hobbes e Spinoza: Scienza e Politica, ed. Daniela Bostrenghi, 689–98. Napoli:
Bibliopolis.

Maimonides. 1963. *Guide of the Perplexed*. 2 vols. Trans. Shlomo Pines. Chicago:
University of Chicago Press.

———. 1972. *A Maimonides Reader*, ed. Isidore Twersky. West Orange, NJ:
Behrman.

Malcolm, Noel. 2002. *Aspects of Hobbes*. Oxford: Clarendon Press.

Malinowski-Charles, Syliane. 2004. *Affects et conscience chez Spinoza*. Hildesheim: Olms.

Manusov-Verhage, Clasina G. 2005. "Jan Rieuwertzs, marchand libraire et éditeur
de Spinoza." In *Spinoza to the Letter: Studies in Words, Texts and Books*, ed. Fokke
Akkerman and Piet Steenbakkers, 237–50. Leiden: Brill.

Martinich, A. P. 1992. *The Two Gods of Leviathan: Thomas Hobbes on Religion and
Politics*. Cambridge: Cambridge University Press.

Matheron, Alexandre. 1969. *Individu et communauté chez Spinoza*. Paris: Editions de
Minuit.

———. 1971. *Le Christ et le salut des ignorants chez Spinoza*. Paris: Aubier.

Meinsma, K. O. 1983. *Spinoza et son cercle*. Ed. Henri Méchoulan and Pierre-
François Moreau. Paris: Vrin.

Melamed, Yitzhak. 2007. Review of Hunter 2005. *Journal of the History of Philosophy*
45:333–34.

Mendes, David Franco. 1975. *Memorias do estabelecimento e progresso dos Judeos Portu-
guezes e Espanhoes nesta famosa citade de Amsterdam. Studia Rosenthaliana 9*.

Meyer, Lodewijk. 2005. *Philosophy as the Interpreter of Holy Scripture*. Trans. Samuel
Shirley. Milwaukee, WI: Marquette University Press.

Moreau, Pierre-François. 1994. *Spinoza: L'Expérience et l'éternité*. Paris: Presses Universitaires de France.

Müller, Johann Heinrich. 1714. *Dissertatio Inauguralis Philosophica de Miraculis*,
Altdorf (Pitts Theological Library, Emory University, Atlanta).

Nadler, Steven. 1998. "Doctrines of Explanation in Late Scholasticism and in
the Mechanical Philosophy." In *The Cambridge History of Seventeenth-Century*

Philosophy, 2 vols., ed. Daniel Garber and Michael Ayers, 1:513–52. Cambridge: Cambridge University Press.

———. 1999. *Spinoza: A Life*. Cambridge: Cambridge University Press.

———. 2002. *Spinoza's Heresy: Immortality and the Jewish Mind*. Oxford: Oxford University Press.

———. 2005a. "Rationalism in Jewish Philosophy." In *A Companion to Rationalism*, ed. Alan Nelson, 100–18. Malden, MA: Blackwell.

———. 2005b. "Spinoza's Theory of Divine Providence: Rationalist Solutions, Jewish Sources." *Mededelingen vanwege Het Spinozahuis* 87.

———. 2006. *Spinoza's Ethics: An Introduction*. Cambridge: Cambridge University Press.

———. 2009a. "The Jewish Spinoza." *Journal of the History of Ideas* 70:491–510.

———. 2009b. "Theodicy and Providence." In *The Cambridge History of Jewish Philosophy: From Antiquity through the Seventeenth Century*, ed. Steven Nadler and Tamar Rudavsky, 619–58. Cambridge: Cambridge University Press.

Novak, David. 1995. *The Election of Israel: The Idea of the Chosen People*. Cambridge: Cambridge University Press.

Nozick, Robert. 1974. *Anarchy, State and Utopia*. New York: Basic Books.

Nussbaum, Martha. 1986. *The Fragility of Goodness: Luck and Ethics in Greek Philosophy and Tragedy*. Cambridge: Cambridge University Press.

Nyden-Bullock, Tammy. 1999. "Radical Cartesian Politics: Velthuysen, De la Court and Spinoza." *Studia Spinozana* 15:35–65.

Otto, Rüdiger. 1994. *Studien zur Spinozarezeption in Deutschland im 18. Jahrhundert*. Bern: Peter Lang.

Pines, Shlomo. 1997. "Spinoza's *Tractatus Theologico-Politicus*, Maimonides, and Kant." In *Studies in the History of Jewish Thought*, ed. W. Z. Harvey and M. Idel, 660–711. Jerusalem: Magnes Press.

Pollock, Frederick. 1880. *Spinoza: His Life and Philosophy*. London: Kegan Paul.

Popkin, Richard. 1984. "Spinoza's Relations with the Quakers in Amsterdam." *Quaker History* 73:14–28.

Popkin, Richard. 1985. "Spinoza and Samuel Fisher." *Philosophia* 15:219–36.

———. 1987. *Isaac La Peyrère (1596–1676): His Life, Work and Influence*. Leiden: Brill.

———. 1995. "The First Published Reaction to Spinoza's *Tractatus*: Col. J. B. Stouppe, the Condé Circle, and the Rev. Jean LeBrun." In *L'Hérésie Spinoziste: La discussion sur le Tractatus Theologico-Politicus, 1670-1677*, ed. Paolo Cristofolini, 6–12. Amsterdam: APA-Holland University Press.

———. 1996. "Spinoza and Bible Scholarship." In *The Cambridge Companion to Spinoza*, ed. Don Garrett, 383–407. Cambridge: Cambridge University Press.

Preus, J. Samuel. 2001. *Spinoza and the Irrelevance of Biblical Authority*. Cambridge: Cambridge University Press.

Ravven, Heidi. 2001a. "Some Thoughts on What Spinoza Learned from Maimonides About the Prophetic Imagination, Part One: Maimonides on Prophecy and the Imagination." *Journal of the History of Philosophy* 39:193–214.

———. 2001b. "Some Thoughts on What Spinoza Learned from Maimonides on the Prophetic Imagination, Part Two: Spinoza's Maimonideanism." *Journal of the History of Philosophy* 39:385–406.

Redondi, Pietro. 1989. *Galileo Heretic*. Princeton, NJ: Princeton University Press.

Reines, Alvin. 1969. "Maimonides' Concept of Mosaic Prophecy." *Hebrew Union College Annual* 40:325–62.

———. 1974. "Maimonides' Concept of Miracles." *Hebrew Union College Annual* 42:243–85.

Revah, I. S. 1959. *Spinoza et Juan de Prado*. Paris: Mouton.

Rosenthal, Michael. 2000. "Toleration and the Right to Resist in Spinoza's *Theological-Political Treatise*: The Problem of Christ's Disciples." In *Piety, Peace and the Freedom to Philosophize*, ed. P. J. Bagley, 111–32. Dordrecht: Kluwer.

———. 2001. "Tolerance as a Virtue in Spinoza's Ethics." *Journal of the History of Philosophy* 39:535–57.

———. 2003. "Spinoza's Republican Argument for Toleration." *Journal of Political Philosophy* 11:320–37.

Roth, Leon. 1924. *Spinoza, Descartes, & Maimonides*. New York: Russell and Russell.

Rutherford, Donald P. 1993. *Leibniz and the Rational Order of Nature*. Cambridge: Cambridge University Press.

Ryan, Alan. 1988. "A More Tolerant Hobbes." In *Justifying Toleration*, ed. Susan Mendus. Cambridge: Cambridge University Press.

Sacksteder, William. 1980. "How Much of Hobbes Might Spinoza Have Read?" *Southwestern Journal of Philosophy* 11:25–40.

Saebø, Magne, ed. 2000. *Hebrew Bible/Old Testament: The History of Its Interpretation*. Vol. I, *From the Beginnings to the Middle Ages*. Göttingen: Vandenhoeck & Ruprecht.

———, ed. 2008. *Hebrew Bible/Old Testament: The History of Its Interpretation*. Vol. II, *From the Renaissance to the Enlightenment*. Göttingen: Vandenhoeck & Ruprecht.

Savan, David. 1986. "Spinoza: Scientist and Theorist of Scientific Method." In *Spinoza and the Sciences*, ed. Marjorie Greene and Debra Nails, 95–123. *Boston Studies in the Philosophy of Science* 91. Dordrecht: Reidel.

Scribano, Emanuela. 1995. "Johannes Bredenburg (1643–1691), confutatore di Spinoza?" In *L'Hérésie Spinoziste: La discussion sur le Tractatus Theologico-Politicus, 1670–1677*, ed. Paolo Cristofolini, 66–76. Amsterdam: APA-Holland University Press.

Sellin, Thorsten. 1944. *Pioneering in Penology*. Philadelphia: University of Pennsylvania Press.

Simon, Richard. 1730. *Lettres choisies*. 4 vols. Amsterdam: R. Leers.

Singer, Charles. 1937–38. "The Pseudonym of Spinoza's Publisher." *Journal of the Warburg Institute* 1:77–78.

Smith, Steven. 1997. *Spinoza, Liberalism, and the Question of Jewish Identity*. New Haven, CT: Yale University Press.

Sommerville, Johann P. 1992. *Thomas Hobbes: Political Ideas in Historical Context*. New York: St. Martin's Press.

Sorkin, David. 2010. *The Religious Enlightenment: Protestants, Jews and Catholics from London to Vienna*. Princeton, NJ: Princeton University Press.

Spinoza, Baruch/Benedictus. [1925] 1972. *Spinoza Opera*. 5 vols. Ed. Carl Gebhardt. Heidelberg: Carl Winters Verlag.

———. 1985. *The Collected Works of Spinoza, Vol. 1*. Trans. Edwin Curley. Princeton, NJ: Princeton University Press.

———. 1999. *Oeuvres*, vol. 3: *Traité Théologico-Politique*. Ed. Fokke Akkerman; trans. Jacqueline Lagrée and Pierre-François Moreau. Paris: Presses Universitaires de France.

———. 2001. *Theological-Political Treatise*. 2nd ed. Trans. Samuel Shirley. Indianapolis: Hackett.

———. 2002. *Complete Works*. Trans. Samuel Shirley; ed. Michael Morgan. Indianapolis: Hackett.

Steinberg, Justin. 2009. "Spinoza on Civil Liberation." *Journal of the History of Philosophy* 47:35–58.

———. 2010. "Spinoza's Curious Defense of Toleration." In *Spinoza's* Theological-Political Treatise: *A Critical Guide*, ed. Yitzhak Melamed and Michael Rosenthal, 210–30. Cambridge: Cambridge University Press.

Stern, Josef. 2005. "Maimonides' Epistemology." In *The Cambridge Companion to Maimonides*, ed. Kenneth Seeskin, 105–33. Cambridge: Cambridge University Press.

Stouppe, Jean-Baptiste. 1673. *La Religion des Hollandois representée en plusiers lettres écrites par un Officier de l'Armée du Roy à un Pasteur & Professeur en Théologie de Berne*. Cologne.

Strauss, Leo. 1947–48. "How to Study Spinoza's Theologico-Political Treatise." *Proceedings of the American Academy for Jewish Research* 17:69–131.

———. 1997. *Spinoza's Critique of Religion*. Chicago: University of Chicago Press.

Tuckness, Alex. 2002. *Locke and the Legislative Point of View: Toleration, Contested Principles, and Law*. Princeton, NJ: Princeton University Press.

Van Bunge, Wiep. 1989. "The Early Dutch Reception of the *Tractatus Theologico-Politicus*." *Studia Spinozana* 5:225–51.

———. 1995. "Van Velthuysen, Batelier and Bredenburg on Spinoza's interpretation of the Scriptures." In *L'Hérésie Spinoziste: La discussion sur le Tractatus Theologico-Politicus, 1670–1677*, ed. Paolo Cristofolini, 49–65. Amsterdam: APA-Holland University Press.

———. 1997 [2003]. "Spinoza's Jewish Identity and the Use of Context." *Studia Spinozana* 13:100–118.

———. 2001a. *From Stevin to Spinoza: An Essay on Philosophy in the Seventeenth-Century Dutch Republic*. Leiden: Brill.

———. 2001b. "Baruch of Benedictus? Spinoza en de 'marranen.'" *Mededelingen vanwege het Spinozahuis* 81.

Vandenbossche, Hubert. 1978. "Adriaan Koerbagh en Spinoza." *Mededelingen vanwege het Spinozahuis* 39.

Van Mansvelt, Regnier. 1674. *Adversus Anonymum Theologo-Politicum Liber Singularis*. Amsterdam: Abraham Wolfgang.

Verbeek, Theo. 1992. *Descartes and the Dutch: Early Reactions to Cartesian Philosophy, 1637–1650.* Carbondale: Southern Illinois University Press.

———. 2003. *Spinoza's Theologico-Political Treatise: Exploring the 'Will of God.'* Hampshire, UK: Ashgate.

Walther, Manfred. 1994. "Spinoza's Critique of Miracles: A Miracle of Criticism." In *Spinoza: The Enduring Questions*, ed. Graeme Hunter, 100–112. Toronto: University of Toronto Press, 1994.

Weissman, A. W. 1908. "Het Tuchthuis en het Spinhuis te Amsterdam." *Oud Holland* 26:35–40.

Whipple, John. 2008. "Hobbes on Miracles." *Pacific Philosophical Quarterly* 89:117–42.

Wolfson, Harry A. 1934. *The Philosophy of Spinoza.* Cambridge, MA: Harvard University Press.

Zac, Sylvain. 1965. *Spinoza et l'interprétation de l'Écriture.* Paris: Presses Universitaires de France.

Index